How Africa Trades

Edited by
David Luke

LSE Press

Published by
LSE Press
10 Portugal Street
London WC2A 2HD
press.lse.ac.uk

Text © The Authors 2023

First published 2023

Cover design by Diana Jarvis

Print and digital versions typeset by Siliconchips Services Ltd.

ISBN (Paperback): 978-1-911712-06-0
ISBN (PDF): 978-1-911712-07-7
ISBN (EPUB): 978-1-911712-08-4
ISBN (Mobi): 978-1-911712-09-1

DOI: https://doi.org/10.31389/lsepress.hat

The full text of this book has been peer-reviewed to ensure high academic standards. For our full publishing ethics policies, see https://press.lse.ac.uk

Suggested citation:
Luke, David (ed) (2023) *How Africa Trades*, London: LSE Press. https://doi.org/10.31389/lsepress.hat License: CC-BY-NC 4.0

To read the free, open access version of this book online, visit https://doi.org/10.31389/lsepress.hat or scan this QR code with your mobile device:

Contents

Extended contents

8. Conclusion: it's in the world's interest to give Africa a new trade deal

David Luke **209**

List of figures, tables and boxes

Figures

Tables

Boxes

Contributors

David Luke is professor in practice and strategic director at the London School of Economics Firoz Lalji Institute for Africa, where he oversees the Africa Trade Programme. He is a former director of the African Trade Policy Centre at the UN Economic Commission for Africa (ECA), where he led the technical work on the protocols that make up the African Continental Free Trade Area (AfCFTA) agreement. His research interests include boosting intra-African trade; the AfCFTA initiative; Africa's multilateral and bilateral trade relationships; and cross-cutting policy areas such as trade, industrialisation and structural transformation; trade, inclusion and gender; trade and public health; and trade and climate change.

Jonathan Bashi is a legal scholar whose work and research interests focus on the correlation between international law, trade and development. His work experience spreads across various sectors, with roles assumed in higher education and in the private sector, as well as in international development, including more recently as a consultant for a UK Aid private sector development programme in the DRC, focusing on building the capacity of cross-border traders' associations in the eastern DRC. He holds a PhD in law from SOAS, University of London, where he is currently a lecturer. He led the research for this book on Africa's trade relations with the UK, India, Turkey, Japan, Russia and Brazil.

Geoffroy Guepie is a research associate at the UMR Transitions Energétiques et Environnementales, Université de Pau, France. He has also served as a researcher at the African Trade Policy Centre at the UN Economic Commission for Africa. Geoffroy's research interests include international economics, trade policies (mainly African regional trade agreements), economic geography and civil conflicts in Africa. He is widely published. He holds a PhD in economics from the Université de Pau. He led the research for this book on EU–Africa trade, regional economic communities, and whether supply chains localised during Covid-19.

Jamie MacLeod is a trade economist whose work spans trade negotiations, policy design and research, and is a policy fellow with the Africa Trade Policy Programme at the London School of Economics Firoz Lalji Institute for Africa. He has worked on trade policy issues with a focus on the African continent for the last 10 years, including with the UN Economic Commission for Africa, the International Trade Centre, the International Labour Organization and the World Bank. He was previously an ODI fellow with the Ghanaian Ministry of Trade and Industry. He holds an MSc in economics for development from the University of Oxford, where he was a Snell scholar. He led the research for this book on Africa's trade and investment flows; the AfCFTA, including negotiations during Covid-19; US–Africa trade; and Covid-19's impact on trade in goods and services, supply chains, digital trade and e-commerce.

Kulani McCartan-Demie is an international consultant with a background in technical assistance and cross-cutting research in economic transformation, trade facilitation, industrial policy and gender mainstreaming. She is the founder and director of the Organisation for Economic Transformation (OET), a think tank specialising in advisory and consultancy services. She has worked on policy design and implementation of inclusive trade facilitation, agro-industries and industrial park development for the likes of UNIDO, GIZ, the UK Foreign, Commonwealth and Development Office and the African Development Bank. Kulani holds an MPhil in development studies with distinction from the University of Cambridge. She led the research for this book on Africa's trade relations with China and on informal cross-border trade during the Covid-19 pandemic.

Colette van der Ven is an international lawyer with expertise in trade and sustainable development. As founder and director of the Geneva-based TULIP Consulting, Colette advises governments and international organisations on how to leverage regulatory frameworks and trade agreements to promote inclusive and green development. Colette is also a visiting lecturer in international economic law at the Graduate Institute in Geneva. Previously, she worked as an international trade lawyer for Sidley Austin, representing governments in international disputes before panels and the Appellate Body at the World Trade Organization. Colette holds a juris doctor from the Harvard Law School and a master's in public policy from the Harvard Kennedy School of Government and is a member of the New York Bar. She led the research for this book on the WTO.

Acronyms

ACP Group	African Caribbean and Pacific Group of Countries
AfCFTA	African Continental Free Trade Area
AfDB	African Development Bank
AGOA	African Growth and Opportunity Act
ARII	Africa Regional Integration Index
ASEAN	Association of Southeast Asian Nations
ATO	African Trade Observatory
AU	African Union
AUC	African Union Commission
AVATT	Africa Vaccine Acquisition Task Team
BIAT	Boosting Intra-African Trade
BRI	Belt and Road Initiative
BII	British International Investment
BSIP	British Support for Infrastructure Projects
CDC	Centers for Disease Control and Prevention
CECPA	Comprehensive Economic Cooperation and Partnership Agreement
CEMAC	Central African Economic and Monetary Community
CEN-SAD	Community of Sahel–Saharan States
COMESA	Common Market for Eastern and Southern Africa
CTD	Committee on Trade and Development
DAC	Development Assistance Committee
DCTS	Developing Country Trading Scheme
DFQF	Duty-Free, Quota-Free
EAC	East African Community
EBA	Everything but Arms

ECA	Economic Commission for Africa
ECCAS	Economic Community of Central African States
ECOWAS	Economic Community of West African States
EPA	Economic Partnership Agreement
EU	European Union
FCDO	Foreign, Commonwealth and Development Office
FCO	Foreign and Commonwealth Office
FOFAC	Forum for China–Africa Cooperation
FTA	Free Trade Agreement
GDP	Gross Domestic Product
GIZ	Deutsche Gesellschaft für Internationale Zusammenarbeit
GNI	Gross National Income
GSP	Generalised System of Preferences
ICBT	Informal Cross-Border Trade
IGAD	Intergovernmental Authority on Development
IMF	International Monetary Fund
IUU	Illegal Unregulated and Unreported
JBIC	Japan Bank for International Cooperation
JSI	Joint Statement Initiative
LDC	Least-Developed Country
MFN	Most Favoured Nation
MoU	Memorandum of Understanding
MPIA	Multi-Party Interim Appeal Arbitration Arrangement
MSME	Micro, Small and Medium-sized Enterprises
NGO	Non-governmental Organisation
NTB	Non-tariff Barrier
OACPS	Organisation of African, Caribbean and Pacific States
OAU	Organisation of African Unity
ODI	Overseas Development Institute
OECD	Organisation for Economic Co-operation and Development
PAPSS	Pan-African Payment Settlement System
PCA	Post-Cotonou Agreement

PRC   Peoples Republic of China

REC   Regional Economic Community

SACU   Southern African Customs Union

SADC   Southern African Development Community

SDR   Special Drawing Right

SDT   Special and Differential Treatment

SEZ   Special Economic Zone

SOE   State-Owned Enterprise

SPS   Sanitary and Phytosanitary

STIP   Strategic Trade and Investment Partnership

STR   Simplified Trade Regime

TBT   Technical Barriers to Trade

TFA   Trade Facilitation Agreement

TICAD   Tokyo International Conference on African Development

TIDO   Trade and Information Desk Officer

TMA   TradeMark Africa

TRIPS   Trade-Related Intellectual Property Rights

UKEF   UK Export Finance

UMA   Union of Arab Maghreb

UN   United Nations

UNDP   United Nations Development Programme

USAID   United States Agency for International Development

USMCA   US–Mexico–Canada Agreement

USTR   The Office of the United States Trade Representative

WAEMU   West African Economic and Monetary Union

WTO   World Trade Organization

Glossary

Aid for trade A subset of official development assistance focused on promoting and supporting international trade.

Development Assistance Committee A group of 24 high-income aid-donating countries comprising Australia, Austria, Belgium, Canada, Denmark, the European Union, Finland, France, Germany, Greece, Ireland, Italy, Japan, South Korea, Luxembourg, the Netherlands, New Zealand, Norway, Portugal, Spain, Sweden, Switzerland, the United Kingdom and the United States.

Duty-free, quota-free Without limit on the amount of trade that is traded without tariffs.

Foreign direct investment An investment from a company in one country into a business in another country.

Groupage trade The aggregation of informal trade wherein groups of traders would bring smaller individual assignments of goods together into a larger, consolidated consignment.

Most favoured nation A common principle in trade agreements based on the idea that countries treat each other with no less 'favour' than they treat other countries in aspects such as tariffs on traded goods or conditions of access for service suppliers.

Non-tariff barriers Restrictions to trade that do not take the form of a tariff, including quotas, embargoes, sanctions, and documentation or standards requirements.

Official development assistance Government aid that promotes and specifically targets economic development and welfare of developing countries.

Regional economic communities (RECs) The geographic groupings of African countries that form the building blocks for regional coordination within the African continent. The term often refers implicitly to the eight African Union-recognised RECs but can include other formations such as the Southern African Customs Union or the Indian Ocean Commission.

Resource curse Used to describe the paradox wherein countries rich in extractive resources, such as petroleum oils or metals, tend to underperform in economic development.

Rules of origin The criteria that a good needs to satisfy to be considered to 'originate' within a country, and therefore eligible to benefit from the trade preferences accorded to that country by partner countries.

Safe trade Sector-specific practices on issues such as border health screening, testing and certification, truck crew sizes, digitalised trade procedures, electronic cargo tracking and information sharing.

Trade and transport corridors Major routes through which people and goods flow between countries.

Trade facilitation Initiatives, programmes or efforts made to expedite the movement, release and clearance of goods, including goods in transit.

Trade integration The process through which two or more states within a broadly defined geographic group reduce economic barriers to trade including tariffs, but also non-tariff issues such as the harmonisation of standards or customs coordination.

Preface

David Luke

Welcome to *How Africa Trades*, which seeks to enhance understanding of the role of trade in Africa's development. It is our expectation that the book will contribute to an extension of the current knowledge base on African trade policy for more informed deliberations on trade as a driver of growth and economic transformation at various levels of policymaking, advocacy, and scholarly and pedagogical pursuits.

Three considerations underpin the idea behind the book. First, it aims to demystify African trade policy, which can be seen as a specialised – perhaps also esoteric – activity best left to 'experts', and to propagate a deeper and broader understanding of how trade impacts the lives of ordinary Africans and the continent's development aspirations. Second, it provides up-to-date information that is easily reachable through open access publication on Africa's trade data, trade negotiations, trade agreements and policy priorities, with analysis to enhance clarity. Third, this book seeks to empower policymakers, stakeholders, scholars and others to interrogate the effectiveness of trade agreements and policy choices including the implementation dimensions from a normative perspective that is pro-development and inclusive and gives precedence to overcoming pervasive poverty on the continent.

The timing of the book is opportune. Spurred by a strong recovery in commodity prices, African economies recovered moderately well from the Covid-19 pandemic-induced recession of 2020–2021. But that also risks sliding into – an unfortunately all too familiar – complacent dependence on the unpredictable fortunes of commodities. The war that started with Russia's invasion of Ukraine on 24 February 2022 exposed Africa's challenges in agricultural productivity, competitiveness, and reliance on food imports, as well as the inherent injustice of international trade rules that distort global food markets. A rebalancing of these rules along with a reset in Africa of policy and strategy to build productive capacities and overcome the boom-and-bust cycles of commodity dependence can help ensure greater resilience to future shocks, sustained growth and much-needed prosperity in the world's poorest continent. This is essential if Africa is to be able to generate the number and quality of jobs needed, with over 170 million of its youth expected to enter the labour market in each of the coming decades, as the population nearly doubles from its current 1.3 billion to 2.5 billion by 2050.

A fitting instrument of reset is the ambitious initiative to create a continent-wide preferential market through the African Continental Free Trade

Area (AfCFTA). If fully implemented, liberalised trade on the African continent offers an incentive and pathway for the restructuring of African economies through diversification and agricultural and industrial development. The AfCFTA further offers a framework for continent-wide reforms to bring trade costs down, undertake border reforms and foster institutions and practices of modern trade governance. A continental market provides a context as well for African countries to follow the playbook of successful development experiences in countries that attained rapid transformation and diminished levels of poverty within a few decades through carefully designed trade policy interventions, effective institutions and other economic and social reforms. As the book explains, though the pandemic delayed the momentum behind the AfCFTA project, it remains at an advanced stage of realisation.

How Africa Trades is being published at a time of global uncertainty and policy fluidity that has characterised the early 2020s. The unpacking of how Africa trades provides a basis for interrogating further the issues at the intersection between trade and major global trends that are expected during the 2020s. For example, as climate action increasingly frames public policies that require accumulative decarbonisation of trade and investment, there is scope to investigate the trade implications of greener production and sustainable growth strategies among African countries. As the efficiencies sought from digitalisation become ubiquitous, driven by more accessible and affordable technologies, there is a need to consider the effect on African trade practices to identify where policy coherence and regulatory alignment can generate positive spin-offs for African countries in a fast-changing global technological landscape. Our assessment of how the Covid-19 pandemic affected African trade in this book includes analysis of trends that were observed in relation to utilisation of digital trade solutions at the peak of the lockdowns.

Still looking into the future, while it is too early to decipher how the war in Ukraine will shape geopolitical alliances, or how its full economic impact will unfold, the 'friend-shoring' of supply chains is one of the likely outcomes. What can we learn from reshoring, in response to supply chain fragilities, in the Covid-19 period? What are the opportunities and risks for African trade and investment flows? And what about other financial flows such as foreign aid flows that support development initiatives? Foreign aid flows are on a downward trajectory in real terms as donor countries prioritise fiscal consolidation following their rapid accumulation of public debt to fight the Covid-19 pandemic while strengthening military and security investments in the light of the emerging geopolitical realities. In the near term, the post-pandemic inflationary spiral will occupy the efforts in donor countries to contain the cost-of-living crisis, adding to the pressure on development assistance budgets. To this extent, trade is – and will continue to be – the largest source of revenue flows into African countries. This raises the stakes for African countries because a reliable revenue stream from trade is critical for development finance and debt management. *How Africa Trades* provides insights for contextualising global developments and Africa's trade policy options in the light of the central role of trade in Africa's aspirations for economic transformation.

The book in outline

The deconstruction of *how* Africa trades is our overriding focus. The first chapter provides an overview of *what* Africa trades, with *whom*, and the biggest challenges this poses for countries that are late developers. In the focus on Covid-19 in this book, the story is told of the relative resilience of petroleum and gold prices amid crashing international commodity markets. Key service sectors such as tourism, logistics, business facilitation and transport experienced a sharp drop as lockdowns took hold. On the whole, intra-African trade that is more diversified performed better. This underscores the gains that could be made from trade reforms under the AfCFTA. Subsequent chapters investigate *where* Africa trades and specifically the *trade regimes* under *which* Africa trades. These chapters assess the state of play in the AfCFTA, and regional trade (Chapter 2), bilateral trade with leading partners (Chapters 3 and 4), and developments under the multilateral umbrella of the World Trade Organization (WTO) (Chapter 5). Some of the ways Covid-19 illustrated how Africa trades is the subject of a deep dive into formal trade (Chapter 6) and informal and digital trade (Chapter 7). The concluding chapter highlights the main messages from the preceding chapters as a call to action by stakeholders and Africa's partners.

Open access publication

Finally, this book is being published on an open access basis. All the datasets used in our analysis are, where possible, publicly available (not behind paywalls), with sources detailed in the reference sections at the end of each chapter. Where website addresses are liable to change, we have used Harvard's perma.cc resource to preserve online sources and ensure they are permanently available to readers. This carries the expectation that readers will use its insights – including what they find themselves in agreement or disagreement with – to engage on issues concerning African trade policy reform. Aside from the inherent virtue of putting the result of social science research within the reach of any reader anywhere in the world, open access publication is especially beneficial to readers in Africa, where the relative cost of books and periodicals is high. Moreover, apart from the output of the UN agencies, the World Bank, the IMF and other organisations, very little independent research is being carried out and published on African trade policy. The two main journals on African trade and related issues that provide much-needed platforms for research, the *Journal of African Trade* and the *Journal of African Transformation*, are sponsored by intergovernmental organisations. For researchers who may wish to dive deeper into the issues covered in this book, most of the sources cited can be accessed on the internet and are not shielded by paywalls. Comments and feedback provided by readers are welcome and useful, and advance open social science. Please send this to Africa@lse.ac.uk. Engaging with the material covered in the book through posts on Twitter (@AfricaAtLSE), Facebook and other social media is also welcome.

Acknowledgements

It takes a village to start a research programme and get a book out. Generous financial support was provided by the London School of Economics and Political Science Firoz Lalji Institute for Africa (FLIA), the LSE Ruth Glass Fellowship Fund, and the Friedrich Ebert Stiftung (FES) Geneva Office. Tim Allen, Martha Geiger Mwenitete, Fadil Elobeid, Tosin Adebisi, Mark Briggs, Laurence Radford and Ikenna Acholonu of the FLIA are unswerving champions of the Africa Trade Policy Programme. Hansjörg 'Hajo' Lanz, Yvonne Bartmann and Sabine Dörfler at FES Geneva readily backed the vision behind pro-development research on African trade policy. Rashid Kaukab of CUTS Geneva, Michelle Moraa Mokaya of TULIP Consulting, Nick Westcott of the Royal African Society and the School of Oriental and African Studies, Lennart Oestergaard of FES Berlin Office, Melaku Desta of the Economic Commission for Africa, Parasram Gopaul of the Mauritius Permanent Mission in Geneva, Michael Amoah, Fadil Elobaid, Elitsa Garnizova, Aggrey Nyondwa and Laurence Radford of LSE joined the editor, contributors and the FES Geneva team at one or both of the workshops that discussed preliminary research findings. several African officials including WTO ambassadors, trade experts at the AfCFTA Secretariat, EAC, ECOWAS, COMESA and SADC, and a variety of specialists on issues covered in the book gave generously of their time for interviews as part of the research. Marios Tokas, a legal consultant, Robert Brock Burton of TULIP Consulting and Michelle Moraa Mokaya helped with inputs for the chapter on the WTO. Melaku Desta, Lennart Oestergaard and Franklyn Lisk of Warwick University read the entire manuscript and provided constructive feedback. Aggrey Nyondwa, Nellie Anderson and Jonathan Terrefe at FLIA assisted in compiling the references. Patrick Dunleavy, Alice Park, Lucy Lambe and Ellie Potts at LSE Press offered valuable insights on the merits of open access publishing and guided the manuscript to publication.

1. Trade and investment flows and a perspective for analysing trade policy in Africa

Jamie MacLeod and David Luke

When a country participates in the global economy, it does so on the basis of foreign exchange inflows and outflows. Even the flow of ideas, in the form of intellectual property rights, entail services trade and foreign exchange. The extent to which exports dominate the inflows of foreign exchange into African countries may be surprising: at \$421 billion in 2019, they eclipsed official development assistance (\$31 billion), foreign direct investment inflows (\$40 billion) and remittances (\$84 billion) (Luke 2020).

Africa's trade, unfortunately, underperforms both in volume and content. Despite having grown in the last couple of decades, it continues to represent an undersized share of world trade. And it remains overly concentrated in fuels, metals and ores. This concentration phenomenon is the case for all but a few African countries. The form of investment inflows into African countries perpetuates these concentrations, which do little to serve the aspirations of structural transformation and industrialisation held by African leaders. That is the story, at least, for most of African trade. Trade within the continent, between African countries, is different. It comprises an unusually large share of manufactures. It is hoped that it is exactly this trade that can be boosted with initiatives like the African Continental Free Trade Area (AfCFTA), and in turn contribute to sustainable economic transformation in the continent.

This chapter elaborates the status of trade in Africa, looking at how much Africa trades, of what and with whom. Trade policy is the principal vehicle through which the role of trade can be improved as a driver for African development. Accordingly, the chapter concludes with an elaboration of the analytical perspective that grounds the approach used to assess trade policy in Africa throughout the book.

How to cite this book chapter:

MacLeod, Jamie and Luke, David (2013) 'Trade and investment flows and a perspective for analysing trade policy in Africa', in: Luke, David (ed) *How Africa Trades,* London: LSE Press, pp. 1–21. https://doi.org/10.31389/lsepress.hat.a License: CC-BY-NC 4.0

1.1 Why African trade matters, but underperforms

Exports dwarf remittances, investment inflows and overseas development assistance from Development Assistance Committee countries – a group of 24 advanced economies – as a source of foreign exchange inflows into African countries. Since the independence of African countries in the 1960s, exports have grown more rapidly than these alternative flows. From 2018 to 2020, exports were worth more than two-and-a-half times as much as the value of remittances, investment inflows and overseas development assistance combined.

Beyond their monetary value, these trade flows are thought to be embedded with continually emerging forms of technology – needed to compete on world markets – and lead to upskilling, capital investments and technological upgrading in the up- and downstream parts of the domestic supply chains that feed into exports. The firms behind these exports are in turn more likely to be more productive, offer higher wages and grant employment opportunities in the formal sector.

Yet, notwithstanding recent growth, Africa's export volumes continue to underperform and fail to live up to their developmental potential. Africa's exports amount to just 2.3 per cent of world trade (Figure 1.2). This world trade share has stagnated for over three and a half decades, before which time it fell from a height of 5 per cent of world trade in the 1970s. Even while Africa's exports soared in the late 1990s and through the early 2000s (as shown in Figure 1.1), they were only keeping pace with a broader worldwide expansion

Figure 1.1: Sources of African foreign exchange flows: exports, FDI inflows, remittances and DAC overseas development assistance (ODA), constant 2020 US$

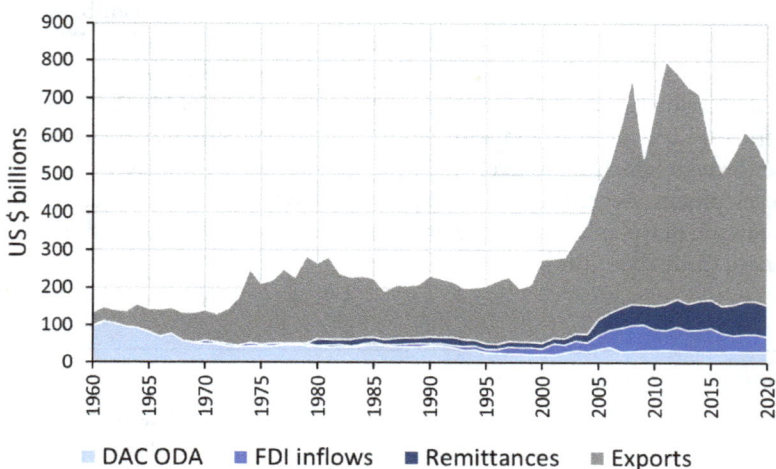

Sources: Authors' calculations based on IMF (2022), UNCTAD (2022), OECD DAC-ODA (2022), Knomad (2022).[1]

Figure 1.2: Africa's exports as a share of world trade: 1960 to 2020

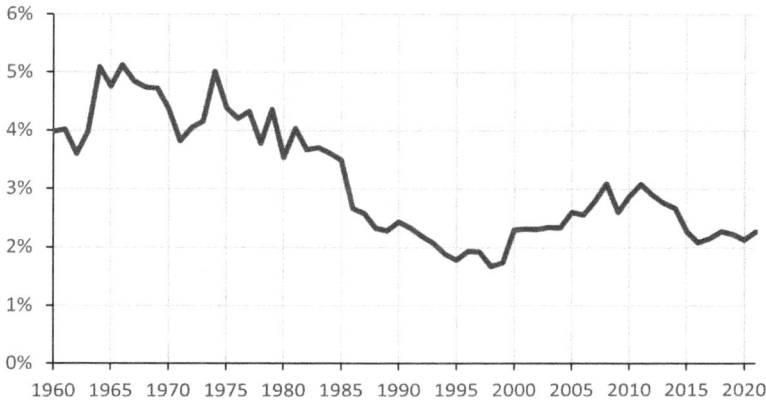

Source: Authors' calculations based on IMF Direction of Trade Statistics (2022).

in trade bolstered by global phenomena such as the accelerated integration of China and other emerging market economies into global trade flows.

What Africa exports also matters. In the most important aspects of concern for policymakers, such as jobs creation and poverty alleviation, not all trade is worth the same. Fuels, ores and basic metals tend to be more capital-intensive and less labour-intensive to produce, and so create fewer jobs. These products are usually more reliant upon foreign capital and expertise and are particularly prone to their extracted value being undermined by illicit financial flows (ECA 2015). Their prices tend to be volatile, exacerbating budgetary planning, and their rents susceptible to elite capture. These much-researched phenomena are well known and have led such goods to be regarded throughout the developmental discourse as the seeds of so-called 'resource-curses'.

Unfortunately, Africa's exports have remained stubbornly concentrated in fuels, ores and metals. The value of exports of these products fluctuates substantially with their prices but has accounted for no less than 60 per cent of Africa's exports in any year since at least 1995, and as much as 89 per cent at its relative height in 2008. Figure 1.3 shows three main 'humps' in Africa's exports over the last 20 years, each coinciding tellingly with heights in global petroleum prices. It also shows that exports of manufactures and foodstuffs have grown too, yet they have done so by only about 1 per cent, on average, in each year over the last decade. That does not nearly suffice for a continent with an economy growing at over 3 per cent and a population increasing at almost 2.5 per cent a year, according to IMF and UN estimates, over this period.

Nevertheless, what Africa exports has considerable strategic significance. Access to fuels and industrial metals is a necessity for the functioning of modern industrial economies elsewhere in the world. Five of the top 30 oil-producing countries in the world are African and the continent has accounted for a little under 10 per cent of the world's supply of petroleum oils in recent years. Two of the top 10 largest exporters of liquified natural gas were African in 2021, with the continent considered to be well positioned to replace Russian gas sources in Europe following the war in Ukraine if infra-structural capacities can be upgraded (Gbadamosi 2022). Africa is also home to many critical minerals increasingly required of emerging digital and green technologies, such as cobalt (which is needed for batteries) and caesium and rubidium (used in mobile cellular global positioning systems). An estimated 42 of the 63 elements used by low-carbon technologies and the so-called Fourth Industrial Revolution are found in Africa (United Nations University – Institute for Natural Resources in Africa 2019).

The other side of trade, besides exports, is of course imports. Though access to imports is important, it attracts less policy attention than exports. Policy-makers tend to care more about boosting exports and the foreign exchange earned by them than about increasing the imports on which that foreign exchange is spent. Imports are seen more as an expression of what a country needs but cannot source domestically, such as refined fuels or stable foods, than the economic structure of that country. As Africa's exports of fuels increased from 2003, so too did Africa's import bill for manufactures. The three ascending 'humps' seen in Africa's exports (Figure 1.3) are replicated in the shape of three softer humps of imports in this period (Figure 1.4). Though admittedly an oversimplification, compounded by other balance of payment flows, Africa's trade represents in general an exchange with the rest of the world of primary fuels, ores and metals in exchange for manufactures, and to a lesser extent foodstuffs.

Figure 1.3: Composition of Africa's exports, constant 2020 US$

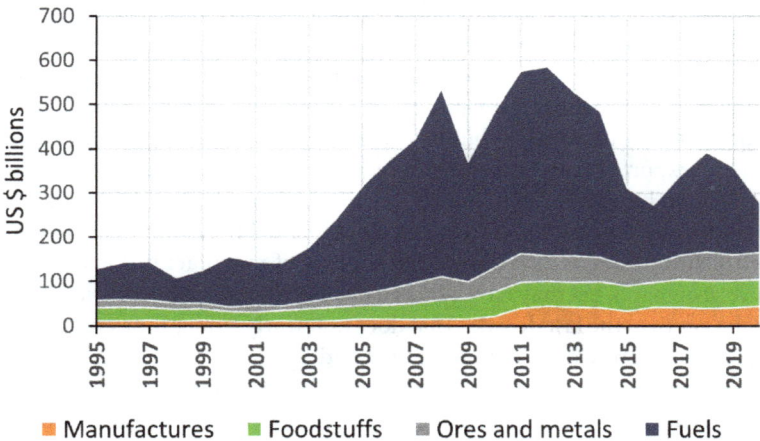

Source: Authors' calculations based on UNCTAD (2022).[2]

Figure 1.4: Composition of Africa's imports, constant 2020 US$

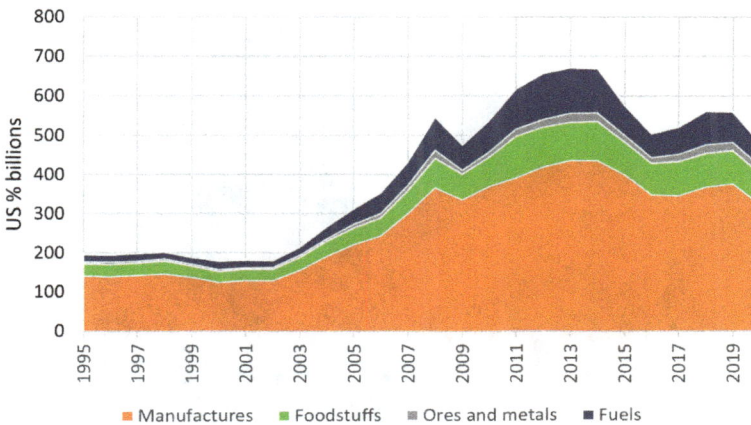

Source: Authors' calculations based on UNCTAD (2022).[3]

1.2 Unpacking how individual African countries trade

African countries differ, and this is true in trade too. In unpacking how we think of Africa's trade, two prevailing features stand out. First, the trade of African countries is dominated by a small number of major economies. The five largest African exporters, between 2016 and 2020, exported more than the next 49 African countries combined. We can think of the economies behind Africa's export volumes in three size categories. The 'big 6' each accounts for a sizeable slice of Africa's exports and at least $25 billion in annual exports. This includes South Africa, Nigeria, Algeria, Angola, Egypt and Morocco. These are denoted in shades of blue in Figure 1.5. Following this, there is a 'middle 12' of medium-sized trading economies, including countries such as Kenya, Ghana, Tunisia and Gabon. These have annual exports greater than $5 billion and collectively represent an important share of exports from the continent but are individually relatively small economies. The 'remaining 36' reflects the nature of most African countries: low trade volumes, and in many instances also small populations with small market economies. Examples of countries within this basket include Chad, Uganda, Niger, Malawi and Comoros.

The second prevailing feature of African trade is its concentration. Most African countries possess an export portfolio heavily concentrated within a single sector. Table 1.1 splits African countries into four types on the basis of the largest economic sector accounting for at least 35 per cent of their exports over the 2016 to 2020 period. Twelve African countries are heavily concentrated in fuels – in half of these, since 2016 more than 90 per cent of

Figure 1.5: Africa's exports, by country, $ billions

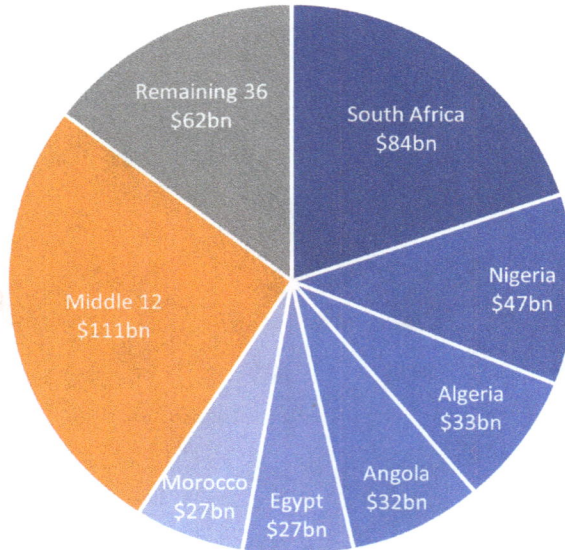

Source: Authors' calculations based on UNCTAD (2022).

Table 1.1: Economic concentration of Africa's exports, by country

Economic concentration	Number of countries	Average annual export value
Foodstuffs	17	$2.1bn
Ores and metals	17	$4.0bn
Fuels	12	$13.3bn
Manufactures	8	$19.9bn

Source: Authors' calculations based on UNCTAD (2022).

their exports have been fuels. This category comprises several large exporters, including Nigeria, Algeria and Angola, but also smaller oil-dependent export-ers, such as Chad, South Sudan and Equatorial Guinea. Seventeen African countries have export portfolios concentrated in ores and metals and another 17 in foodstuffs. These non-oil-exporting countries tend to account for much smaller values of exports, and include most of the 'remaining 36' countries mentioned in Figure 1.5. A final eight African countries have achieved a degree of industrialisation, allowing manufacturing to represent the largest economic sector in their exports. This latter category comprises a mix of large industrial economies – such as South Africa, Egypt, Morocco and Tunisia – but also smaller ones that have managed to develop export bases or integrate into the industrial value chains of their larger neighbours, including Lesotho, Eswatini, Mauritius and Djibouti.

Industrialisation remains the exception for African countries, but also a prevailing goal. Unfortunately, the picture of over-concentration found in Africa's aggregate trade is reflected at the disaggregated level for most African countries. Too many have export portfolios that are highly concentrated in the primary sectors, though in different instances these comprise not just the fuel sector but also ores and metals, and foodstuffs too. The largest African exporters tend to be those that have achieved a degree of industrialisation, or merely found themselves host to large stocks of hydrocarbons.

1.3 Trade with whom?

The trade that flows into and out of a country flow to or from somewhere. In the aggregation of total trade flows, some countries and regions are better represented than others; they account for a larger share of total trade flows. Yet some countries are important because of *what* they trade, too. For instance, African countries are a known source of rare earth minerals and supply chain inputs, including metals, agricultural commodities and petroleum oils.

The relative significance of partner markets evolves over time. While world trade has grown in general terms in recent decades, much of this growth owes to certain countries and regions. As Figures 1.6 and 1.7 demonstrate, the EU is Africa's most important source of imports, accounting for 26 per cent of all imports into African countries, followed by China (16 per cent) and intra-African trade (15 per cent), on average between 2018 and 2020. The US (5 per cent) and the UK (2 per cent) are important, but much less significant sources of imports into African countries (Figure 1.6). For the UK, its relatively small share in Africa's total imports in recent years is the result of a long relative (though not absolute) decline in importance since the 1990s, a period in which the UK accounted for a far greater share of the continent's trade (Figure 1.6). Africa's imports from the EU, China and other African countries ballooned from the early 2000s. This was a period marked by rapidly rising commodity prices – granting African countries increasing foreign reserves with which to fund such imports. This was also, notably, the period in which China joined the WTO, allowing its gradual – but spectacular – integration into world supply chains.

The destination of Africa's bilateral exports closely mirrors, in order of economic importance, Africa's imports. The EU is Africa's most important destination for exports – accounting for 26 per cent of all African exports in terms of value, followed by intra-African trade (18 per cent) and China (15 per cent), between 2018 and 2020 (Figure 1.9). The US (5 per cent) and the UK (3 per cent) are smaller export destinations.

Though the general rising trend in Africa's imports follows that of Africa's exports, it is much less 'smooth'. The total of Africa's exports experienced

Figure 1.6: Origin of Africa's imports, constant 2020 US$

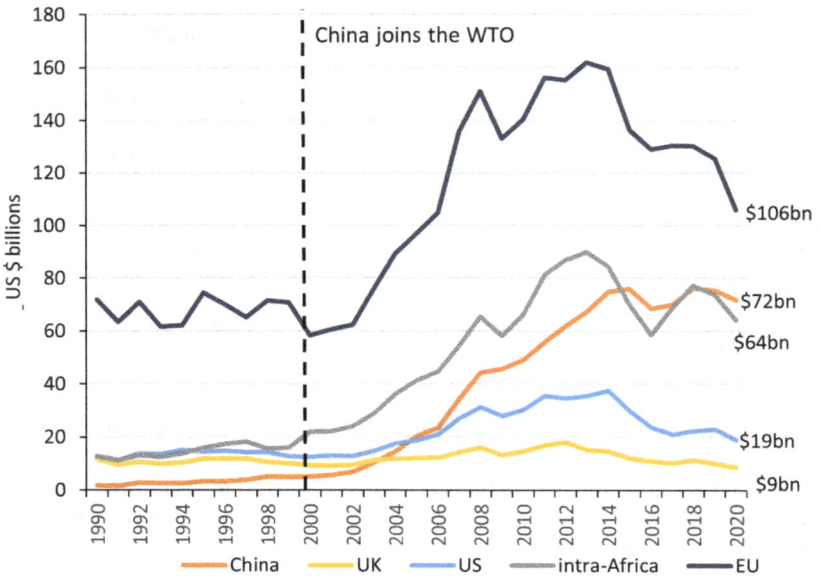

Source: IMF (222).

Figure 1.7: Share of Africa's imports, three-year average (2018–2020)

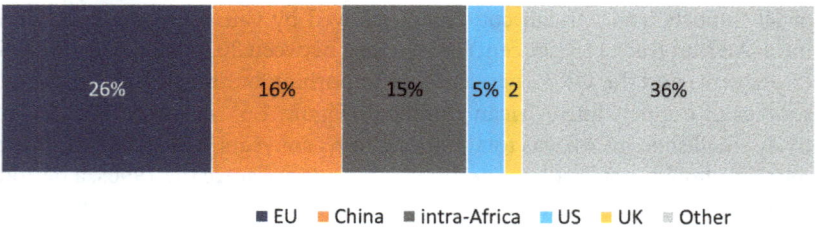

| 26% | 16% | 15% | 5% | 2 | 36% |

■ EU   ■ China   ■ intra-Africa   ■ US   ■ UK   ▨ Other

Source: IMF (2022).

repeated shocks, notably in 2009, 2015 and 2020 (Figure 1.8). These correspond with oil price shocks and belie the heavy concentration of African exports in petroleum fuels. This explains, too, the declining share of African exports destined for the US, which, since the early 2010s, have been replaced by domestic US sources of shale oil.

Despite accounting for around 17 per cent of the total world population, only about 3 per cent of global GDP occurs in the African continent. Africa is, economically, a small portion of the global economy. Accordingly, in few partner markets is Africa a major export destination or import supplier. Africa accounts for just 3.9 per cent of China's trade, 2.2 per cent of the EU's trade, 2.2 per cent of the UK's trade and 1.1 per cent of US trade (Figure 1.10).

Figure 1.8: Destination of Africa's exports, constant 2020 US$

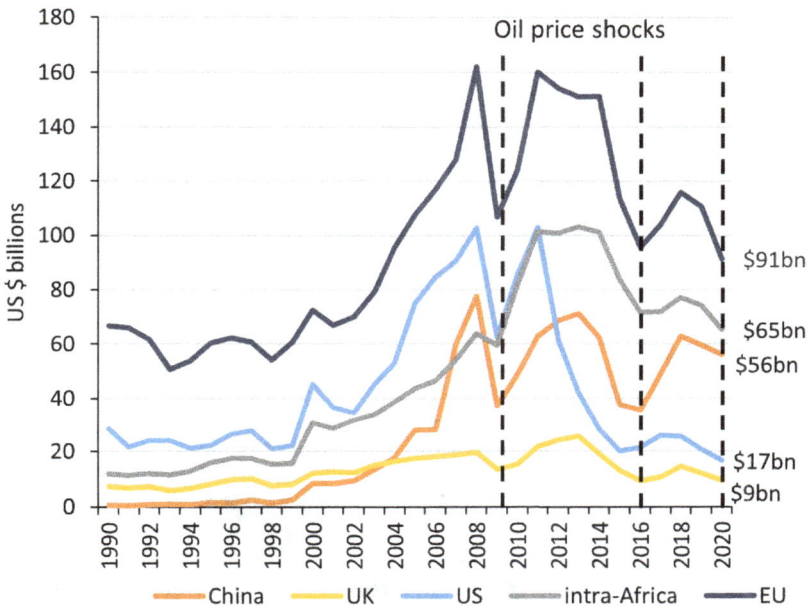

Source: IMF (2022).

Figure 1.9: Share of Africa's exports, three-year average (2018–2020)

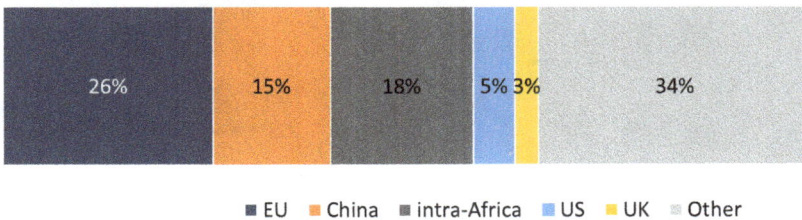

Source: IMF (2022).

1.4 Investment: a mirror of trade

Africa's investment story in general holds a mirror up to that of its trade. Though the total foreign direct investment (FDI) stock in African countries has increased considerably since the early 2000s, this has not substantially exceeded rising global trends, leaving Africa's share of the world stock of FDI relatively stable since the early 1990s (Figure 1.11). This experience closely matches that seen of Africa's total trade in Figures 1.2 and 1.3, in which recent growth has kept apace with broader global trends, rather than representing a 'catch-up' with the rest of the world.

Figure 1.10: Relative importance of Africa to its top trading partners, share of Africa in total trade, by partner

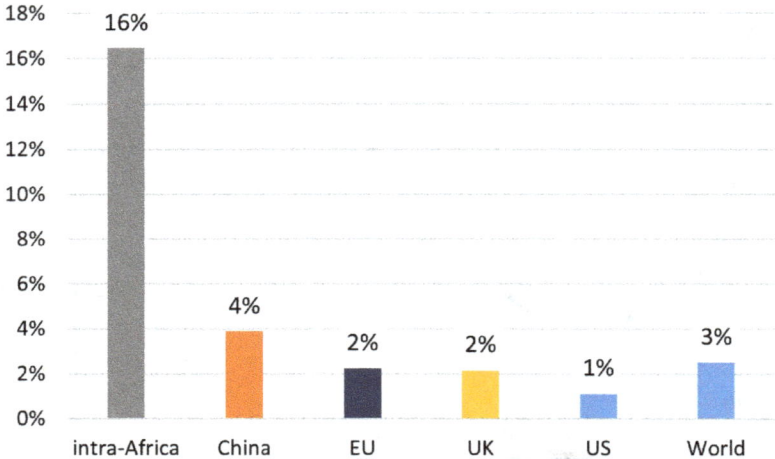

Source: IMF (2022).

Figure 1.11: Africa's inward foreign direct investment stock, constant 2020 US$

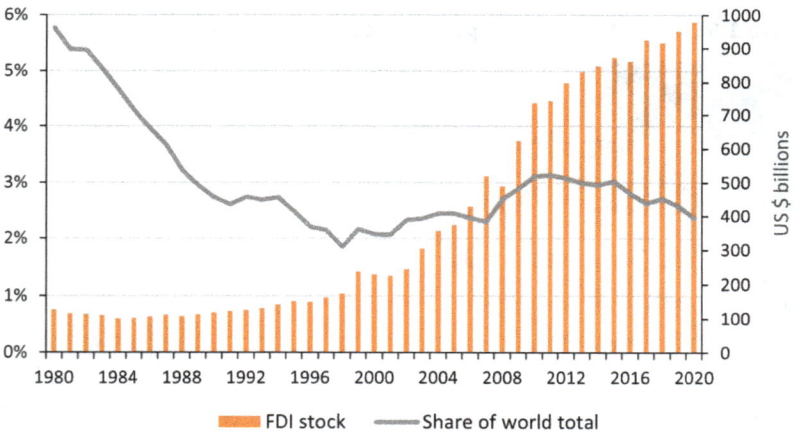

Source: Authors' calculations based on UNCTAD (2022).

Though comprehensive investment data from all sources does not exist, a demonstrative vignette can be seen through three large economies, the US, the EU and China, which issue bilateral and sectorally disaggregated FDI stock and net flows data. Investment stocks, in the case of African countries, mirror trade statistics, reflecting a concentration in the mining and extractive

Figure 1.12: US outward foreign direct investment stock in Africa as compared to US investment stock in all countries, by sector, 2020

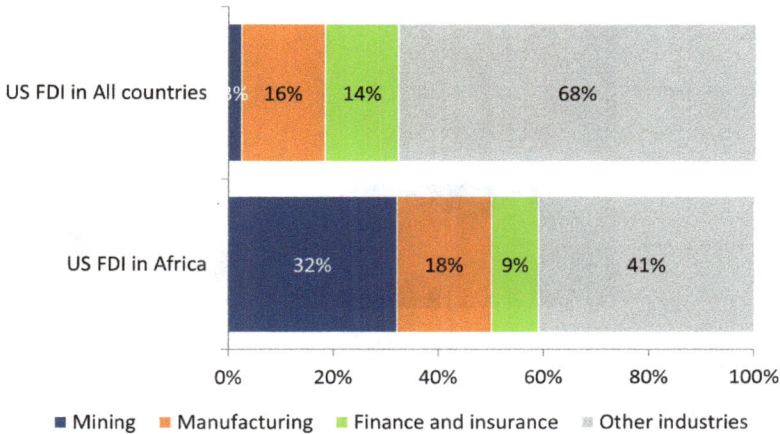

Source: Authors' calculations based on Bureau of Economic Analysis US Department of Commerce (2022).

sectors, associated with fuels and metals. The mining sector is the main sectoral destination for US investments in Africa, accounting for 32 per cent of all US investments in the continent, despite mining accounting for only 3 per cent of outward US investments in all countries (Figure 1.12). In most instances, investment stock is also concentrated in just a small number of African countries. Egypt, Nigeria and South Africa alone account for 59 per cent of US investment stock on the continent.

EU investments into Africa are similarly concentrated in the mining sector, which accounted for almost half of all EU net direct investments abroad in Africa between 2013 and 2020 (Figure 1.13). By comparison, just 7 per cent of EU investments in all other countries are in the mining sector. EU investments into African countries are, however, relatively better represented than investments from the US in Africa's manufacturing sector, which accounted for 41 per cent of all EU net direct investments abroad in Africa between 2013 and 2020. The vignette expressed by Chinese outward foreign direct investment data in sub-Saharan Africa is similar, being heavily concentrated in the energy and metals sectors, but also transport (Figure 1.14).

Africa's share of world investment stocks continues to be undersized and concentrated in the extractive primary sectors. As such, prevailing investment flows in general reinforce Africa's commodity dependency rather than contribute to its structural transformation and sustainable development. This is also reflected in evidence that suggests that the impact of FDI in the extractive sector on the number of jobs created is on a downward trajectory, which is mainly due to the capital-intensity of the investments (Keppel 2021).

Figure 1.13: EU net direct investments abroad in Africa as compared to EU investments in all countries, by sector, 2013–2020

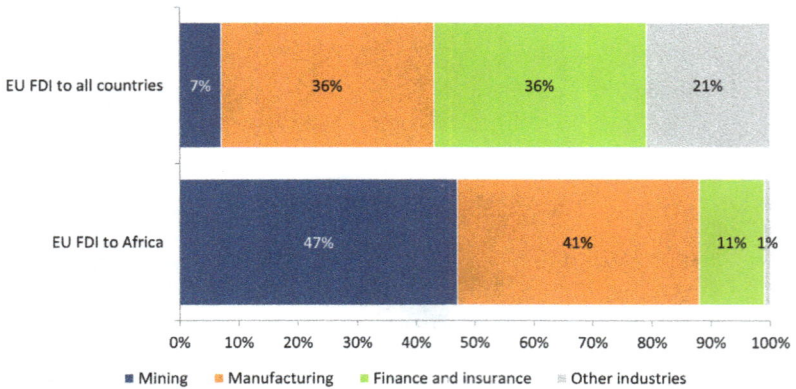

Source: Authors' calculations based on Eurostat (2022).

Figure 1.14: China outward foreign direct investment in sub-Saharan Africa, by sector

CHINA OFDI IN SUBSAHARAN AFRICA BY SECTOR

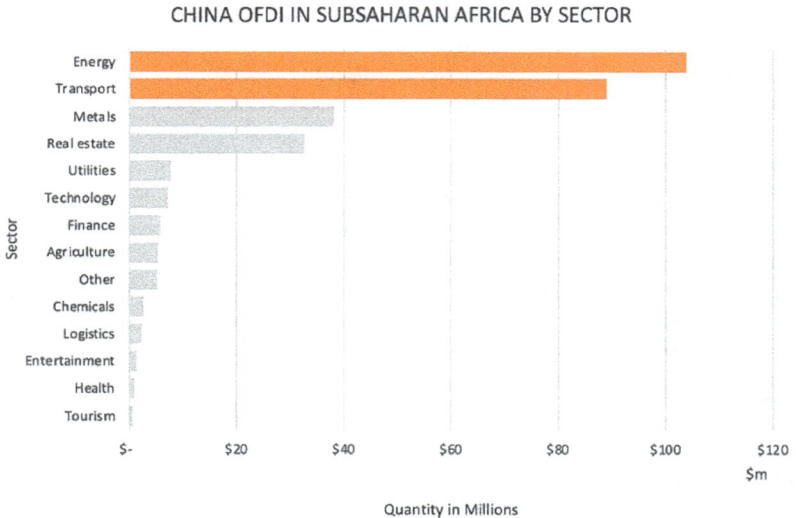

Quantity in Millions

Source: Yu (2021).

1.5 Africa's trade in services

Services account for around two-thirds of the global economy but when it comes to trade they are worth less than a third of the value of trade in goods.

In many respects, finding ways to facilitate trade in services is the 'promised land' of the future of trade. Until the Covid-19 crisis, global trade in services had been growing at a faster pace than trade in goods for at least 15 years. In Africa, too, exports of services had been growing twice as fast as had exports of goods since 2005, doubling from $62 billion to $124 billion in 2019 (Figure 1.16). While impressive, this slightly lagged behind the global growth in services exports, with Africa's share of total world services exports falling from 2.3 per cent to 2 per cent over this period. This is smaller than the share of Africa's exports in the world goods trade, which itself is small at 2.5 per cent in 2019. To put services trade into perspective, the ratio of African services to goods exports was just over a quarter in 2019. Northern Africa is the biggest regional exporter of services in Africa, accounting for about 43 per cent of Africa's services exports, followed by Eastern Africa (22 per cent), Western Africa (21 per cent), Southern Africa (10 per cent) and Central Africa (4 per cent) (Figure 1.15). However, services exports have been growing fastest in Western and Eastern Africa in recent years, while they have stagnated in Southern Africa.

In usual years, travel services, including business travel and tourism, account for the largest share of Africa's services exports, followed by transport services, such as sea and air passenger and freight transport. In 2019, African exports in these two sectors were worth a combined $82 billion and accounted for two-thirds of all African services exports (Figure 1.17). Though Africa's travel and transport services grew steadily from 2005 to 2019, they were surpassed by growth in the more indefinite categories (which derive from the IMF's classification system for international cross-border transactions) of 'other business services' and 'other' services. Within these categories there has been impressive growth in African financial services, telecommunication services, computer services, research and development, professional and management consulting services, and cultural and technical services exports. At the end of Figure 1.17 is an unmissably sharp drop in African services exports, corresponding to the impact of the Covid-19 pandemic – a subject further interrogated in Chapters 6 and 7 of this book.

Figure 1.15: Regional contribution to Africa's services exports, 2020

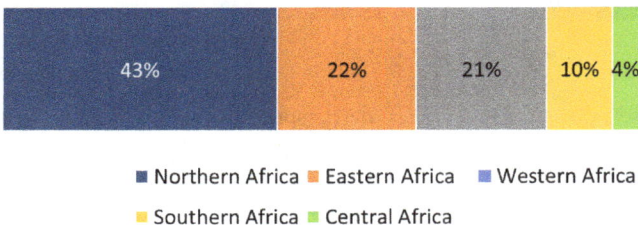

| 43% | 22% | 21% | 10% | 4% |

■ Northern Africa ■ Eastern Africa ■ Western Africa
■ Southern Africa ■ Central Africa

Source: Authors' calculations based on UNCTAD (2022).

Figure 1.16: Africa's services exports over time, 2005–2020

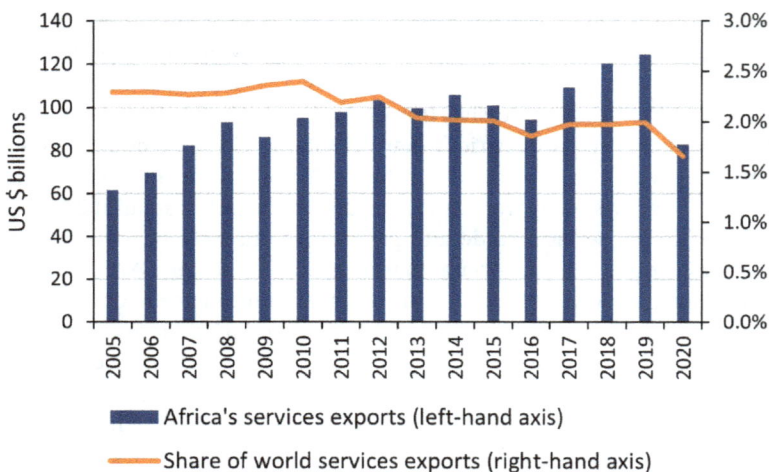

Source: Authors' calculations based on UNCTAD (2022).

Figure 1.17: Composition of Africa's services exports, constant 2020 US$

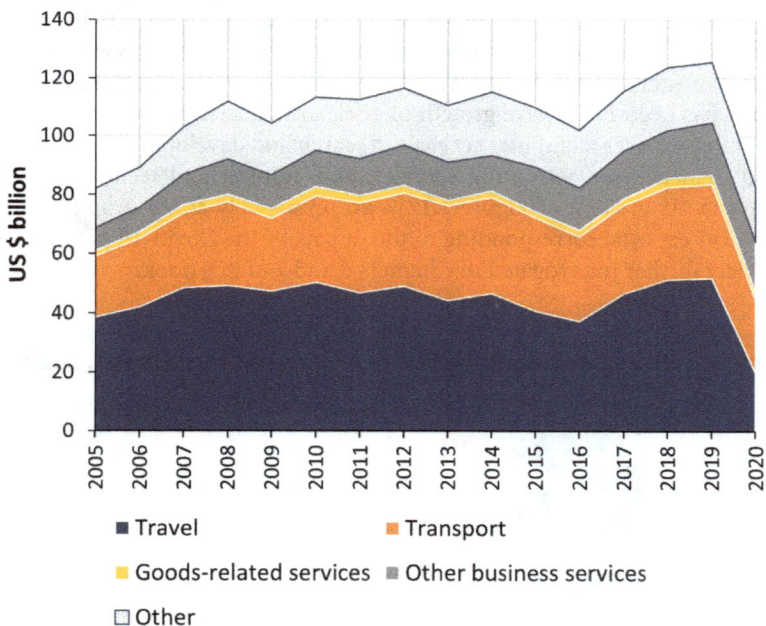

Source: Authors' calculations based on UNCTAD (2022).

1.6 Intra-African trade is different

The exact contours of Africa's exports differ depending on their destination. For Africa's exports to many of its larger and more developed markets, such as the EU, the US and the UK, exports are concentrated in fuels, followed by manufactures (Figure 1.18). Africa's exports to emerging market economies like China and India tend to be even more strongly concentrated in fuels, ores and metals, with these products collectively accounting for 87 per cent of African exports to China between 2016 and 2020, for instance. Yet the demarcations are not always clear-cut and vary considerably when considering several smaller export destinations. Canada, Korea and Japan, although in the 'most developed' bracket of export destinations, import mostly fuels, ores and metals from Africa. Similarly, the share of manufactures is relatively high in African exports to several emerging market economies, such as Turkey and Brazil. To large fuel exporters, such as countries of the Middle East and Russia, Africa exports few fuels.

Intra-African trade is different, however. Within the continent, manufactures are the largest type of export – accounting for 45 per cent of all formal intra-African trade. Foodstuff exports are also more significant, amounting to a fifth of trade between African countries. These 'formal' figures furthermore miss much African trade that flows across contiguous borders informally and unrecorded. Recent estimates are that such informal trade flows account for the equivalent of between 7 and 16 per cent of formal intra-African trade flows (ECA 2021). Much of that comprises foods and basic consumer goods. It is for this reason that intra-African trade is so interesting for African trade policymakers. If initiatives like the African Continental Free Trade Area (AfCFTA) can be used to boost intra-African trade, and even encourage the formalisation of informal trade between African countries, then it can contribute to Africa's sustainable economic transformation better than Africa's prevailing trade flows can.

1.7 Analytical perspective for understanding trade policy in Africa

The chapters that follow assess new developments in African trade policy. It is these trade policies that would seek to improve the trade flows so far discussed so that they might better contribute to sustainable economic development. They aspire to bring out insights and information that would be less accessible from only publicly available sources, while casting an analytical lens on these developments to identify political economy and strategic considerations. In so doing, it gives special attention to developments in trade policy instigated or catalysed by the emergence of, and reactions to, Covid-19. If this book were a camera, it would begin with a zoom lens, focusing in on regional topics close to home, including the status of the AfCFTA and

Figure 1.18: Composition of Africa's exports, by destination, five-year average (2016–2020)

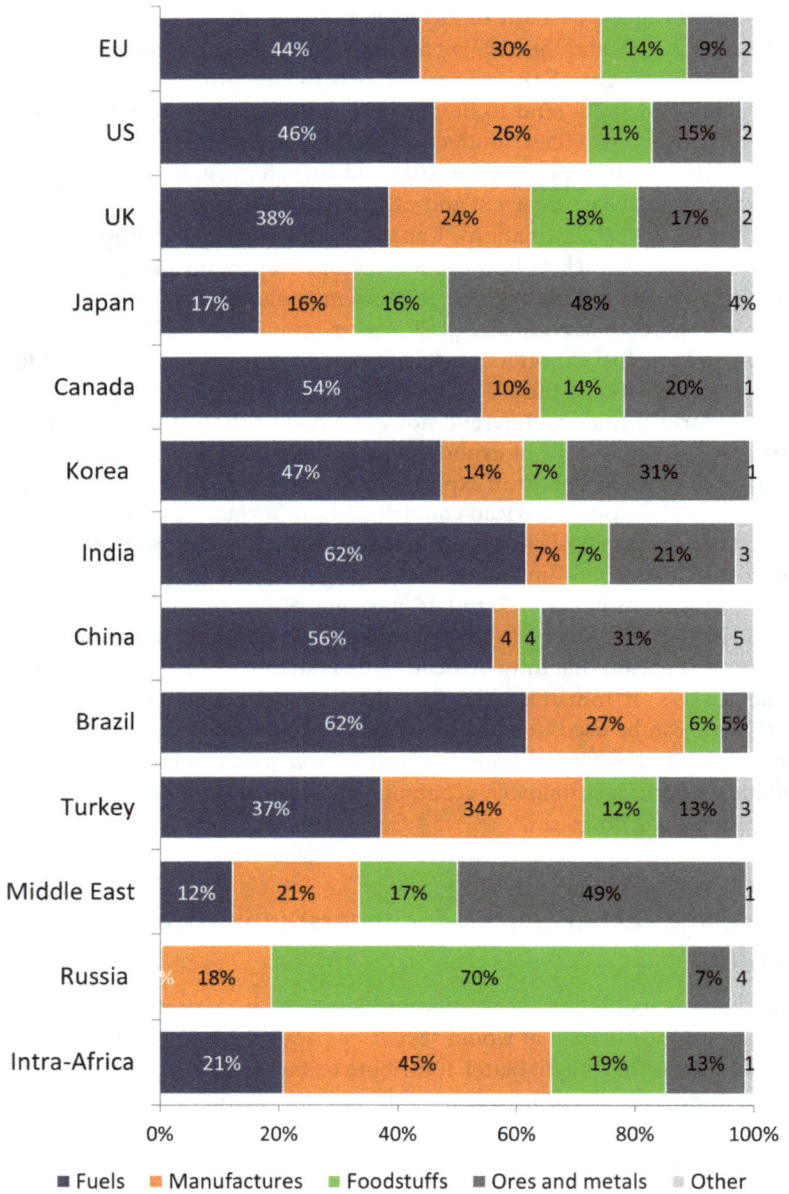

Destination	Fuels	Manufactures	Foodstuffs	Ores and metals	Other
EU	44%	30%	14%	9%	2
US	46%	26%	11%	15%	2
UK	38%	24%	18%	17%	2
Japan	17%	16%	16%	48%	4%
Canada	54%	10%	14%	20%	1
Korea	47%	14%	7%	31%	1
India	62%	7%	7%	21%	3
China	56%	4	4	31%	5
Brazil	62%	27%	6%	5%	
Turkey	37%	34%	12%	13%	3
Middle East	12%	21%	17%	49%	1
Russia	%	18%	70%	7%	4
Intra-Africa	21%	45%	19%	13%	1

Source: UNCTAD (2022).[4]

Figure 1.19: Phases of the negotiations cycle within the context of trade policy

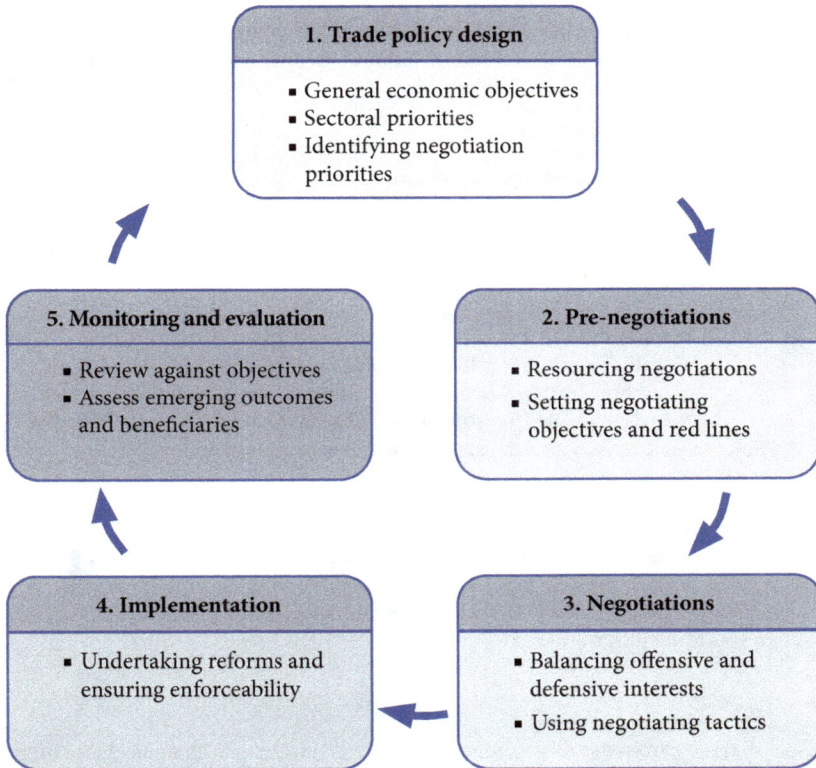

1. Trade policy design

- General economic objectives
- Sectoral priorities
- Identifying negotiation priorities

5. Monitoring and evaluation

- Review against objectives
- Assess emerging outcomes and beneficiaries

2. Pre-negotiations

- Resourcing negotiations
- Setting negotiating objectives and red lines

4. Implementation

- Undertaking reforms and ensuring enforceability

3. Negotiations

- Balancing offensive and defensive interests
- Using negotiating tactics

Source: Authors' elaboration.

trade policy developments within Africa's regional economic communities. It would then scan out to bilateral trade developments with a selection of significant African trading partners – the EU, China, the US and the UK. Finally, it would deploy a wide-angle lens to bring in developments in multilateral trade policy issues, and particularly developments at the World Trade Organization. Any photographer knows that it takes more than focus alone to produce a picture. At each level of focus, the book applies a deliberate analytical perspective to analyse key issues as they pertain to stages within the trade policy cycle (Figure 1.19). This perspective is less about theoretical approaches and more about agency and policy.

In many instances, African trade policy remains in the design phase – clarifying objectives and identifying priorities. This would include, for instance, efforts in coordinating African trade policy with respect to China. In more advanced areas, implementation or monitoring and evaluation are

Figure 1.20: Good governance principles for trade policymaking

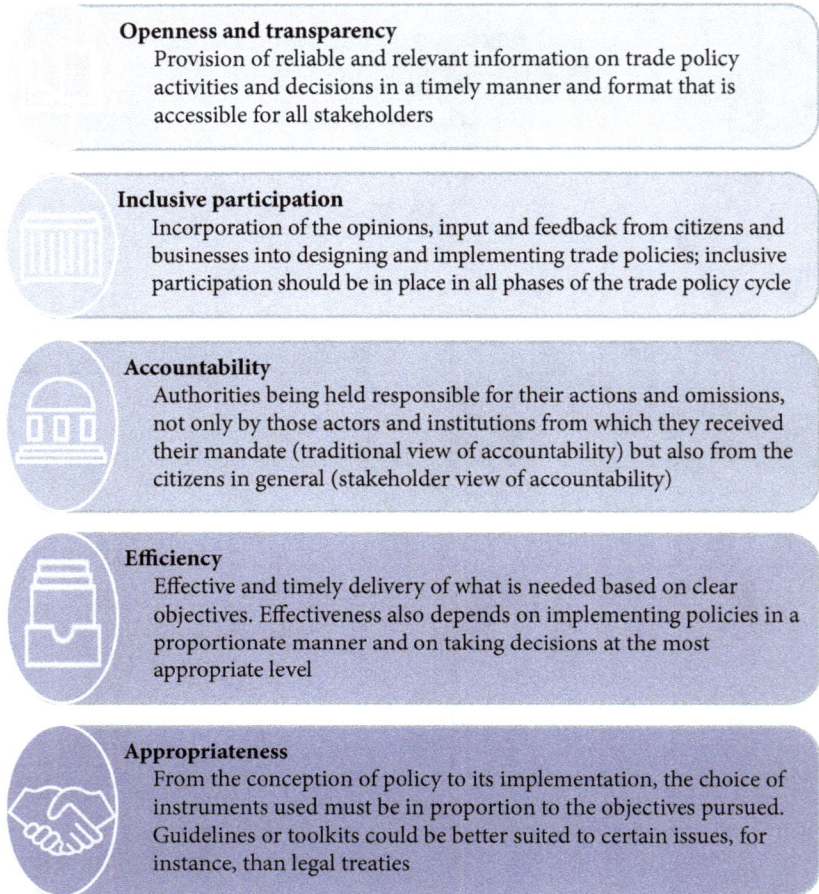

Openness and transparency
Provision of reliable and relevant information on trade policy
activities and decisions in a timely manner and format that is
accessible for all stakeholders

Inclusive participation
Incorporation of the opinions, input and feedback from citizens and
businesses into designing and implementing trade policies; inclusive
participation should be in place in all phases of the trade policy cycle

Accountability
Authorities being held responsible for their actions and omissions,
not only by those actors and institutions from which they received
their mandate (traditional view of accountability) but also from the
citizens in general (stakeholder view of accountability)

Efficiency
Effective and timely delivery of what is needed based on clear
objectives. Effectiveness also depends on implementing policies in a
proportionate manner and on taking decisions at the most
appropriate level

Appropriateness
From the conception of policy to its implementation, the choice of
instruments used must be in proportion to the objectives pursued.
Guidelines or toolkits could be better suited to certain issues, for
instance, than legal treaties

Source: Based on De Lombaerde, Estevadeordal and Suominen (2008).[5]

the issues of significance. As discussed in following chapters, a topic like the AfCFTA finds itself in limbo between the negotiations and implementation phases of the trade policy cycle. An appreciation of the phase within the trade policy cycle helps to concentrate analysis on the pressing issues at each stage, which can vary from aspirational vision setting and policy cohering to reflective evaluation and policy adjustments.

In unpacking how Africa trades, this book aims to go beyond merely describing African trade policy, however; it aspires to provide a normative assessment in relation to pro-development and equitable outcomes. Figure 1.20 outlines the evaluative standards against which African trade policy is considered. These are the principles that can best help guide trade policymaking towards sustainable and inclusive development outcomes while identifying red flags. To begin with, the trade policymaking process must be open and transparent to allow stakeholders – such as businesses, civil society organisations, researchers and other areas of government – to understand the issues at stake and the decisions being made on their behalf. Inclusiveness ensures that, once they are aware of trade policy issues, the opinions of stakeholders are integrated into each phase of trade policy, while accountability anchors decisions made by authorities therein onto the interests of those stakeholders. Trade policy, and particularly trade negotiations, are prone to delays; efficiency demands promptness in achieving trade outcomes. Finally, the appropriateness of instruments used to realise trade policy is important. Badly chosen tools – such as a binding treaty when guidelines would have suited – can result in poorly performing trade policy outcomes.

Finally, the analytical perspective deployed in the book also strives to provide a performative assessment of African trade policy. Here the focus moves from the normative perspective of what *should* be the policy orientation to the effectiveness in *how* policy is delivered. Figure 1.21 provides a demonstrative array of stratagems that might be used in effectively delivering the negotiations part of trade policy. When African trade policy is performing well, it shapes and influences outcomes such as impactful decisions and treaties or, for that matter, deflects away from unhelpful trivialities and distractions. Doing so skilfully, however, requires considerable negotiating resources and capacities that are lacking in most least-developed and even developing countries. In practice, owing to their level of development and available resources, African countries can often find themselves on the back foot, fielding trade policy priorities advanced by other partners rather than articulating and achieving their own.

Figure 1.21: Negotiation stratagems for effective trade policy

1. *Organising to influence*: creating, staffing, funding, and directing institutions in ways that influence the trade negotiation process.
2. *Selecting the forum*: identifying the most promising forum in which to pursue one's objectives and then ensuring that negotiation take place there.
3. *Shaping the agenda*: adding or removing issues from the agenda, dividing the larger agenda into modules for parallel negotiations, and establishing some high-level principles to govern the process.
4. *Building coalitions*: identifying potential winning and blocking coalitions and then devising plans for building supportive coalitions and breaking or forestalling opposing ones.
5. *Leveraging linkages*: linking and de-linking issues or sets of negotiations to create and claim value.
6. *Playing the frame game*: crafting and promulgating a favourable framing of 'the problem' and 'the options'.
7. *Creating momentum*: channelling the flow of the negotiation process in promising directions by establishing appropriate stages to demarcate the process, as well as by instigating or taking advantage of action-forcing events.

Source: Devereau, Lawrence and Watkins (2006).

Summary

Though trade can be a powerful economic tool, it underperforms in the African continent in contributing to development. Africa's share of world trade continues to be undersized, despite growing in recent years. It critically remains concentrated in the primary sectors, and particularly fuels, and as such struggles to contribute to structural transformation and sustainable development in the continent. This scenario is mirrored by foreign direct investments into Africa, which are similarly undersized and concentrated in the mining and fuel industries. African trade flows must change, and it is trade policy that can be the instrument of this change. This chapter concluded by introducing the analytical perspective for trade policy analysis used throughout the rest of the book to identify what is working, and what is not, in African trade policy. By better understanding African trade policy, its interactions with the policies of trading partners, and its successes and failures, we hope to lead to improvements in it to better service African development.

Notes

[1] FDI inflow data is available, and so presented, only from 1970 and remittance data from 1980.

[2] Foodstuffs is SITC 0 + 1 + 22 + 4, ores and metals is SITC 27 + 28 + 68 + 667 + 971, manufactures is SITC 5 to 8 less 667 and 68, and fuels is SITC 3.

[3] Foodstuffs is SITC 0 + 1 + 22 + 4, ores and metals is SITC 27 + 28 + 68 + 667 + 971, manufactures is SITC 5 to 8 less 667 and 68, and fuels is SITC 3.

[4] Foodstuffs is SITC 0 + 1 + 22 + 4, ores and metals is SITC 27 + 28 + 68 + 667 + 971, manufactures is SITC 5 to 8 less 667 and 68, and fuels is SITC 3.

[5] As cited in Gerout (2022).

References

Bureau of Economic Analysis US Department of Commerce (2022) 'U.S. Direct Investment Abroad: Balance of Payments and Direct Investment Position Data'. https://perma.cc/T5QK-Y42E

De Lombaerde, Philippe; Estevadeordal, Antoni; and Suominen, Kati (2008) *Governing Regional Integration for Development*, London: Routledge.

Devereau, Charan; Lawrence, Robert; and Watkins, Michael (2006) 'Negotiating Trade Agreements', in *Case Studies in US Trade Negotiations: Making the Rules*, Institute for International Economics. https://perma.cc/2R67-N2JJ

ECA (2015) *Illicit Financial Flows: Report of the High Level Panel on Illicit Financial Flows from Africa*, Addis Ababa: ECA Publications. https://perma.cc/R38E-9NDZ

ECA (2021) 'Assessing Regional Integration in Africa X: Africa's Services Trade Liberalization & Integration under the AfCFTA', Addis Ababa: Economic Commission for Africa. https://perma.cc/MVE4-V7KY

Eurostat (2022) 'European Union direct investments (BPM6)'. https://ec.europa.eu/eurostat/web/economic-globalisation/globalisation -in-business-statistics/foreign-direct-investments

Gbadamosi, Nosmot (2022) 'Can African Oil and Gas Replace Russia's?', *Foreign Policy*, 16 March. https://perma.cc/NG78-9JF3

Gerout, G. (2022) *Negotiating Institutions: Putting in the Right Foundations*, Addis Ababa: Economic Commission for Africa Publications.

IMF (2022) 'Direction of Trade Statistics'. https://perma.cc/ZNL3-PSWX

Keppel, Robert (2021) 'Africa's Employment Challenges: The Ever-Widening Gaps', Friedrich Ebert Stiftung, 9 September. https://perma.cc/4NF2-6GZZ

Knomad (2022) 'Remittances Data'. https://perma.cc/V2J9-4B22

Luke, David (2020) 'Why Trade Matters for African Development', Africa at LSE, 27 July. https://perma.cc/H3ZX-NSMV

OECD DAC-ODA (2022) 'Development Finance Data'. https://perma.cc/G6Y9-FN5N

UNCTAD (2022) 'UNCTAD Statistics'. https://perma.cc/R6RN-JT9R

United Nations University – Institute for Natural Resources in Africa (2019) 'Africa's Development in the Age of Stranded Assets', Discussion Paper. https://perma.cc/N9F2-WCBC

Yu, Shirley (2021) 'Why Substantial Chinese FDI Is Flowing into Africa', Africa at LSE, 2 April. https://perma.cc/2EHF-VNCA

2. The AfCFTA and regional trade

Jamie MacLeod, David Luke and Geoffroy Guepie

Trade is central to Africa's development but it underperforms, mainly because of what Africa trades and the inherent limitations of commodity concentration. However, in the relative diversification of intra-African trade can be found some promising green shoots that point to a viable route for realising Africa's aspirations towards industrialisation and economic transformation. Trade policy has been described as the principal driver of the vehicle that can be used to travel along this route. Africa's regional economic communities (RECs) are the uncelebrated heroes of the effort to establish and utilise common arrangements for cross-border trade and related regional initiatives to overcome mutual supply-side constraints. Changing metaphors, if this book were a camera, it would employ its zoom lens to begin by focusing in on regional topics close to home, including the status of the African Continental Free Trade Area (AfCFTA) and the RECs before scanning out to consider other trade relationships. Accordingly, this chapter begins with a focus on the AfCFTA before turning the spotlight on the intriguing role of the RECs as enablers of Africa's integration, not only in relation to trade but through ambitious regional plans and policies that encompass energy, infrastructure, transport corridors and sectoral value chains.

2.1 Why has the AfCFTA assumed such importance in African trade policy?

The AfCFTA has succeeded in crafting an explanatory narrative that is strong and communicable. It can be seen repeatedly in the words chosen by heads of state, ministers and negotiators, and representatives of the African Union, whenever they speak on the subject. Rarely does such a speech fail to reference the size of the AfCFTA marketplace (around 1.3 billion people with a combined GDP of around $3 trillion, depending on sources). This is seen as a vehicle for 'creating a market large enough to attract investors from across the world' and reflecting the importance of 'industrial value in Africa', in the words of South African President Ramaphosa at the opening session of the 2021 Intra-Africa Trade Fair. 'A large part of the growth and prosperity that we seek on the continent will come from us trading more among ourselves', according to Ghana President Nana Akufo-Addo, in his address at the commissioning of the AfCFTA Secretariat in August 2020.

The policy rationale behind the AfCFTA project might be thought to have five core parts. The first of these is that the AfCFTA represents a large and attractive marketplace. Most individual African countries are small (Figure 2.1). Twenty-two have populations under 10 million and a further 22 have populations under 30 million. The annual GDP of the median African country is just $16 billion, roughly equivalent to the output of a British city like Bristol. To the extent that it reflects a consolidated market, the AfCFTA by comparison comprises 1.3 billion people and an annual output of $3 trillion, like India and equivalent to about the seventh or eighth largest economy in the world. The enormous size of the collective African market is seen to be valuable in attracting investors and achieving competitive economies of scale. While large today, what is perhaps more enticing is how the African marketplace is expected to grow further. This is the second part of the rationale. In his statement at the July 2019 summit of the AU, which launched the operational phase of the AfCFTA, AU Commission Chairperson Moussa Faki Mahamat reminded heads of state that 'the growth of the African economy should be twice as fast as that of the developed world'. Ten of the top 20 fasting growing economies are expected to be African in 2023, according to IMF estimates as of April 2022. Over the longer term, the African population is expected to grow to 2.75 billion by 2060, with an increasing middle-class market and a combined annual output of $16 trillion (Figure 2.2).

The third part of the AfCFTA rationale is its perceived potential to contribute to the long-overdue industrialisation and economic diversification of African countries. Many economic policymakers see manufacturing-based industrialisation as a critical step in their countries' development, and as a means of reducing their dependencies on primary commodities. Yet trade outside the continent – dominated by primary products like fuels and metals – has struggled to drive such industrialisation. Conversely, the intra-African trade that would be stimulated by the AfCFTA is seen as a more conducive vehicle for industrialisation. It comprises a far greater share of manufactures, as well as agricultural goods (Figure 2.3), and embodies a higher technology content (Saygili, Peters and Knebel 2018). While only 20 per cent of Africa's exports outside the continent are manufactured goods, 45 per cent of trade within the continent, between African countries, comprise manufactured goods.

Attempts to model the expected impact of the AfCFTA by the World Bank (2020), IMF (Abrego 2019), UNECA (2021) and UNCTAD (2017) all expect Africa's manufacturing sector to be a major beneficiary. The World Bank (2020) estimated manufacturing output to rise by $56 billion, compared to a $17 billion increase for the natural resources sector (though less than an anticipated $147 billion increase in services). The IMF (2019) forecast that '60 percent of the increase in overall income comes from higher manufacturing

Figure 2.1: A giant fragmented market: African countries by population

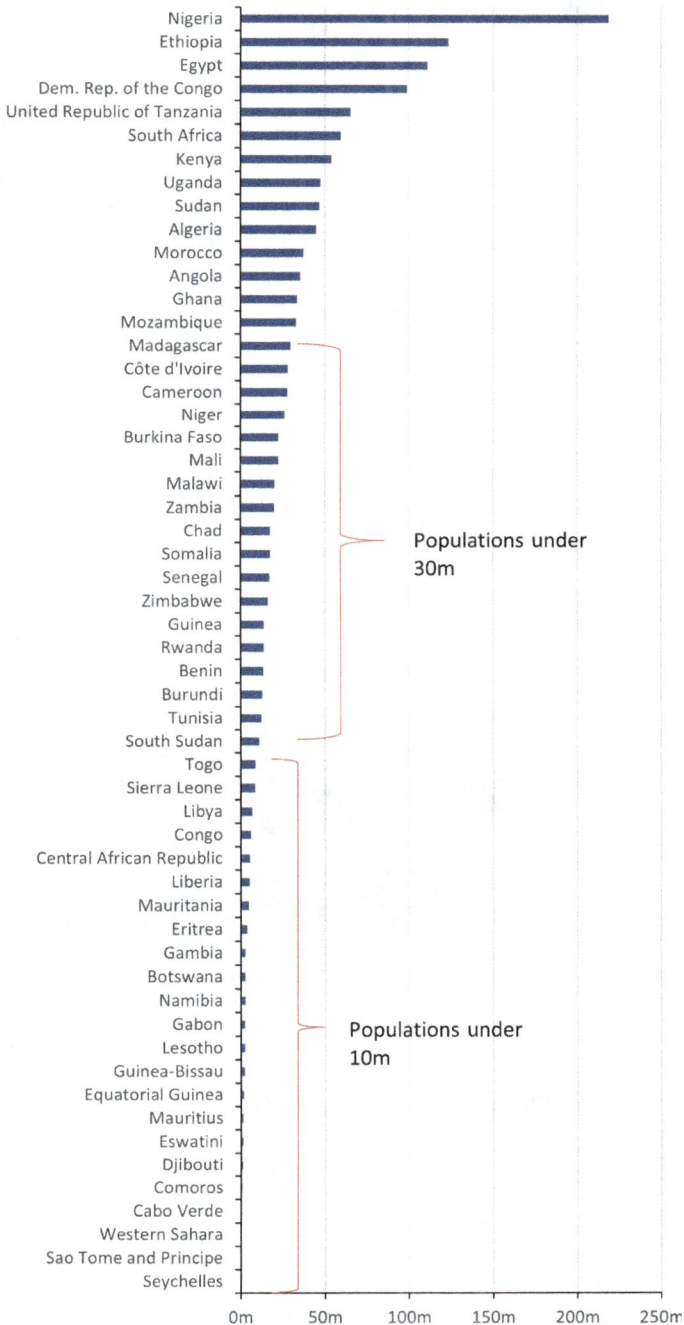

Source: Authors' calculations based on UN Department of Economics and Social Affairs (2019).

Figure 2.2: A growing, and maturing, market: African population and middle-class share, 2000–2060

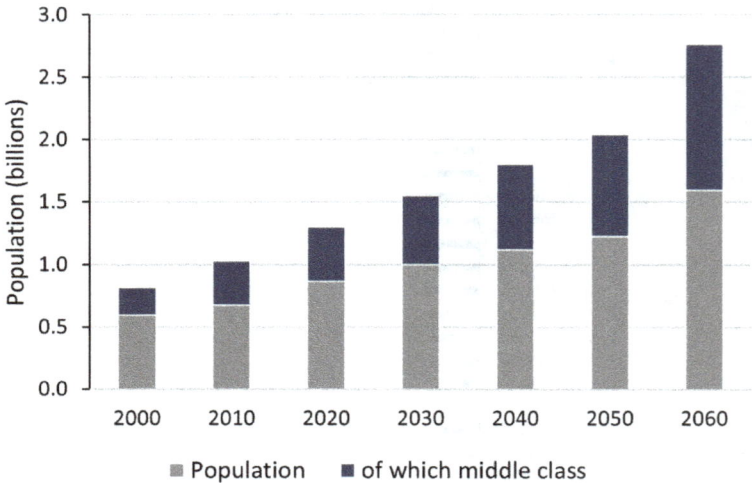

Source: AfDB (2011).

Figure 2.3: Exports within the continent are more conducive to development: intra- and extra-African exports, composition, 2018–2020

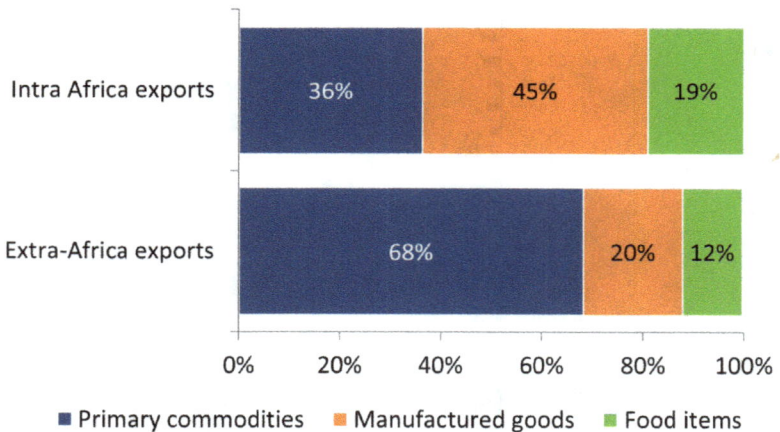

Source: Authors' calculations based on UNCTAD (2022).[1]

output'. The Economic Commission for Africa (ECA 2021) found that 'approximately two-thirds of the intra-African trade gains would be realized in the manufacturing sector' (Figure 2.4), while UNCTAD (2017) reported that 'the largest employment growth rates are found in manufacturing industry'. This is a significant finding in view of the demographic pressure for jobs.

Figure 2.4: Industry to gain most: distribution of absolute gains in intra-African trade, by main sectors, with AfCFTA, implemented as compared to baseline (i.e. without AfCFTA) – US$ billions and % – 2045

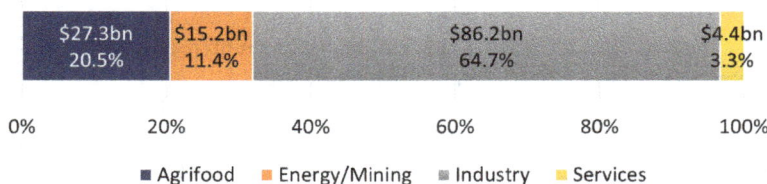

$27.3bn 20.5%	$15.2bn 11.4%	$86.2bn 64.7%	$4.4bn 3.3%

0%	20%	40%	60%	80%	100%

■ Agrifood   ■ Energy/Mining   ▪ Industry   ■ Services

Source: ECA and the Centre for International Research and Economic Modelling (CIREM) of the Centre d'Etudes Prospectives et d'Information Internationales (CEPII) calculations based on MIRAGE CGE model, as cited in ECA (2021).[2]

Table 2.1: The importance of looking beyond tariffs: AfCFTA benefits by impact channels in different models (percentages)

	World Bank (real income)	IMF (welfare)
Tariffs	0.22%	0.07%
Tariffs + NTBs	2.4%	2.6%
Tariffs + NTBs + trade facilitation	7%	

Source: Extracted from World Bank (2020) and IMF (2019).

The fourth part of the rationale for the AfCFTA speaks to its form. The AfCFTA is a deep trade agreement, extending beyond merely tariff reductions that might amount to a traditional free trade agreement. Instead, the AfCFTA includes provisions on trade facilitation, non-tariff barriers, trade in services, and behind-the-border regulatory issues such as competition policy, investment and intellectual property rights.

While the average tariff encountered on intra-African exports amounts to about 6.1 per cent, the ad valorem equivalent for non-tariff barriers is much larger, at an estimated 14.3 per cent (ECA, UNCTAD, AUC and AfDB 2019). It is unsurprising, therefore, that most of the models that estimate the impact of the AfCFTA attribute relatively more importance to trade facilitation and addressing non-tariff barriers than to tariff reductions. The World Bank (2020) expects the combined effect of a reduction in tariffs and non-tariff barriers to amount to more than 10 times the increase in real income that would be expected by a reduction in tariffs alone. Approaching the question in a different way methodologically, the IMF (2019) estimates the effect of reducing tariffs and non-tariff barriers to be 37 times the increase in welfare that would result from a reduction in tariffs alone (Table 2.1). Not all aspects of the AfCFTA can be easily or reliably modelled. Yet, as the modelled estimates suggest, the agreement is about far more than a reduction in tariffs. While some of the issues that extend beyond tariffs may take longer to negotiate and implement, dealing with them amounts to core parts of the AfCFTA offering.

The fifth and final part of the rationale for the AfCFTA is that it can be a tool for cohering Africa trade policy. As the economic significance of the African continent has grown, third parties have increasingly looked to formalise their economic engagements with African countries through trade and other arrangements. Notable examples include the EU's economic partnership agreements, the United States' bilateral negotiations with Kenya, and a free trade agreement between Mauritius and China and Mauritius and India. To use the language of the AU's Agenda 2063, in pursuit of 'the Africa we want', it is argued that Africa can achieve more if it will 'speak with one voice and act collectively to promote our common interests and positions in the international arena'. With a single voice, Africa has the economic heft and pooled technical capacities to negotiate trade deals better than individual countries alone can. An example can be drawn from the ASEAN group of 10 Southeast Asian countries. As a group, it found itself more attractive to partners seeking trade agreements, providing the impetus for negotiating various ASEAN+1 agreements (Mikic and Shang 2019). The consolidated economic size of a country grouping in negotiations makes it more attractive to partners, giving it clout with which to press for more preferential negotiated outcomes.

AfCFTA: failure to launch?

For several years since its inception in 2018, AfCFTA has been stuck somewhat between the 'negotiations' and 'implementation' phases of the trade policy cycle (Figure 2.5). At several points, AU summits have celebrated the *near* completion of the AfCFTA, yet effective implementation has been elusive. In March 2018, African leaders from 44 countries signed the Agreement Establishing the African Continental Free Trade Area and declared the 'launch' of the AfCFTA at the 10th Extraordinary Session of the AU Summit. In May 2019, the threshold of 22 depositions of ratification of the AfCFTA was reached, allowing the agreement to 'enter into force', followed by a 12th Extraordinary Session of the AU Summit, which launched the 'operational phase' of the AfCFTA in July 2019, while a 13th Extraordinary Session held virtually in Johannesburg in December 2020 announced that the 'commencement of trading' under the AfCFTA would start in January 2021.

Despite a small number of publicity consignments aligned with the formal commencement of trading (Kwofi 2021), trade under the AfCFTA has yet to start substantively (as of early 2023). Negotiators repeatedly failed to keep apace, and live up to, the timelines aspired to by their leaders. The culprit blocking the finalisation of the negotiations, and the effective commencement of trading under the AfCFTA, has been the long-delayed conclusion of a small number of vital technical components of the agreement. The main blockage has been the rules of origin. In the March 2018 summit that launched the AfCFTA, a deadline was given to conclude the remaining unfinished rules of

Figure 2.5: Missed deadlines: is the AfCFTA stuck between negotiations and implementation?

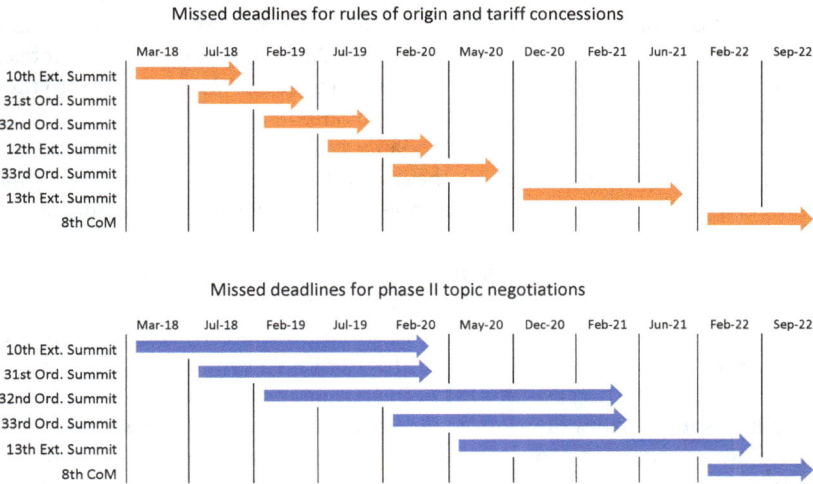

Missed deadlines for rules of origin and tariff concessions

	Mar-18	Jul-18	Feb-19	Jul-19	Feb-20	May-20	Dec-20	Feb-21	Jun-21	Feb-22	Sep-22
10th Ext. Summit											
31st Ord. Summit											
32nd Ord. Summit											
12th Ext. Summit											
33rd Ord. Summit											
13th Ext. Summit											
8th CoM											

Missed deadlines for phase II topic negotiations

	Mar-18	Jul-18	Feb-19	Jul-19	Feb-20	May-20	Dec-20	Feb-21	Jun-21	Feb-22	Sep-22
10th Ext. Summit											
31st Ord. Summit											
32nd Ord. Summit											
33rd Ord. Summit											
13th Ext. Summit											
8th CoM											

origin within a 'built-in agenda' by the next AU summit in July 2018. Consecutive AU summits granted six-month extensions to this deadline (or those for the submission of tariff schedules of concessions that depended upon the rules of origin) until May 2020, at which point the focus of the continent was on Covid-19. The December 2020 summit, which announced the commencement of trading under the AfCFTA, further reissued another six-month deadline for the finalisation of the rules of origin by May 2021, which was again missed. In February 2022, the AfCFTA Council of Ministers granted another deadline extension – the seventh in four years – until September 2022 for the conclusion of the rules of origin.

Given the persistence of delays to finalise the remaining rules of origin, efforts have been made to circumvent them. The December 2020 AU summit, which intended to launch the start of trading under the AfCFTA, aimed to do so based on only the 'agreed rules of origin' at the time, which amounted to around 81 per cent of tariff lines. The February 2022 AU summit reiterated that decision, endorsing the 'Provisional Application of Rules of Origin'. But this circumvention approach – to move ahead with implementation with incomplete rules of origin – makes it difficult for countries to submit tariff offers that comply fully with the modalities for tariff liberalisation that require countries to liberalise 90 per cent of tariff lines. Negotiators are hesitant to submit schedules for tariff lines for which they do not yet know the rules of origin that will govern all the products covered by those offers.

It is mainly for this reason that only 29 countries, as of December 2022, had been able to submit tariff offers that complied fully with the modalities for tariff liberalisation. The relatively low number of tariff offers implied that many countries had been hesitant to commit fully in the absence of clarity on what the rules of origin would entail for the remaining products. In turn, the 29 countries that had submitted compliant tariff offers at that point were hesitant to progress towards the implementation of those offers until they were matched by the remaining countries. At least some of the countries that were yet to ratify the AfCFTA Agreement were hesitant to do so until they knew the concluded rules of origin. As policy attention remained on these technical components of the phase I negotiations, the focus shifted during 2022 to the phase II negotiating issues. By the end of the year, protocols on intellectual property rights, investment and competition policy were in the final stages of completion.

Why have these rules of origin issues proven so problematic to conclude? The breadth of pre-existing rules of origin governing intra-African trade within different regional economic communities already varied considerably prior to the commencement of the AfCFTA negotiations, indicating a divergence in 'starting positions'. In 2018, negotiators also opted to negotiate product-specific rules of origin rather than general ones. Such specific rules were always going to prove more 'time consuming to negotiate, potentially adding several years to the time taken to negotiate the [Af]CFTA]' (ECA, AUC and AfDB 2017). Negotiators also decided against the approach of using 'temporary' general rules of origin until more detailed product-specific rules could be determined, as would have followed the approach used in the negotiations for the Greater Arab Free Trade Area that involved several North African countries that were also negotiating the AfCFTA. In theory, 'hybrid' transitional rules of origin were permitted in the language of the agreement (Protocol on Trade in Goods, Annex II, Article 42I), though they were never substantively operationalised in practice.

Negotiators knew of the complexity and time-consuming process required to negotiate product-specific rules of origin. They would also have been aware that such rules can be more protective and complex to implement. Many would have decided that these costs were outweighed by the opportunity for greater nuance in designing rules that would cover particularly sensitive products. In many instances, we can identify exactly where these sensitivities have been by where the rules of origin negotiations have dragged on longest. Negotiations have persisted over specific rules of origin for a notably small number of highly sensitive sectors, including textiles and apparel, automobiles, sugar and edible oils. Tariffs on these products tend to be higher (Gourdon et al 2021), meaning that there is more that negotiators may be sensitive about protecting. Even with product-specific rules of origin, the sensitivity of these sectors has made compromise difficult. Negotiators, struggling to make concessions in these areas, have instead erred towards brinkmanship – holding fast to entrenched positions. Yet the risk of this approach, as shown in Figure 2.5, has been continual slippages in implementation, and the erosion of the momentum behind the AfCFTA.

Unlocking regional leadership could offer a solution. In their regional economic communities, economic powers such as Kenya and South Africa liberalised more rapidly or fully than their neighbours, emphasising their leadership roles and corresponding responsibilities. For instance, Kenya immediately allowed duty-free imports into its market from its neighbours when the East African Community customs union was established in 2005, while permitting its own exports to be progressively liberalised over a longer five-year period. If Africa's regional powers could again show greater leadership, creativity and ultimately compromise in realising the start of trade under the AfCFTA, it could help to generate the momentum needed to get trade flowing across and transforming the continent.

Eventually, even once the rules of origin and the tariff schedules are concluded, countries will also need to take practical steps to put the agreement into operation within their customs administrations, including through the gazetting of new tariff structures, notification of specimen stamps and signatures, and in some instances training for customs officers. The AfCFTA Secretariat is aware of the gatekeeper role played by Africa's customs administrations and has hosted several meetings of the heads of customs authorities across the state parties to the AfCFTA. These have sought to identify bottlenecks and solutions to the practical start of trading under the AfCFTA. The World Customs Organization was supporting through the provision of technical support for the digitalisation of the new AfCFTA tariff schedules to enhance transparency and the accessibility of economic operators.

Agenda-shifting to create pockets of progress

In lieu of progress in concluding the remaining technical aspects of the AfCFTA negotiations, a well of pressure has spilled over into other areas where advancements with the AfCFTA can be made. First, attention has turned to institution-building. Principally, this has included the establishment of the AfCFTA Secretariat as the central institution driving the AfCFTA, as envisaged by Article 13 of the Agreement Establishing the AfCFTA. In February 2020, Wamkele Mene, the former chief AfCFTA negotiator of South Africa, was appointed as the secretary-general of the AfCFTA Secretariat by the 33rd Ordinary Session of the Assembly of the Heads of States and Government of the African Union. The AfCFTA Secretariat building was officially opened in Accra, Ghana, in August 2020. As of early 2022, reportedly 60 per cent of the 31 positions comprising the first phase of recruitments at the AfCFTA Secretariat had been filled. A second phase of recruitment aims to bring the staff complement of the Secretariat to 296 at an estimated staff annual cost of $29 million.

Institution-building has also entailed the creation of a committee structure for implementation – and continued negotiations, where relevant. Each protocol under the AfCFTA has had a committee established for it. There is, for instance, a committee for trade in goods and for trade in services. Under each committee have been established sub-committees governing the annexes of the protocols. Under the committee on trade in goods, sub-committees exist covering trade facilitation, customs cooperation, trade transit, non-tariff barriers, technical barriers to trade and rules of origin. Typically, such sub-committees identify work programmes to implement the commitments relevant to them under the AfCFTA. The sub-committee on non-tariff barriers, for instance, has set out a work programme involving capacity-building, promotion of the online non-tariff barrier mechanism, and facilitation of the resolution of reported non-tariff barriers.

One area of AfCFTA institution-building to have received a large amount of effort has been the creation of the AfCFTA dispute settlement body. Five meetings of the dispute settlement body were held between April 2021 and February 2022. For comparison, in this period, the committee on trade in goods met just four times. These dispute settlement committee meetings focused on constituting the dispute settlement mechanism and its Appellate Body. This would suggest that there is an appetite from negotiators to establish the AfCFTA as a relatively strict rules-based system, in contrast to experiences at the regional level that have often involved more ad hoc derogations and dispensations negotiated between ministers (ECA, AUC and AfDB 2017).

The second area of agenda-shifting has been in the creation of new areas of the negotiations. There are two major new areas of the negotiations that were not previously envisaged at the launch of the AfCFTA negotiations. The first of these followed the decision by the AU heads of state and government at their assembly in February 2020 to create a mandate for negotiations on e-commerce. A subsequent decision in January 2021 endorsed the (missed) deadline of December 2021 for the conclusion of those negotiations, effectively bringing the negotiations on e-commerce alongside the timeline for the other phase II negotiations on competition policy, intellectual property rights and investment. In April 2021, the AfCFTA Secretariat announced it was considering a further additional protocol under the AfCFTA on women and youth. A committee on women and youth was established to drive these negotiations in June 2021 before the February 2022 summit formally decided to adopt such a protocol within the scope of the AfCFTA.

Notable by their absence have been efforts to include equivalent areas of negotiations on trade and the environment or labour within the AfCFTA. The AfCFTA still retains only minimal references to the environment (van der Ven and Signe 2021), being overshadowed by significant trade policy momentum in this area in the multilateral arena, in which progress is being on topics such as plastics pollution and the Trade and Environmental Sustainability Structured Discussions. Labour remains a further area untouched by negotiators (beyond the agreement preamble) (MacLeod 2022). Despite the importance of agriculture for the continent, the agreement contains no specific provisions on this critical sector.

The third area of agenda-shifting has been the creation of new instruments in the wider AfCFTA orbit (Figure 2.6). What might be considered the 'first set' of these were the 'operational instruments' promoted by the AU in the launch of the 'operational phase' of the AfCFTA at the summit of July 2019.

Figure 2.6: AfCFTA ecosystem of projects, programmes and activities

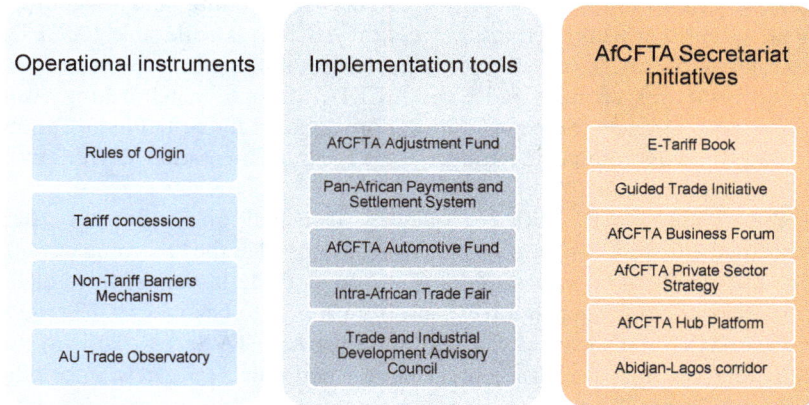

Operational instruments	Implementation tools	AfCFTA Secretariat initiatives
Rules of Origin	AfCFTA Adjustment Fund	E-Tariff Book
	Pan-African Payments and Settlement System	Guided Trade Initiative
Tariff concessions		AfCFTA Business Forum
	AfCFTA Automotive Fund	AfCFTA Private Sector Strategy
Non-Tariff Barriers Mechanism	Intra-African Trade Fair	AfCFTA Hub Platform
AU Trade Observatory	Trade and Industrial Development Advisory Council	Abidjan-Lagos corridor

Source: Elaboration based on Assembly Decision Assembly Decision Assembly/ AU/4(XXXIII) of 10 February 2020, Assembly/AU/Dec. 831(XXXV) of 6 February 2022, and the AU-AfCFTA website.[3]

These include the AU Trade Observatory (ATO) and the Pan-African Payment Settlement System (PAPSS). A beta version of the ATO was made operational in December 2020, while the PAPSS was commercially launched in January 2022.

This wider orbit of tools was expanded in the February 2022 AU summit with the 'AfCFTA Implementation Tools', which additionally include an AfCFTA Adjustment Facility, AfCFTA Automotive Fund, Intra-African Trade Fair, and Trade and Industrial Development Advisory Council. The AfCFTA Adjustment Facility, designed and financed by the African Export–Import Bank (Afreximbank), was launched in February 2022 to help countries to implement the AfCFTA and adjust to trade under it. The AfCFTA Automotive Fund, which was originally proposed to unlock concessions in the negotiations for rules of origin for automobiles, involves an Afreximbank-sponsored $1 billion sector-specific fund. The Intra-African Trade Fair, in its third iteration, has established a business trade show platform. The Trade and Industrial Development Advisory Council provides technical advice to the AfCFTA Secretariat.

The AfCFTA Secretariat itself also manages its own growing set of projects and initiatives. These include an E-Tariff Book, showing verified tariffs for products under the AfCFTA, an AfCFTA Business Forum, an AfCFTA Private Sector Strategy, an AfCFTA Hub Platform, and efforts to support trade specifically on the Lagos–Abidjan corridor. The most notable addition to the AfCFTA Secretariat's toolkit of initiatives was the Guided Trade Initiative, announced by the AfCFTA Secretariat in July 2022. Covering Ghana, Kenya, Cameroon, Tanzania, Mauritius, Rwanda, Tunisia and Egypt, and notably no Southern African countries, it seeks to provide hands-on support to businesses to get trade flowing under the AfCFTA. Its stated objectives include 'demonstrat[ing] that the AfCFTA is functioning' and to 'giv[ing] hope to the continent that trading under the AfCFTA is achievable' (AfCFTA Secretariat 2022a). It amounts to a deliberate 'solutions-based approach' to unblock the lack of trade under the AfCFTA through 'matchmaking businesses and products for export and import between interested State Parties in coordination with their national AfCFTA Implementation Committees' (AfCFTA Secretariat 2022b).

The Guided Trade Initiative officially launched on 7 October 2022 (though the first consignments under it were shipped in the preceding weeks). The first goods to be traded under the Guided Trade Initiative were coffee, from Rwanda to Ghana, and batteries, from Kenya to Ghana (AfCFTA Secretariat 2022b). The expressed intention of the AfCFTA Secretariat with the Guided Trade Initiative has been to 'prompt' and provide a 'gateway' for official trade under the AfCFTA using the formal AfCFTA trading documents, such as certificates of origin and import–export declaration forms (AfCFTA Secretariat 2022b). It also aims to be a learning device for 'feedback on the effectiveness of the legal and institutional national systems in the participating countries', to 'test the readiness of the private sector to participate in trade under the AfCFTA' and to 'identify possible future interventions' (AfCFTA Secretariat 2022c).

Principally the initiative helps to show that (at least some heavily assisted) trade can begin to flow in some form under the AfCFTA. In the words of the AfCFTA Secretariat, 'the Guided Trade Initiative has proven that AfCFTA is truly operational' (AfCFTA Secretariat 2022c). Yet the Guided Trade Initiative is not the AfCFTA regime provided for in the AfCFTA Agreement (Tralac 2022). The AfCFTA cannot substantively operate at scale until the remaining technical parts of the agreement are concluded (Tralac 2022).

The negotiations on the remaining technical aspects of the AfCFTA phase I negotiations must be finished for substantial volumes of trade to flow under the AfCFTA, and for it to contribute to transformative development. The Guided Trade Initiative can benefit by providing a 'demonstrative effect' to show that the AfCFTA can work that there is appetite for trade under it. It can also help to take pressure away from negotiators and the AfCFTA Secretariat in the slightly embarrassing situation in which heads of state had announced the commencement of trade under the AfCFTA on 1 January 2021, only for that trade not to flow. Care should be taken, however, that, by giving negotiators space to breathe, the Guided Trade Initiative does not allow them to further procrastinate. Care must also be taken to ensure that the Guided Trade Initiative does not become the new reality for continent-wide trade in goods in place of the more substantial actual AfCFTA regime (Tralac 2022).

Beyond these initiatives launched at AU summits, the AfCFTA continues to be the centre of an expanding range of other complementary initiatives. An African Collaborative Transit Guarantee Scheme was launched by Afreximbank in March 2021 to help mitigate cross-border transport frictions. The

AfCFTA Secretariat has been involved in a consultative study of the Lagos–Abidjan corridor, with a view towards improving border management and logistics along this important West African artery. The range of initiatives now included under the umbrella of the AfCFTA suggests a growing understanding of the AfCFTA not merely as a traditional trade agreement but as an ecosystem of programmes and activities to support trade in Africa. The necessity for this is long understood. The decision by the 18th Ordinary Session of the AU Assembly in January 2012 to endorse the establishment of the AfCFTA, effectively launching the negotiations for the AfCFTA, was made within a broader decision that endorsed the Boosting Intra-African Trade (BIAT) Action Plan. Though the BIAT has achieved less attention, the approach to the AfCFTA has entailed a broader ecosystem of trade support.

Partners' role in getting the AfCFTA going

Negotiations entail sensitivities over fundamental economic decisions that can make countries cautious about donor influence, and more hesitant towards support that might directly affect the negotiations. This is not unmerited: when donors offer bilateral 'capacity-building' workshops and training they often draw from the experiences and ideological approaches of their countries. Negotiators understand this and apportion caution and trust accordingly.

Policymakers have relied upon several 'trusted' technical institutions during the negotiations. In the June 2015 AU summit decision that launched the AfCFTA negotiations, African heads of state explicitly called for technical assistance and capacity-building from the Economic Commission for Africa (ECA), the African Development Bank (AfDB) and the African Export-Import Bank (Afreximbank). The ECA and AfDB were further included in the AfCFTA Continental Task Force, established by the first meeting of the African Ministers of Trade in May 2016 to support the AfCFTA through analysis, studies and preparatory documentation. In this role, these partners have been privileged with observer status within the AfCFTA negotiations and the responsibility to respond to specific requests from negotiators, including technical notes and presentations on issues within the negotiations. The AUC also signed a memorandum of understanding with the International Trade Centre on 15 July 2015 to provide a framework for cooperation on trade issues, though this was broader in scope than the AfCFTA (African Union 2015). It has been through these established international organisation relationships that donors have often sought to provide arms-length support to the AfCFTA. The European Commission, UK Aid, GIZ and Global Affairs Canada have each channelled considerable development assistance in support of the AfCFTA through these partners, as well as directly with the AUC.

The establishment of the AfCFTA Secretariat has shifted the focus of partners' attention as this new institution has sought to garner donor resources and cement its own relationships. In March 2021, the United Nations Development Programme (UNDP) and the AfCFTA Secretariat signed a new partnership to bring in UNDP expertise to support implementation of the AfCFTA (UNDP 2021). The AfCFTA Secretariat has since signed additional agreements with the UK on 16 September 2021, the China Ministry of Commerce on 25 October 2021, the African Regional Standards Organisation on 30 November 2021, the World Customs Organization on 22 February 2022, and the International Trade Centre on 25 May 2022. This expansion of formal partners with the AfCFTA Secretariat reflects growing trust in, and popularity of, the AfCFTA among donors and the organisations they work through. It is also demonstrative of a clear shift away from the AUC towards the AfCFTA Secretariat as the central node in the expanding AfCFTA-related universe of projects, initiatives and programmes.

The inherently sensitive nature of trade negotiations makes it difficult for development partners to support the AfCFTA negotiations directly, other than through arm's length support provided via technical partners or the Secretariat to the negotiations. Where donors can provide more direct and visible support is at the country level. The AfCFTA is ultimately an agreement between states, each of which must contend with national-level implementation challenges alongside specific actions to take advantage of the agreement. Nevertheless, and despite the recent growth of interested donors and partners, the mandate of the AfCFTA Secretariat is large. Substantively more support will be required to achieve all that the AfCFTA promises to offer. As is always the case in issues that attract a breadth of supportive partners, coordination among and between partners will become an increasingly important job for the AfCFTA Secretariat to manage. Donors should take care to not make this more difficult than needs be, including by acceding to the direction of the AfCFTA Secretariat rather than by enforcing donor priorities that can unduly distract scarce coordinating resources.

According to trade modelling, the AfCFTA offers opportunities to all African countries – including those that are less developed or in more fragile economic contexts (Songwe, MacLeod and Karingi 2021; World Bank 2020). What those models cannot reflect, however, is that many of African's lesser-developed countries will face bigger challenges in utilising these opportunities. Africa's development partners have a continuing role to play in supporting the lesser-developed countries of the continent to design, and more crucially implement, strategies to seize market opportunities created by the AfCFTA.

Commitment to the AfCFTA not yet translating into trade

The ideological battle for the AfCFTA has already been won. More importantly, it has also weathered the threats and distractions of the severe crisis of Covid-19 (see Chapter 6) and the emergence of the Ukraine crisis in 2022. Much of the narrative that sustained policy interest in the AfCFTA through Covid-19 was framed as it forming part of African countries' pandemic recovery strategy. However, slippages to the deadlines for the conclusion of the AfCFTA negotiations, and cascading implementation delays, have in practice meant that the AfCFTA is not yet operating to enable this.

So far, efforts have been made to 'go around' the problem of the persisting unconcluded technical parts of the negotiations. This has included AfCFTA institution-building, the expansion of negotiations into new areas (such as e-commerce and women and youth in trade), and complementary programmes, projects and initiatives. Perhaps notably, this approach has also involved the creation of an AfCFTA Guided Trade Initiative to hand-hold trade in a few initial consignments between participating countries. This 'circumvention' approach is understandable: the AfCFTA and its stakeholders need to show progress to those that have been investing political capital in the project. Yet such an approach can only persist for so long before an existential crisis emerges in the substantive implementation of the AfCFTA.

Meaningful trade under the AfCFTA remains the Rubicon to be crossed. All stakeholders in the AfCFTA can help by focusing on this goal. This includes development partners, the priorities of which can at times serve as distractions. The AfCFTA Guided Trade Initiative is a welcome and innovative start. Yet possibly the most potent solution lies with the regional hegemons of the continent (including South Africa, Kenya, Nigeria and Egypt). These critical central stakeholders have the most important role to play in brokering – and offering – compromises to get the final technical parts of the AfCFTA Agreement finished and substantive trade flowing.

As attention to the broader and more complementary parts of the AfCFTA ecosystem has grown, the AfCFTA Secretariat has established itself as the central coordinating node within this system. A critical demarcation of the responsibilities of the AfCFTA Secretariat is yet to emerge with respect to the role of the AUC Department of Trade and Industry, which traditionally served as a coordinating platform for trade policy between African countries; however, the AfCFTA Secretariat is increasingly absorbing donor attention and support. In theory, at least, the AUC might be expected to remain an important home of broader trade and industrial policy initiatives in alignment with the AfCFTA. Yet such initiatives can easily overlap with the growing remit of the AfCFTA Secretariat and the AfCFTA appears to be taking over as the most important and exciting institution for trade development on the continent. An example can be drawn from the continental e-commerce strategy under development at the AUC but involving policy directions that would be broached by negotiators under the ambit of the AfCFTA negotiations on e-commerce.

It is also unclear how the responsibilities of the AfCFTA Secretariat will align with, or overlap, those of Africa's pre-existing regional economic communities. While the 2008 Protocol on Relations between the RECs and the AU governs this relationship at the AU level, whether that extends to the AfCFTA Secretariat or whether an equivalent legal framework is required is still being clarified. In September 2021, the AfCFTA Secretariat held its first Coordination

Meeting of the Heads of Regional Economic Communities on the Implementation of the AfCFTA, seeking to identify a mechanism for collaboration between the AfCFTA Secretariat and the regional economic commissions.

When starting an automobile in cold weather, the ignition sometimes requires a few attempts before the engine roars to life. That needn't necessitate throwing away a good car. When the AfCFTA gets going – which it will – it will contribute to transforming trade in the African continent and driving long-overdue African industrialisation. The wait will be worth it. In the meantime, Africa's regional economic powers have a leadership role to play in getting the AfCFTA moving without further delay. The collective size of the leading economies in each of Africa's five regions accounts for more than half of the continent's GDP. If they can show the leadership required to make compromises in the rules of origin and get trade flowing, the AfCFTA will have the impetus it needs to truly take off.

2.2 The regional economic communities (RECs) as building blocks of trade integration

For more than 60 years – and since the late 19th century, in the case of SACU, which is one of the oldest customs unions in the world – African countries have set up various institutional arrangements to guide and support trade integration and economic cooperation between them. These span the spectrum from free trade areas to customs and monetary unions. They are collectively referred to as regional economic communities (RECs). Each REC has its specific historical origin, institutional structure, and political and economic rationale. Their operations are necessarily confined to relatively small economies with relatively small volumes of cross-border trade, if also increasingly diversified, as noted in the previous section. They are constrained by institutional capacities, resources, overlapping mandates and, in some contexts, challenging border management facilities and practices. Yet the RECs have been persistent enablers of trade integration in Africa.

Table 2.2 gives a breakdown of shares in both intra-REC trade and REC trade in African trade. Only SADC, SACU and EAC come close to attaining a quarter of intra-community or intra-African trade shares. However, the literature suggests that the overall effect of the regional trade agreements on African trade is positive (Candau, Guepie and Schlick 2019). But a trade liberalisation programme alone is not enough to boost trade flows. It must be accompanied by complementary measures and supply-side measures, along with political stability and reduced political risk (Mayer and Thoenig 2016; Ngepah and Udeagha 2018). In their regional planning and long-term vision frameworks, the RECs to their credit have long recognised the broad multisectoral orientation of their mission. This section begins with a categorisation of the RECS to pin down their main roles before turning to how they have functioned as enablers of trade integration, concluding with an overall

Table 2.2: African RECs' performance in continental and global trade (average 2018–2020), percentage

RECs	Intra-REC trade as percentage share of total REC trade	REC trade with Africa as percentage share of REC total trade
Arab Maghreb Union (UMA)	3.66	9.08
Common Market for Eastern and Southern Africa (COMESA)	7.15	15.71
Community of Sahel–Saharan States (CEN-SAD)	6.58	10.27
Economic Community of Central African States (ECCAS)	2.47	13.56
East African Community (EAC)	12.56	23.57
Economic Community of West African States (ECOWAS)	9.09	14.27
Intergovernmental Authority on Development (IGAD)	8.94	17.58
Southern African Development Community (SADC)	20.37	23.76
Southern African Customs Union (SACU)	13.71	24.56

Source: Authors calculation with UNCTAD trade[4] data downloaded 29 March 2022.

assessment of the RECs in relation to the framework for trade policy analysis outlined in the previous chapter.

Towards a categorisation of the RECs

Africa is littered with a variety of economic cooperation arrangements that have a broad range of objectives. Some, like the Mano River Union, encompassing Guinea, Côte d'Ivoire, Liberia and Sierra Leone, aspire to coordinate development planning and consolidate peace and security among countries that have been plagued by violence and instability. The Mano River Union also leads cross-border projects, including some that cover trade facilitation, but otherwise has little role in trade policy. The Lake Chad Basin Commission, with Cameroon, Chad, Central African Republic, Niger and Nigeria as the members, manages a shared water body resource and coordinates sustainability initiatives against the treat of climate change and desertification.

Table 2.3: Categorisation of the status of the 11 RECS

REC	Legacy	Customs and monetary union	Customs union	Free trade area	General economic cooperation
AMU					X
CEMAC	X	X			X
CEN-SAD					X
COMESA			X		X
EAC			X		X
ECCAS				X	X
ECOWAS			X		X
IGAD					X
SACU	X	X	X		X
SADC				X	X
WAEMU	X	X			X

Source: Authors' elaboration.

Eleven RECs can be identified and categorised into monetary unions, customs unions, free trade areas, and general economic cooperation arrangements (see Table 2.3). Two of the 11, ECCAS and SADC, are FTAs and three, COMESA, ECOWAS and EAC, have evolved over time into customs unions. Three, CEN-SAD, IGAD and UMA, are general economic cooperation arrangements that incorporate trade integration among their objectives. Some also serve as forums for coordinating political and diplomatic objectives such as regional peace and security. In three cases, the monetary and customs unions are coterminous. These are the West African Economic and Monetary Union (WAEMU), the Economic and Monetary Union of Central Africa (CEMAC) and the Southern Africa Customs Union (SACU). WAEMU and CEMAC are legacy arrangements and operate among the former French colonies in West and Central Africa. SACU is also a legacy arrangement of Apartheid South Africa's regional sphere of influence. However, one of its members, Botswana, does not participate in the monetary union.

Under a 2008 Protocol on the Relations between the African Union and the Regional Economic Communities, eight of the 11 were officially recognised by the African Union as building blocks of economic integration. These are AMU, COMESA, CEN-SAD, EAC, ECCAS, ECOWAS, IGAD and SADC. (African Union 2008). A close reading of the protocol and its 2021 revision (African Union 2021) suggests that conferment of this recognition was aimed at establishing a representative group of the RECs with which the AU could engage on a range of policy matters. To be sure, the eight that were

Figure 2.7: Overlapping REC memberships and mandates

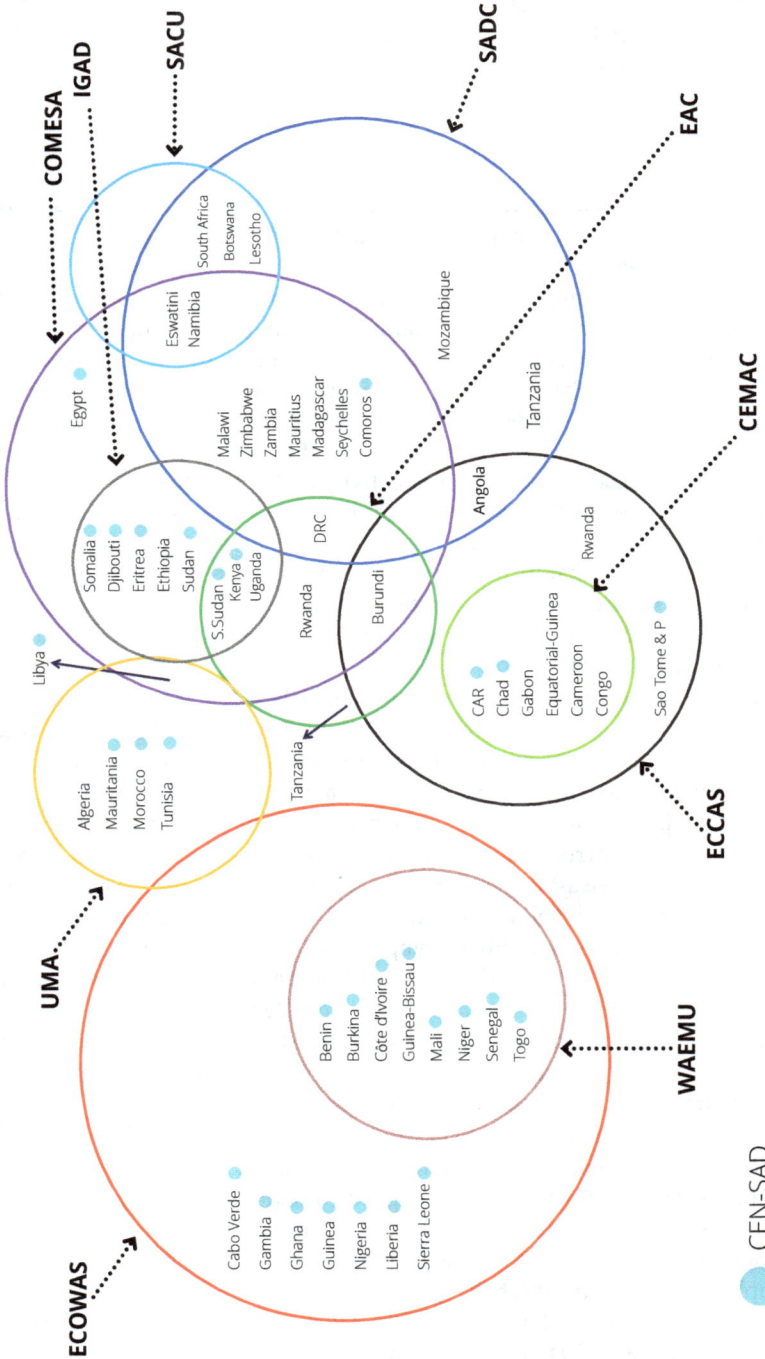

Source: Authors' elaboration.

recognised are representative of the regions. But they still exhibit a 'spaghetti bowl' (Bhagwati 1995) or perhaps 'rice bowl' effect, with overlapping REC memberships and mandates, as shown in Figure 2.7.

The enabling role of the RECs

Covering some 30.2 million square kilometres, Africa is the world's second largest and second most populous continent, after Asia on both counts. It is a massive continent, intensely Balkanised, with 54 countries and over 107 land borders. It has a complex history and legacy and equally complex development challenges. Inevitably, political interest will drive countries with common problems to band together to find common solutions. Evidence in the literature suggests that the benefits from trade integration arrangements are derived not only from reduced transaction costs that arise from the provisions of trade agreements but also from collateral advantages. This may include institutional quality, enhanced productivity and productive capacities. From this perspective, trade integration strategies may be said to be driven by endogenous factors that are integral to the design of trade agreements and exogenous factors that include the wider requirements for successful integration (Baier, Bergstrand and Egger 2007; Kohl et al. 2016). Understood as such, the RECs play a wide-ranging enabling role as reflected in the breadth of policy issues they seek to address.

The Africa Regional Integration Index (ARII),[5] which measures the level of economic integration within the RECs and their member states on five dimensions (trade integration, productive integration, macroeconomic integration, infrastructural integration and free movement of peoples), provides clarity on where the gaps are deepest. Of the five dimensions that are analysed, productive and infrastructural dimensions are those in which African countries and RECs are the least integrated. On a 0–1 scale, the 'RECs' productive integration scores are all below 0.5, with ECOWAS (0.22) being the least productively integrated region. This is compounded by infrastructure and logistics deficits that limit the growth and spread of regional value chains. Another index that measures progress in infrastructure development found that more than three-quarters of the African countries have a composite infrastructure index[6] below 0.5 (African Development Bank Group 2020). Specifically, regarding transport infrastructure, only Egypt (0.55) and the Seychelles (0.52) have a transport index above 0.5.

The RECs have not been oblivious to these gaps. Their strategic planning frameworks, which are generally aligned to national planning programmes and the African Union's Agenda 2063, provide well-thought-out roadmaps for responding to the deficiencies. The unavailability of resources and implementation capacity challenges mean that these plans are effectively wish lists. The African Development Bank (AfDB) estimated Africa's infrastructure needs to be $130–170 billion a year, with a financing gap (infrastructure needs minus the total financing available from all sources) in the range of $68–$108 billion. The shortfall extends across energy, transportation, and water and sanitation infrastructure (Economic Commission for Africa 2021). Despite that, the plans provide insights into the RECs' prioritisation of the challenges they face. The EAC's Vision 2050, for example, identifies:

> the development pillars and enablers that would create jobs to absorb the expected expansion of workforce in the next decades ... They include infrastructure and transport network that is easy, fast and cheap means both for people and goods for regional competitiveness; energy and information technology that are accessible to citizens; and industrialization that is built on structural transformation of the industrial and manufacturing sector through high value addition and product diversification based on comparative and competitive advantages of the region. (EAC 2015)

As shown in Table 2.4, the SADC, ECOWAS and EAC vision documents have almost identical architectures with prominent pillars on interconnectivity and infrastructure, sustainable development and industrialisation.

On some projects and sectors, progress is being achieved. The Economic Commission for Africa (ECA), for example, reports that the roads in the Trans-African Highway – a network with nine highways amounting to 56,683 kilometres connecting all regions of the continent – are about 60 per cent complete, and the remaining 40 per cent comprises missing links. Africa's transport corridors are mainly road-based, although recent years have seen an increase in the rehabilitation and development of railways. The ECA estimates

Table 2.4: Main pillars in RECs vision frameworks

ECOWAS Vision 2050	SADC Vision 2050	EAC Vision 2050
A secure, stable, and peaceful region	Industrial development and market integration	Infrastructure development
Governance and rule of law	Infrastructure development in support of regional integration	Industrialisation
Economic integration and interconnectivity	Social and human capital development	Agriculture, food security and rural economy
Transformation and inclusive and sustainable development		Natural resources and environment management
Social inclusion		Tourism, trade, and services development

Africa's entire railway network at about 75,000 kilometres on a surface of 30.2 million square kilometres, translating to a density of about 2.5 kilometres per 1,000 square kilometres. This is far below the density in other regions or the world average of 23 kilometres per 1,000 square kilometres (Economic Commission for Africa 2021).

Various corridor organisations work closely with the RECs to manage the trade and transport corridors. For example, in West Africa, the Abidjan–Lagos Corridor Organization oversees the 1028-kilometre route between Abidjan, Accra, Lomé, Cotonou and Lagos. In East Africa, the Northern Corridor Transit and Transportation Coordination Authority presides over a multimodal trade route that runs from Kenya's Mombasa port on its Indian Ocean coast to Burundi, the eastern DRC, Rwanda, South Sudan and Uganda in the interior. In Southern Africa, the Walvis Bay Corridor Group is responsible for three corridors operating from Namibia's port at Walvis Bay on the Atlantic Ocean. These are the Trans-Kalahari Corridor that links Walvis Bay to Botswana's capital, Gaborone, and beyond to South Africa's Gauteng Province, which is the country's industrial heartland, and Zimbabwe; the Walvis Bay–Ndola–Lubumbashi Development Corridor encompasses the transport hubs of Livingstone, Lusaka and Ndola in Zambia, Lubumbashi in the southern DRC, and Zimbabwe; and the Trans-Cunene Corridor links Walvis Bay to southern Angola via Tsumeb and Ondangwa to Oshikango in Namibia and the Santa Clara border post in Angola. These organisations plan, coordinate and advocate for business opportunities and competitive transportation and promote health and safety standards. The latter emerged as an important necessity during the Covid-19 pandemic. Notable results have been achieved. In East Africa, for example, TradeMark Africa, a consortium of development partners that works closely with the EAC, reported that, through its support programmes and related interventions, border crossing and transit time decreased significantly between Mombasa and the entry points to Burundi, the eastern DRC, Rwanda and Uganda.[7]

Assessing the RECs

In relation to the framework for trade policy analysis, the legacy RECs, the FTAs and customs unions have progressed well beyond the design phase, having established programmes that are both endogenous and exogenous to trade integration which continue to evolve. Innovations have also been introduced in COMESA, EAC, SADC and ECOWAS, such as simplified trading regimes that enable small-scale traders to move their wares across borders under regulations that require minimum paperwork. As noted in the previous chapter, informal cross-border trade, while difficult to estimate, accounts for a significant part of cross-border trade flows. As will be seen in Chapter 6, during the Covid-19 pandemic the RECs were proactive in taking measures to ensure safe trade.

However, on services, which are a dominant driver of growth and development, the evidence suggests that the RECs have been less focused on them than on trade in goods, which has been prioritised in the trade liberalisation agenda of the RECs (Economic Commission for Africa 2021). SADC and EAC have negotiated deeper commitments on services, the latter building upon an agreement that allows free movement of persons. ECOWAS maintains a long-standing regime on free movement of persons that facilitates cross-border services flows. Transport and travel services are on average (2017–2019) the most traded services on the continent, accounting for over three-quarters of services exported and imported between African countries.[8] The approach to services liberalisation under the AfCFTA will build upon progress that has been made by the RECs.

Resources and capacities remain perennial concerns. The massive financing gap on infrastructure was noted. The RECs are further challenged by overlapping commitments of some members to different trade agreements. As Asche (2021, pp. 39–40) has observed:

> [M]ultiple memberships are technically feasible [if] the overlapping RECs in question do not exceed the stage of preferential or free trade areas. Already at the FTA stage, overlaps become inconvenient as they necessitate continuous controls at the internal borders for certificates of origin and customs duties for goods that entered the community at ports with different external tariffs. Otherwise, internal border controls could be abolished for goods traded among members. When a regional community strives to become a customs union, overlapping trade arrangements become technically impossible as there can only be one common external tariff and export regime.

WAEMU and ECOWAS in West Africa are examples where the former's common external tariff has been aligned with that of the latter to ensure the coherence of the ECOWAS customs union. However, Burundi and Rwanda in EAC and ECCAS, which are respectively a customs union and an FTA (with negotiations for a common external tariff at an advanced stage in ECCAS, which will make it a customs union), are examples of the challenges to the coherence of customs unions arising out of overlapping memberships. The FTAs and customs unions are also littered with carve-outs for sensitive products that challenge the expected norms. As will be discussed in Chapters 3 and 4, bilateral partners are sometimes complicit in compounding the policy and regulatory difficulties faced by the RECs by pursuing trade deals that result in picking regional arrangements apart.

However, while the legacy RECs, FTAs and customs unions have reached an advanced stage in trade policy cooperation, CEN-SAD, IGAD and UMA can be located at the design stage. With political momentum behind the AfCFTA, it is not clear what added value CEN-SAD can offer its member states since the original vision was to create a preferential trade area encompassing countries north and south of the Sahara.[9] IGAD has veered towards a broad economic cooperation agenda. UMA remains stunted by a long-running diplomatic stand-off between Algeria and Morocco over the status of the Western Sahara.

Summary

Intra-African trade and integration are long held objectives of policy leaders on the African continent. Though the inaugural summit of the Organisation of African Unity in 1963 spoke about 'the possibility of establishing a free trade area' (OAU 1963), the AfCFTA, which was established 55 years later, marks the greatest practical effort towards this goal. The AfCFTA is a flagship project of the AU Agenda 2063, to boost intra-African trade and through doing so diversify African economies, while contributing to their long-overdue indus-trialisation. It amounts to the crystallisation of decades of policy deliberation into an actionable and legally enforceable instrument.

As we have seen, the RECs have a practical function in enabling trade inte-gration and connecting a continent that is as vast in size as Africa. They are massively under-resourced, but they help to find and apply common solutions to mutual supply constraints. In the preamble to the AfCFTA Treaty, and again in Article 5 of the AfCFTA Framework Agreement, the eight AU-recognised RECs are designated as the AfCFTA's 'building blocks', meaning that their best practices and achievements are to be followed and incorporated into AfCFTA implementation. Article 12 confers an advisory role on them in AfCFTA deliberations. This complements the role accorded to the RECs as partners in the implementation of AU programmes.

However, the ignition of the AfCFTA project is stutter-starting. Several 'launch' attempts and an increasing breadth of complementary projects, tools and initiatives within the growing AfCFTA ecosystem conceal the fact that trade is yet to substantively flow under the arrangement. The Guided Trade Initiative is to be welcomed as a gateway for formal trade under the AfCFTA but is not a substitute. The real risk of this is to the remarkable polit-ical momentum behind the AfCFTA, which, having weathered the Covid-19 storm, remains strong.

Notes

[1] Primary commodities is SITC 2 + 3 + 4 + 68 + 667+ 971, food items is SITC 0 + 1 + 22 + 4 and manufactured goods is SITC 5 to 8, less 667 and 68.

[2] The choice to present the results in 2045 is justified by the fact that the AfCFTA reform is implemented over time between 2021 and 2035 but also to give enough time for all the variables to adjust following full implementation of the AfCFTA reforms in the model.

[3] The distinction between 'operational instruments' and 'implementation tools' is not always clear. The African Union Assembly Decision Assembly/ AU/Dec. 831(XXXV) of 6 February 2022 identifies four 'Implementation Tools': (1) the AfCFTA Adjustment Fund, (2) the Pan-African Payments and Settlement System, (3) the AfCFTA Automotive Fund and (4) the Inter-African Trade Fair. The African Union Assembly Decision Assembly/ AU/4(XXXIII) of 10 February 2020 identifies five 'operational tools': (1) rules of origin, (2) the AU Trade Observatory, (3) the Trade in Goods Password Protected Dashboard, (4) the Pan-African Payments and Settlements System and (5) the NTB Monitoring, Reporting and Elimination Mechanism. The AU-AfCFTA website lists four 'operational Instruments': (1) the Pan-African Payments and Settlement System, (2) non-tariff barriers tools, (3) the AfCFTA Adjustment Fund and (4) the Automotive Fund.

[4] Trade = imports + exports.

[5] See https://www.integrate-africa.org for more details.

[6] The composite infrastructure index is an African Development Bank Index, which is a composite index of nine indicators grouped within four pillars (transport, electricity, ICT, water and sanitation).

[7] See www.trademarkafrica.com

[8] Calculation based on WTO-OECD Balanced Trade in Services Dataset (BaTiS) – BPM6.

[9] This point also applies to the Tripartite Free Trade Area initiative between COMESA, ECA and SADC.

References

Abrego, Lisandro; Amado, Maria Alejandra; Gursoy, Tunc; Nicholls, Garth; and Perez-Saiz, Hector (2019) 'The African Continental Free Trade Agreement: Welfare Gain Estimates from a General Equilibrium Model', IMF, Working Paper WP/19/124. https://perma.cc/2QF8-XGY6

AfCFTA Secretariat (2022a) 'The AfCFTA Initiative on Guided Trade', Press Release https://perma.cc/4384-NU3C

AfCFTA Secretariat (2022b) 'What Is the AfCFTA Guided Trade Initiative All About?', Press Release. https://perma.cc/N4F8-4K8T

AfCFTA Secretariat (2022c) 'Towards the Commencement of Commercially Meaningful Trade under the African Continental Free Trade Area (AfCFTA)', Information Note.

AfDB (African Development Bank) (2011) 'Africa in 50 Years' Time: The Road towards Inclusive Growth', African Development Bank Group, Tunisia. https://perma.cc/F5MH-CMRX

African Development Bank Group (2020) 'The Africa Infrastructure Development Index (AIDI)', Abidjan: AfDB. https://perma.cc/4D6H-BCXL

African Union (2008) 'Protocol on the Relations between the African Union and the Regional Economic Communities'. https://perma.cc/SV8V-ZSJZ

African Union (2015) 'The African Union Commission Signs an MoU with the International Trade Center', Press Release No. 163/2015, 15 July. https://perma.cc/7J7F-S3MP

African Union (2021) 'Revised Protocol on the Relations between the African Union and the Regional Economic Communities'. https://perma.cc/Z2VK-J5PD

Asche, Helmut (2021) 'Regional Integration, Trade and Industry in Africa', in Seck, Diery; Elu, Juliet; and Nyarko, Yaw (eds) *Advances in African Economic, Social and Political Development*, Switzerland: Springer. https://doi.org/10.1007/978-3-030-75366-5

Baier, Scott; Bergstrand, Jeffrey; and Egger, Peter (2007) 'The New Regionalism: Causes and Consequences', *International Economics*, vol.109, no.1, pp.9–29. https://doi.org/10.3917/ecoi.109.0009

Bhagwati, Jagdish (1995) 'US Trade Policy: The Infatuation with Free Trade Agreements', in Bhagwati, Jagdish and Krueger, Anne (eds) *The Dangerous Drift to Preferential Trade Agreements*, Washington, DC: AEI Press.

Candau, Fabien; Guepie, Geoffroy; and Schlick, Julie (2019) 'Moving to Autarky, Trade Creation and Home Market Effect: An Exhaustive Analysis of Regional Trade in Africa', *Applied Economics*, vol.51, no.30. https://doi.org/10.1080/00036846.2019.1566691

EAC (2015) 'East African Community Vision 2050', Arusha: EAC. https://perma.cc/W8M2-8PNA

ECA; AUC; and AfDB (2017) 'Assessing Regional Integration in Africa VIII: Bringing the Continental Free Trade Area About', Addis Ababa: ECA Publications. https://perma.cc/LC8X-BW8N

ECA; UNCTAD; AUC; and AfDB (2019) 'Assessing Regional Integration in Africa IX: Next Steps for the African Continental Free Trade Area', Addis Ababa: ECA Publications. https://perma.cc/T5KV-ZCCQ

Economic Commission for Africa (2021) 'Assessing Regional Integration in Africa X: Africa's Services Trade Liberalization & Integration under the AfCFTA', Addis Ababa: Economic Commission for Africa. https://hdl.handle.net/10855/46739

Gourdon, Julien; Khiahin, Dzmitry; de Melo, Jaime; and Mimouni, Mondher (2021) 'Closing In on Harmonizing Rules of Origin for

AfCFTA: Anatomy of Reconciliations and Remaining Challenges', Geneva: ITC. https://perma.cc/5QGM-6U6P

Kohl, Tristan; Brakman, Steven; and Garretsen, Harry (2016) 'Do Trade Agreements Stimulate International Trade Differently? Evidence from 296 Trade Agreements', *The World Economy*, vol.39, no.1, pp.97–131. https://doi.org/10.1111/twec.12272

Kwofi, Maclean (2021) 'Kasapreko, Ghandour Begin Export under AfCFTA', Graphic Online, 26 February. https://perma.cc/42XM-VKFW

MacLeod, Jamie (2022) 'Human Rights and the AfCFTA: Taking Stock and Navigating the Way Forward', FES, 24 May. https://perma.cc/QDS7-3H9G

Mayer, Thierry and Thoenig, Mathias (2016) 'Regional Trade Agreements and the Pacification of Eastern Africa', International Growth centre, Working Paper. https://perma.cc/U8EX-WALU

Mikic, Mia and Shang, Weiran (2019) 'ASEAN at 50 and Beyond', in Luke, David and MacLeod, Jamie (eds) *Inclusive Trade in Africa: The African Continental Free Trade Area in Comparative Perspective*, London: Routledge. https://perma.cc/C8WC-V72X

Ngepah, Nicholas and Udeagha, Maxwell Chukwudi (2018) 'African Regional Trade Agreements and Intra-African Trade', *Journal of Economic Integration*, vol.33, no.1, pp.1176–99. https://doi.org/10.11130/jei.2018.33.1.1176

OAU (1963) 'Resolutions Adopted by the First Conference of the Independent African Heads of State and Government (CIAS/Plen.2/Rev.2)', Addis Ababa. https://perma.cc/88B2-8GBA

Saygili, Mesut; Peters, Ralph; and Knebel, Christian (2018) 'The African Continental Free Trade Area: Challenges and Opportunities of Tariff Reductions', UNCTAD, Research Paper No. 15. https://perma.cc/B2F3-JGSV

Songwe, Vera; MacLeod, Jamie; Karingi, Stephen (2021) 'The African Continental Free Trade Area: A Historical Moment for Development in Africa', *UNECA, Journal of African Trade*, vol.8, no.2, pp.12 – 23. https://doi.org/10.2991/jat.k.211208.001

Tralac (2022) 'The AfCFTA Secretariat's Guided Trade Initiative Has Been Launched: How Will It Work and Where Does Trade under AfCFTA Rules Now Stand?', Special Trade Brief. https://perma.cc/76PA-QMAP

UN Department of Economics and Social Affairs (2019) '2019 Revision of World Population Prospects', New York. https://perma.cc/7A4Y-J6GY

UNCTAD (2022) 'UNCTAD Statistics'. https://unctadstat.unctad.org/EN

UNDP (2021) 'AfCFTA and UNDP Announce New Partnership towards Inclusive Growth in Africa', 30 March. https://perma.cc/HQJ4-KVS6

van der Ven, Colette and Signe, Landry (2021) 'Greening the AfCFTA: It Is Not Too Late', Brookings, 16 September. https://perma.cc/GEX3-VGH3

World Bank (2020) 'The African Continental Free Trade Area: Economic and Distributional Effects', Washington, DC: World Bank. https://perma.cc/6U4H-STC4

3. Africa's trade arrangements with the European Union and China

David Luke, Kulani McCartan-Demie and Geoffroy Guepie

Having focused on regional trade issues close to home on the continent in the previous chapter, this book's metaphorical zoom lens scans out in this chapter to consider bilateral trade developments with Africa's two most economically significant trading partners. These are the EU and China, which together account for a little under half of both Africa's exports and imports. As geographical neighbours, Europe and Africa have a long trade history, while China is a relative newcomer to trading with Africa. Aside from this obvious point of contrast, Africa's trade arrangements with the EU and China cannot be more different. Specifically, while the EU has established an explicit policy structure for its trade relations with Africa, only a loose policy framework is in place to guide trade and investment flows between China and African countries. In this chapter, we show that, from a pro-development perspective, there is scope for improvement in both the EU's and China's trade offers to Africa.

3.1 Africa–EU trade

Formal compacts for trade and economic cooperation between Europe and Africa can be traced back to the early years of economic integration in Europe and the independence era in Africa. From the 1960s, the cooperation was formally codified in successive agreements in the form of the Yaoundé, Lomé and Cotonou Conventions and in similar country-specific pacts with North African countries. These covered development assistance, finance and trade. From the start, European trade policy established a clear division between Africa north and south of the Sahara, with separate market access concessions to the countries in these configurations. The lofty objectives of trade coopera-

How to cite this book chapter:

Luke, David; McCartan-Demie, Kulani and Guepie, Geoffroy (2023) 'Africa's trade arrangements with the European Union and China', in: Luke, David (ed) *How Africa Trades*, London: LSE Press, pp. 51–76. https://doi.org/10.31389/lsepress.hat.c License: CC-BY-NC 4.0

tion included diversification from commodity dependence. However, in over 60 years of preferential trade arrangements, the structure of trade between the two continents has hardly changed. Morocco, Egypt, Tunisia and South Africa are partial exceptions (see Chapter 1) and, in each case, more diversified trade is the outcome of significant European investment in non-extractive sectors. With a colonial legacy of little intra-African trade along with weak infrastructure to connect African countries, and against the reality of nearby Europe as a dominant, stable and mature market, preferential trade between Europe and its former African colonies locked in a powerful incentive to maintain the status quo. It is a status quo that is contested by the rapid rise of China as a competitor to Europe in Africa and the Chinese approach of combining trade with financing for infrastructure development and forays into manufacturing.

Fast-forward to 2021, when the European Union took three important steps that will shape its trade relations for the foreseeable future. First, it announced a new Open, Sustainable and Assertive Trade Policy (European Commission 2021a) to reaffirm European trade principles and reset its trade ambitions. This followed the unilateralism of the Trump years, the systemic traumas of Brexit, and a changing geopolitical landscape. Second, it concluded additional negotiations with sub-Saharan countries and other ex-colonies in the Caribbean and Pacific for a Post-Cotonou Agreement. Third, it launched a Global Gateway Initiative as a strategic plan for investment in infrastructure with digitalisation, climate and energy, transport, health, education and research as related priority areas to counter China's rising geopolitical influence and its Belt and Road Initiative. This section reviews these developments and implications for the EU–Africa trade relationship in relation to the analytical framework outlined in Chapter 1. The section begins with an outline of the trade regimes under which Africa trades with the EU.

The EU trade regimes

Figure 3.1 provides a map of the different arrangements governing trade relations between the EU and Africa. The arrangements are based on geography (such as whether the African country is in North Africa or below the Sahara), level of development (whether it is a least-developed or a developing country) or whether the country has opted out of any arrangement with the EU and trades under the general WTO baseline (most favoured nation, MFN) terms. This translates into five preferential schemes alongside MFN:

- **Everything but Arms (EBA):** applicable to 33 least-developed countries (LDCs), providing duty-free, quota-free market for their exports to the EU on a unilateral basis.
- **Economic Partnership Agreements (EPAs):** applicable to 14 countries in five different regional blocs, which are generally not consistent with the membership of the established regional economic communities.

Figure 3.1: EU trade regimes by African country

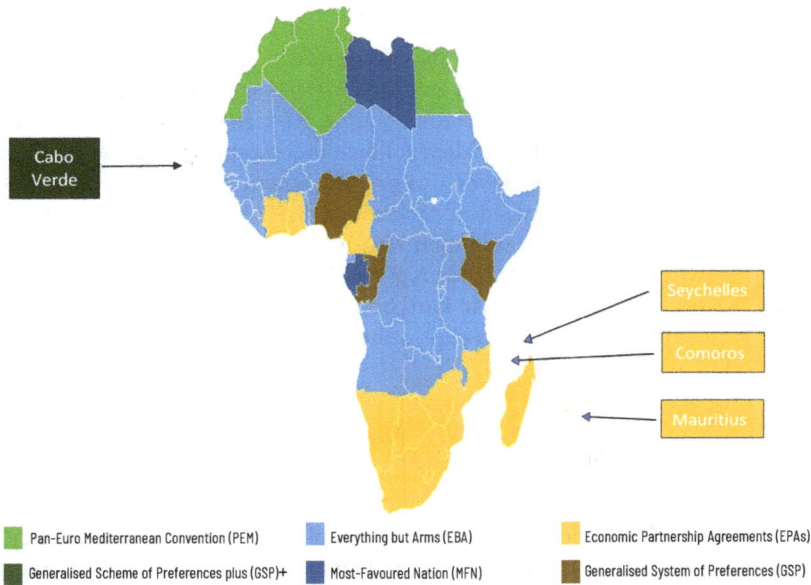

Source: Authors' compilation.

The EPAs are reciprocal but include asymmetrical aspects that accord a small degree of special differential treatment to participating African countries.

- **Generalised System of Preferences (GSP)-Plus:** a scheme valid until 2023 applicable to the Cabo Verde islands on Africa's north-west coast, which, as a recently graduated LDC, is not eligible for EBA. The market access arrangements are like EBA but require the beneficiary country to implement international human rights, labour and environmental conventions.
- **GSP:** applicable to the Republic of Congo, Kenya and Nigeria and provides for full or partial removal of customs duties on two-thirds of tariff lines on products within the EU market.
- **Euro-Mediterranean Association Agreements:** country-specific and applying to Algeria, Egypt, Morocco and Tunisia. Like the EPAs, they are reciprocal, semi-asymmetrical free trade area agreements.
- **Most-Favoured Nation (MFN) (WTO terms):** applying to Libya and Gabon.

The rules of origin underpinning market access for trade in goods are moderate but differing under the preferential arrangements. For instance, the EU grants more liberal rules of origin in the textile and apparel sector to countries that are trading under interim or regional EPAs. Most EU agreements do not grant 'cumulation', in which the value from inputs of other African countries embedded in a good would be considered to originate under the agreement. This is a disincentive for fostering export value chains between countries confined to different trade regimes.

The stringent provisions of the EU's food safety (sanitary and phytosanitary) measures are known to limit gains for African agricultural and fisheries exports to the European market. For example, African exports to the EU in the fish and beef sectors have fallen following compulsory regulations that are expensive to fulfil. Regulations to prevent bovine spongiform encephalopathy (BSE) are being applied to African countries in which BSE has never been diagnosed (Luke and Suominen 2019). Moreover, the EU's hotchpotch arrangements in the different trade regimes are detrimental to Africa's integration efforts since they result in hard borders for EU trade between several African countries. This is discussed in the section 'Assessing the EU-Africa trade arrangements'.

Open, sustainable and assertive trade policy

On 18 February 2021, the European Commission published the communication 'Trade Policy Review: An Open, Sustainable and Assertive Trade Policy'. This policy articulation, prepared at the height of the pandemic, elaborates current and continuing evolutions in the EU's trade policy, many aspects of which have important implications for African countries. The 'open and sustainable' component instrumentalises trade policy to contribute to a green deal and a digital transformation of the EU economy over the next decade. The 'assertive' aspect speaks to a 'geopolitical EU' that desires to chart its own course on the global stage, exercising leadership and engagement to safeguard a multilateral rules-based trading order centred on the WTO while assertively defending its interests and values. The EU is styled as a 'global economic power' with a responsibility to champion multilateral cooperation in line with the openness and attractiveness of its single market and its active trade with partners around the world.

Openness and engagement are described as a 'strategic choice' that lead to more prosperity, competitiveness and dynamism. The policy commits the EU to collaborate with partners to advance a positive agenda on economic recovery from the pandemic, green growth and digitalisation but to 'work autonomously when it must'. While the war in Ukraine has renewed the Western Alliance, which was fractured by the abrasive policies of the Trump administration, it is also clear that, despite the demonstrable interest of the Biden administration in strengthening the transatlantic relationship, the intent of the document was to put a marker down that the EU is an independent actor and will behave as such when necessary.

The policy established six medium-term priorities as follows:

1. Reforming the WTO
2. Supporting the green transition and promoting responsible and sustainable value chains

3. Promoting the digital transition and trade in services
4. Strengthening the EU's regulatory impact
5. Deepening the EU's partnerships with neighbouring, enlargement countries and Africa
6. Reinforcing the EU's focus on implementing and enforcing trade agreements and ensuring a level playing field for EU businesses

For Africa, which is specifically referenced in the document, two distinct facets of the new policy stand out. First, for the first time, the EU made sustainability an explicit and central pillar of its trade policy. This implies a commitment to leverage the EU's global power and strong trade relationships to support sustainable and fair trade as well as to increase the ambition of its trading partners to address climate change. This is both an opportunity and a challenge for Africa. The opportunity is that a new focus on sustainable and fair trade is consistent with Africa's industrial development ambitions for capturing and retaining more value from commodities along the supply chain. If this is backed by the approach that the EU rolled out in its Global Gateway Initiative (discussed below), it could help to foster economic diversification and inclusive growth. The challenge, however, is that the EU could pivot towards protectionism by introducing new measures and tariffs such as the already announced carbon border adjustment mechanism (European Commission 2019). This is aimed at avoiding the risk of carbon leakage in certain sectors with a high carbon emission intensity where the EU increases its climate ambition and partners do not. Unfortunately, Africa, which bears little responsibility for the climate crisis, could find its exports from these sectors penalised in the EU market.

The second facet of the new policy is recognition that most future growth will take place outside the EU and trade plays a key role in connecting Europe to these high growth regions. Africa is viewed as one of these regions. Recognising the problematic effects that are reinforced by its own fragmented trade regimes in Africa, the policy points to a continent-to-continent trade agreement as a solution, not for the immediate future but as a long-term prospect. In the meantime, the EU plans to 'widen and deepen' the EPAs and Euro-Mediterranean Agreements to tap into the robust growth that is expected. This is in line with another priority of the policy, which is to 'implement and enforce trade' existing agreements. With respect to these Africa agreements, this means in effect that the EU wants to enforce the rendezvous clauses embedded in many of them for adding investment, services, intellectual property rights and government procurement, among others.

As already noted, the EU's fragmented approach and the different trade regimes are detrimental to Africa's trade integration efforts. This led Concord, the European NGO Confederation for Relief and Development, to ask:

> Where does this leave the African Continental Free Trade Area and the continent-to-continent approach and where does it leave the local and regional attempts to strengthen intra-African

trade.… It is crucial that the EU allows [the] countries to make their own assessments as to when they would be ready to negotiate such issues with the EU and that the EU does not pressure them to prematurely take up far-reaching liberalisation commitments for which they are not ready. Triggering the rendezvous clauses and broadening and deepening the [agreements] would also mean that the … countries involved would drift further away from the other countries in their regions. The EU's offensive interests in Africa should not prevail over the development needs of African countries. (Concord, European NGO Confederation for Relief and Development 2021)

The other priorities identified in the Open, Sustainable and Assertive Trade Policy communication complete the EU's 'positive agenda' for engaging with its trading partners. These are WTO reform, updated rules for the digital economy including digital delivery of trade in services, and maintaining leadership in global regulatory cooperation.

The Post-Cotonou Agreement

The latest in the series of trade, development, finance and governance compacts with sub-Saharan countries was initialled on 15 April 2021 as part of an overall agreement between the EU and the Organisation of African, Caribbean and Pacific States (OACPS). Known as the Post-Cotonou Agreement (PCA), it establishes a development cooperation framework between the EU and the ex-colonies for the next two decades. What is striking about the agreement is the relative marginalisation of core trade policy issues, the EU having taken the view that its trade regimes with these countries were already well established in initiatives like the EPAs. Accordingly, the negotiations on behalf of the EU were led by the Directorate for International Partnerships, not the Directorate for Trade. As such the focus was on a broader set of issues on which there was already broad consensus, such as economic growth, climate change, mobility and migration, business environment, and private sector support. Multilateral commitments in the UN Agenda 2030, its UN Sustainable Development Goals and the Paris Agreement are the main frame of reference. With this broad focus, the agreement reads like a manual for economic development, unlike previous iterations of compacts between the EU and the same group of countries, which centred on trade. The agreement took over 30 months to negotiate. This relatively long period can be explained both by the Covid-19 pandemic, which led to repeated postponement of face-to-face negotiations, which were eventually replaced by virtual formats, and resistance from some OACPS countries to some aspects of a good governance agenda that the EU put on the table. These concerned human and sexual rights and the death penalty, which predictably revealed disagreements (Ishmael 2021).

The PCA has four main parts: an umbrella agreement with general objectives and principles and three region-specific protocols for each of the three regional parties: Africa, the Caribbean and the Pacific. The umbrella agreement addresses trade in broad and hortatory terms in relation to the positive benefits of trade and sustainability, trade in services, trade facilitation, business environment, investment, and private sector development. It calls for a 'high level of environmental, social and labour protection' in their trade relations and developing low-carbon productive capacities. It reaffirms the desire of the parties to 'build on their existing preferential trade arrangements and Economic Partnership Agreements (EPAs) as instruments of their trade cooperation' and 'broadening the scope of EPAs and encouraging the accession of new Member States'.

The Africa Protocol commits the parties to 'support ... the implementation of the African Continental Free Trade Area' while also claiming that:

> the implementation of EPAs, the African Continental Free Trade Area and other applicable trade agreements are complementary and mutually supportive while contributing to the deepening of the regional and continental integration process as part of the AU's trade and structural transformation agenda.

Cooperation at the WTO is highlighted but there is no mention of unlocking the Doha Round impasse including support for African priorities such as trade distortions in agriculture (for more on which see Chapter 5). While the principle of special and differential treatment for developing countries in relation to WTO rules is recognised, it is considered only in the areas in which there is already consensus at the WTO, such as cooperation to ensure clarity in sanitary, phytosanitary and other standards and compliance with trade facilitation commitments.

Prominence is also given to business environment reforms, barriers to trade, non-tariff measures and reducing trade costs. For example, under Article 10 on Business Environment and Investment Climate, the PCA states that:

> parties shall improve national and regional regulatory frameworks and simplify business regulations and processes, reduce and streamline administrative formalities, reinforce cooperation and build capacities to implement effective competition policies. They shall adopt open, transparent, and clear regulatory frameworks for business and investment, with protection for property rights.

Under the same article, the parties agreed to support financial sector reforms through measures that promote the improvement of access to finance and financial services, especially for micro, small and medium-sized enterprises (MSMEs), the development and interconnectivity of financial markets, and the integration of capital markets to ensure the efficient allocation of savings to productive investment and the private sector. They agreed to foster competition between financial service providers, to develop viable banking and non-banking financial sectors and to strengthen mobile and digital financial services in view of increasing access to finance, especially for MSMEs. The agreement recognises African industrial development aspirations, noting in Article 14 that:

> the parties shall promote the transformation of African economies and their transition from commodity dependence to diversified economies through the local treatment and processing of raw materials, added-value manufacturing and integration into regional and global value chains.

In Article 21 the parties commit to support efforts to increase trade in manufactured goods through linkages to markets and trade facilitation, including for enhanced quality standards and infrastructure. Article 13 on investment commits the parties to:

> undertake to work jointly to unlock sustainable and responsible investment from domestic and foreign, public and private sources. They shall pay particular attention to sectors that are essential for economic development, have high potential for sustainable job creation particularly in value-adding sectors and foster environmental sustainability.

The reforms that are proposed are in line with Africa's industrial development aspirations and can help to drive diversification and ramp up exports. But the agreement contains no specific commitments on investment flows, which is perhaps the most critical factor for driving economic transformation. The Global Gateway Initiative provides for a financial envelope to support the agenda outlined in the PCA and its Africa Protocol. But this, too, is vague on actual commitments.

The EU Global Gateway Initiative

The EU Global Gateway Initiative (European Commission 2021b) was launched on 1 December 2021 as the EU's financial offer to support economic development around the world. It can be seen as the EU's answer to back its claim to be a global economic power and autonomous actor on the world stage and its response to China's Belt and Road Initiative. The Global Gateway differentiates itself from the Belt and Road Initiative as being underpinned by European values and multilateral policy frameworks. This was made clear by the president of the European Commission at the launch of the initiative:

> COVID-19 has shown how interconnected the world we live in is. As part of our global recovery, we want to redesign how we connect

the world to build forward better. The European model is about investing in both hard and soft infrastructure, in sustainable investments in digital, climate and energy, transport, health, education and research, as well as in an enabling environment guaranteeing a level playing field. We will support smart investments in quality infrastructure, respecting the highest social and environmental standards, in line with the EU's democratic values and international norms and standards. The Global Gateway Strategy is a template for how Europe can build more resilient connections with the world. (European Commission 2021c)

The financial model is based on the tools in the EU multi-annual financial framework 2021–2027 for budgetary allocations over this period. Over €300 billion has been pledged during the six years to 2027 from the EU's budget and planned investment by European financial and development finance institutions such as the European Investment Bank and the European Bank for Reconstruction and Development. This suggests a repacking of existing instruments rather than new EU development financing. Some of this support will go through a new institution, the European Export Credit Facility. Having observed the approach taken by China's state-backed financial institutions, the new facility:

> would help ensure a greater level playing field for EU businesses in third country markets, where they increasingly have to compete with foreign competitors that receive large support from their governments, and thus facilitate their participation in infrastructure projects. (European Commission 2021b)

The delivery model is what is described as 'Team Europe':

> The Global Gateway will bring together the EU, Member States with their financial and development institutions, including the European Investment Bank (EIB), and the European Bank for Reconstruction and Development (EBRD) and seek to mobilise the private sector in order to leverage investments for a transformational impact. The EU Delegations around the world, working with Team Europe on the ground, will play a key role to identify and coordinate Global Gateway projects in partner countries.

Half of the amount pledged for the Global Gateway (€150 billion) is earmarked for Africa, according to announcements made at an EU–AU summit in February 2022 (see Box 3.1). It is noteworthy that trade was conspicuously absent from the seven clusters of the summit agenda. How the Global Gateway funds will be accessed and disbursed remains unclear and the impact that the initiative will make on the ground remains to be seen.

Box 3.1: 2022 EU–AU Summit

In February 2022, the EU hosted the sixth EU–AU summit with the objective of forging a common vision for a renewed partnership in building back from the pandemic. Forty African leaders and the 27 EU leaders attended. The agenda had seven clusters as follows: financing sustainable and inclusive growth; climate change, energy transition and infrastructure; peace and security; private sector and economic integration; education, mobility, and migration; agriculture and sustainable development; and health systems and vaccine production. Among the main announcements were:

- An investment package of €150 billion to help build more diversified, inclusive, sustainable and resilient economies around core areas of the Global Gateway Initiative.

- An EU pledge to provide 450 million Covid-19 vaccine doses to African countries in coordination with the Africa Vaccine Acquisition Task Team (AVATT) platform, by mid-2022, and to provide support to the African CDC to ramp up the pace of vaccination.

- Further action on debt relief and liquidity support beyond the Debt Service Suspension Initiative to fight the pandemic-induced recession including through the new allocation of IMF special drawing rights (SDRs).

However, what has become clear is that the renewal of the Atlantic Alliance under the Biden administration includes an allied effort to counter China's dominant role in infrastructure investment and delivery in the developing world. Hence,

> the EU is committed to working with like-minded partners to promote sustainable connectivity investments. Global Gateway and the US initiative Build Back Better World will mutually reinforce each other. This commitment to working together was reaffirmed at COP26 … where the EU and the United States brought together like-minded partners to express their shared commitment to addressing the climate crisis through infrastructure development that is clean, resilient, and consistent with a net-zero future. (European Commission 2021c)

Assessing the EU–Africa trade arrangements

The three main policy initiatives that have framed the EU's engagement with Africa since 2021 made important new commitments to a green transition, sustainable value chains, industrial development, and soft and hard infrastructure. These commitments in the Open, Sustainable and Assertive Trade Policy, in the Africa Protocol of the PCA, and in the Global Gateway are staples in the diet of African aspirations, as can be found in manifestoes such as Agenda 2063: The Africa We Want (AU Commission 2015). What is missing from EU policy are the trade arrangements that are essential to deliver the desired outcomes.

In the multiple trade regimes that are in place, the EU and (most) African countries have established a structured framework for their trade relations. However, the EU trade arrangements are neither efficient nor appropriate from a development perspective. The effect of the EU's varying trade regimes is a fragmentation of African markets, with gaps in coverage and hard borders for EU trade between African countries within the same customs union. This is the case, for example, in the Economic Community of West African States (ECOWAS), which has achieved the status of a customs union, with its 15 member states implementing a common external trade regime. Côte d'Ivoire and Ghana concluded separate interim EPAs with the EU, thereby undermining ECOWAS's, and indirectly the continent's, integration programme.

Similarly in the case of the South African Development Community (SADC), the EPA group within this REC contains only seven of the 16 SADC member states that are implementing an EPA. The different rules of origin that apply to the different trade regimes do not help to foster integrated supply chains between countries. On top of this, the EU has begun to move forward into deepening its reciprocal trade regimes with the North African and EPA countries to encompass services, intellectual property rights and government procurement. The risk is that, if care is not taken, this will deepen divisions between trade regimes among African countries, making African trade policy harmonisation even more difficult (Luke, Mevel and Desta 2020; Luke, Mevel and Desta 2021; Luke and Suominen 2019).

This matters because, as demonstrated in Chapter 1, intra-African trade, although accounting for only a small share of Africa's total trade, is more diversified and with higher value-added content than Africa's exports to the EU and other trading partners outside the continent. It follows that, as a matter of sequencing, the harmonisation of trade rules between African countries must first be achieved to underpin intra-African trade with predictability and certainty and to incentivise trade growth and smoother trade flows. This is indeed the rationale of the AfCFTA, which aims to create a preferential trade area throughout the African continent.

The Africa Protocol of the PCA makes the claim that the EU's trade arrangements with African countries are 'complementary and mutually supportive' and contribute to the 'deepening of the regional and continental integration process as part of the AU's trade and structural transformation agenda'. The empirical evidence does not support this. Analysis by the Economic Commission for Africa (ECA) based on economic modelling for trade in goods found that implementation of the EU reciprocal agreements ahead of the AfCFTA would result in losses in trade – or trade diversion – between

African countries. On the other hand, if the AfCFTA were fully implemented before the reciprocal agreements, this negative impact would be mitigated. Trade gains by both African countries and the EU would be preserved while intra-African trade would expand, significantly benefitting trade in industrial goods. This points to the need for a strategic sequencing of trade policy, prioritising the AfCFTA first (Mevel et al. 2015).

The 2021 ECA modelling results, which took liberalisation of trade in goods and services along with reduction of non-tariff measures into account, further affirms the need for correct sequencing. This study found that the share of intra-African trade would nearly double following the AfCFTA reforms. Most of the gains will accrue to the industrial and agri-food sectors as well as services, which are critical for Africa's transformation (UNECA 2021). As such, AfCFTA implementation should be prioritised over reciprocal trade deals with third parties. In time, this approach will ensure substantial benefits for both Africa and its advanced country partners. The challenge for Africa is to find an alternative pathway that better aligns incentives and sequences trade openings with the EU and other advanced partners. Two considerations should illuminate any such pathway.

First, as shown in Chapter 1, the EU's trade relationship with Africa is highly asymmetrical. The EU accounts for a much larger share of Africa's exports than Africa represents in the EU's exports, but Africa's exports to the EU are overly concentrated in fuels and metals. For a transitional period benchmarked against milestones in AfCFTA implementation and the gains emerging from it, a good development case can be made for unilateral market access that is duty-free and quota-free to all African countries, with cumulative rules of origin regime. This will require multilateral legitimisation through a new WTO waiver. One element in overcoming the current paralysis at the WTO, which is discussed in Chapter 5, must be recognition that its 'one size fits all' rules require reimagination to meet the 21st-century realities and challenges facing late developers, such as African countries. Given the weight of the combined number of EU and African members of the WTO, and the precedent established by the US's African Growth and Opportunity Act (AGOA), which provides sub-Saharan African countries with duty-free access to the US market (discussed in Chapter 4), securing a waiver should not be an insurmountable feat. In AGOA, the United States, in contrast to the EU, applies a uniform preferential trade regime for all sub-Saharan countries that meet the eligibility criteria. However, the US approach also maintains different trade arrangements with North African countries.

Concessions to Africa, as the world's least-developed continent, that allow non-reciprocal access to the EU and other advanced country markets for a fixed transitional period are strongly pro-development. They incentivise African countries to seek trade opportunities with each other and mitigate the risks of trade diversion. By ensuring the right sequencing for the AfCFTA, this will also help Africa to build productive capacities and achieve its potential for strong and diverse growth in intra-African trade with inclusive and transformational consequences. African integration is in the interest of the EU and the rest of the world. Reduced non-tariff barriers, lower intra-African tariffs, improved trade facilitation, and integrated markets create a large, prosperous, peaceful and more dynamic environment for trade and investment opportunities for Africa's partners as well as for African own enterprises to grow.

At the European Parliament, if not at the Commission, there is strong support for a radical change in EU trade policy towards Africa, as a resolution adopted by the Parliament in June 2022 made clear:

> Members believe that the EU needs a whole new basis for its economic partnership with Africa, based on a level playing field, equality, mutual respect and understanding. This is a unique opportunity to re-launch trade relations between the two continents, to engage in a renewed, mutually beneficial and sustainable partnership based on solidarity and cooperation, and to reshape economic and trade relations with a view to empowering Africa. (European Parliament 2022)

In relation to the framework for trade policy analysis outlined in Chapter 1, plurality in European politics and society is reflected in the efforts of the EU Commission to engage its European constituencies at various stages of the policy process. The Open, Sustainable and Assertive Trade Policy, for example, is based on extensive intra-European consultation. Under the EU institutional arrangements, the Commission has executive responsibility for trade policy, which provides a basis for active engagement and enables it to take a strategic view of European interests. With far more resources, the EU Commission is better equipped not only to leverage linkages between development finance, investment and trade but also to set and shape the agenda and outcomes. On the African side, notwithstanding AU strictures to 'to engage external partners as one … speaking with one voice' (AU Commission 2018), the AU Commission has no mandate to act on behalf of member states in trade negotiations. Ad hoc arrangements are put in place to coordinate negotiations. This leaves the African countries vulnerable to being outmanoeuvred in trade negotiations and more broadly in engagement with its partners. The same vulnerability is inherent in Africa's trade relations with China.

3.2 Africa–China trade

China's economic activities in Africa covering trade, investment, infrastructure, construction, manufacturing, and development finance have expanded rapidly over the last two decades. Unlike the EU, which since the 1960s has established an explicit policy structure for its trade relations, or the US's Africa Growth and Opportunity Act (AGOA), only the most basic policy framework is in place for facilitating trade and investment flows between China and African countries. This is not withstanding the rapid trade growth that has seen China rise to become Africa's second most important trade partner after the EU, as shown in Chapter 1.

On the African side, trade policy interest has centred mainly in trade promotion and access to technology for boosting productive capacities. This includes clarification of sanitary and phytosanitary (SPS) regulations, the setting up of 'green lanes' to fast-track agricultural exports to China, and emerging e-commerce initiatives, along with securing access to China's technological know-how in sectors such as transport, energy and telecommunications. On China's side, its trade interests follow the well-established pattern of engagement through an overwhelming concentration on natural resource imports from Africa (see Chapter 1) and export of manufactures. But Chinese financing and response to demand for infrastructure development support, along with investment in manufacturing, have been a prominent part of the relationship, which other partners are almost enviously trying to emulate. As a 'late developer' itself, there is understandable appreciation in China of the contribution that good infrastructure and affordable energy can make to competitiveness and industrial development. Forty-three African countries signed up to China's flagship trillion-dollar Belt and Road Initiative (BRI).

China–Africa trade relations is the focus of this section, with issues such as finance and manufacturing only touched upon as part of framing the highlights of the trade relationship. It is a relationship that has evolved from what may be described as 'speed dating' to a 'steady courtship'. This is the result of both China's reassessment of its global economic strategy and African countries' awakening to the geopolitical stakes at play in their relationship with China.

From speed dating to a steady courtship

After three decades of China's *zǒuchūqū* 'Go Out' policy, Chinese president Xi Jinping in 2021 unveiled a 'dual circulation' strategy that pledges to reduce overseas capital outflows and rebalance growth towards domestic consumption (PRC 2021). This is a response to slower growth in the Chinese economy and an effort to 'level up' against burgeoning inequalities. The new approach translates into reduced development financial flows from China to Africa (see Table 3.1), compounded by mounting African debt and growing concerns over debt servicing.

At the Eighth Forum for China–Africa Cooperation (FOFAC-8), China announced a US$20 billion reduction in nominal terms of its Africa financial envelope. This was preceded by dampening enthusiasm for project financing by China's largest policy banks, China Exim Bank, and the China Development Bank, which sharply reduced global lending from $75 billion in 2016 to just $4 billion in 2020 (Olander 2020). Official policy for the foreseeable future is a deepening and intensification of private sector investment with

Table 3.1: China's financing commitments (loans and grants) announced at the Forum for China–Africa Cooperation (FOCAC), 2006–2021

Date	Amount (US $ billions)
2006	5
2009	10
2012	20
2015	35
2018	60
2021	40

Source: Authors' compilation based on FOCAC (n.d.).

targeted support to smaller and medium-scale projects as opposed to large-scale infrastructure deals (PRC 2021). It is not clear how the new approach will impact the ambitious BRI (Box 3.2).

As China restructures its financial engagement, its relationship with Africa appears to be maturing into a steady courtship from the hot flush of speed dating. Meanwhile, the US, EU, Japan and other OECD countries that failed to keep up with Chinese development financing and infrastructure investments in Africa announced new programmes such as the EU's Global Gateway Initiative and the US's 'Build Back Better World' (B3W) initiatives. These initiatives are aimed at ensuring that China's courtship is not exclusive since decoupling between Africa and China is not a realistic proposition (Yu 2022).

However, Beijing's shift from lavishing African countries with state-backed capital has potentially opened policy space for trade promotion and support for utilising Chinese market access provisions to boost exports into China, as announced at FOCAC-8 in 2021. Trade promotion featured heavily in President Xi's opening speech at FOCAC-8. In a bid to reach a declared target of $300 billion in non-oil imports from Africa by 2024, the president announced the introduction of 'green lanes' for African agricultural exports to China, more efficient inspection and quarantine procedures, and expansion of the scope of products enjoying zero-tariff treatment for the least-developed countries (LDCs) under the duty-free, quota-free (DFQF) scheme. It remains to be seen whether these measures will be sufficient to triple China's imports from Africa within three years to reach the target.

Trade policy arrangements

> When we talk about China-Africa trade, we need to emphasise how insignificant Africa is to China in strictly numerical value. (Olander 2021)

Box 3.2: The Belt and Road Initiative: vested interests and African incentives

There is a clear plan on the Chinese side and every policy and investment decision China makes towards the African continent is geared to the pursuit of Chinese interests ... Do African policymakers recognise and have a response to this (not necessarily bad policy shift)? There is no Chinese actor in Africa that is there for altruistic reasons, there are always vested interests. (Moore 2021)

It is never about what China wants to do, it is about what Africa wants to do. (Foreign Minister Wang, 2021)

The Belt and Road Initiative (BRI) is not a foreign aid project but rather a Chinese economic and strategic project to help secure trade, investment opportunities and natural resources for Chinese domestic enterprises 'with the assumption that closer economic ties spill over to closer strategic ties'. (Hwang 2021)

China trades more with countries in Asia ($3.06 trillion) than anywhere else in the world. Asia accounts for more than half of China's total trade. Africa's share of China's $6 trillion global trade in 2021 was only 4 per cent, according to China Customs Administration data (Olander 2022; see Figure 3.2). China satisfies its appetite for commodities through imports from across the world – not just Africa. Except for a handful of select commodities with strategic importance for the digital and green economy, such as cobalt and manganese, that are in high demand for Chinese manufacturing, it does not rely on Africa's natural resources as a single supply source for its industry. However, nearly all of China's imports of cobalt and manganese are from Africa.

While commodity trade remains dominant, a subset of China's trade relations with Africa is Chinese investment in manufacturing in several countries mainly driven by relatively lower labour costs (Calabrese, Huang and Nadin 2021; Oya 2021). Some investments in the manufacturing sector have been criticised for their trade diversion, value capture and opportunistic use of preferential agreements such as AGOA and EBAs, as opposed to contributing to industrial upgrading and domestic value addition for African firms and enterprises (Calabrese and Tang 2020). But the picture is more complex: not all Chinese 'geese' are seeking new locations in Africa for production as part of global networks and value chains. Some firms in the flock are local market-seeking geese producing specifically for the regional market and

Figure 3.2: Top 10 countries and regions in China's imports (percentage share), 2021

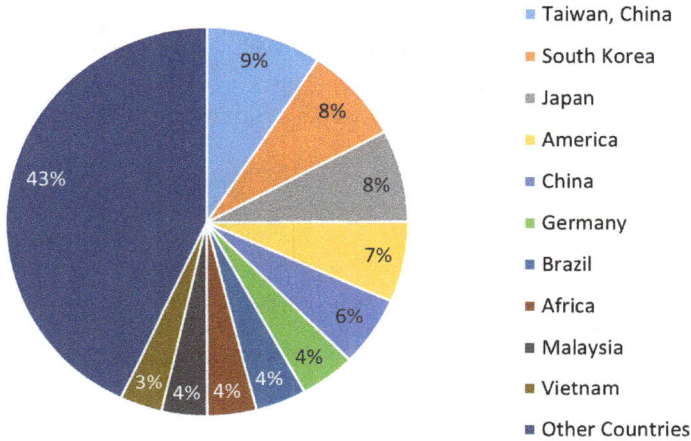

Source: Authors' calculations based on China Customs Administration (2021).

following a mass-customisation approach to reach African consumers. For example, smartphones produced and sold by the Chinese manufacturer Transsion Holdings account for the largest market share in Africa. Others are raw material-seeking geese, or small geese creating cluster investments. However, the flock offers a range of development opportunities and challenges for economic transformation in Africa (Bräutigam, Xiaoyang and Xia 2018, p.3; Bräutigam, 2021).

The Chinese market is national, but its provincial expression and the provincial level opportunities do not yet appear to be fully understood by African policymakers. For example, Zhejiang, a coastal province, which is home to the port of Yiwu, is one of the major distribution hubs for commodities in the world and the second largest port for African goods. When the provincial governor of Zhejiang embarked on a tour of three African countries, policymakers overlooked the importance of the visit, although Zhejiang's GDP approaches half of that of the entire African continent and is home to Alibaba, the financial and e-commerce conglomerate (Olander 2021). On the other hand, Hunan, a central Chinese province, provided the destination of a large red chilli pepper import deal signed with Rwanda (Olander 2021).

> No matter what happens in the announcements of trading arrangements and the opening up of market access through tariff free agreements ... not many African countries are in a position to take advantage of these arrangements. (Oya 2021)

Table 3.2: Summary of key China–Africa trade policy measures

Duty Free Quota Free (DFQF) scheme	• Commenced in 2010 and renewed in 2015 • Covers 97 per cent of tariff lines • 33 African LDCs are eligible under the scheme
Sanitary and phytosanitary measures (SPS) and product specific standards	• 11 African countries have signed SPS agreements with China, starting from 1998 onwards
E-commerce initiatives	• The Silk Road E-commerce initiative • Two African member states are operating on Alibaba Electronic World Trade platform: Ethiopia and Rwanda
China's economic and trade cooperation zones in Africa (ETCZs)	• Five (out of 20 planned) national level ETCZs confirmed: the China–Egypt TEDA Suez; the China–Ethiopia Eastern Industry Zone; the Nigeria Lekki Free Zone; China-Tanzania ETCZ; and Zambia–China ETCZ
Free Trade Areas (FTAs)	• Mauritius-China FTA operational as of 2021
'Green Lanes' scheme	• Established in 2021 at FOCAC-8 to speed up the inspection and quarantine procedure for African agricultural exports to China. • Expected to help reach $300 billion in total imports from Africa in the next three years.

Source: Authors' elaboration.

African countries are generally in the initial trade policy design stage, with a focus on clarifying basic regulatory issues such as SPS, 'green lane' schemes to speed up inspection and quarantine processes for African produce, e-commerce transactions and the establishment and operation of SEZs (see Table 3.2).

As previously noted, only the most basic framework is in place for trade engagement between Africa and China. These are, first, the obligatory WTO most favoured nation (MFN) privileges that cover both China and African countries that are WTO members. Second are the concessional arrangements for the least-developed countries through the duty-free, quota-free (DFQF) initiative for these countries. Third is a free trade area agreement signed in 2021 between China and Mauritius. Since it considers itself a developing country, China does not offer a GSP preferential trade scheme to the African countries that are not classified by the UN as least developed. Indeed, until 2014, China itself was a beneficiary of the GSP schemes offered by several OECD countries. Today, New Zealand, Australia and Norway still grant China GSP status (Huld 2021).

China's SPS rules have been a thorny issue in its trade relationship with Africa. Although Chinese SPS requirements are implemented in line with WTO approved SPS protocols, many African exporters lack the capacity to meet additional measures required by Chinese importers and formalised in Chinese customs processes (Anam 2021; see Box 3.3). This has proved to be such an irritation on the African side that President Xi was forced to address it at the 2021 FOFAC. Some African countries have SPS arrangements with China to export fresh agricultural products. Since 1998, 11 African countries have signed such agreements (Development Reimagined 2021a).

The Duty-Free Quota-Free (DFQF) scheme for 33 African LDCs[1] with diplomatic relations with China was established in 2010 (UNCTAD 2012). It covers up to 97 per cent of tariff lines with rules of origin that require regional value cumulation of no less than 40 per cent (UNCTAD 2016). Since China has no preferential scheme for non-LDCs, meeting the RVC requirement presents a challenge for supply chains that connect African LDCs and non-LDCs. Another issue is that the same product from an African LDC and non-LDC may face different tariffs. For example, there is a 10 per cent duty on floriculture, horticulture and other agricultural produce from Kenya, making them more expensive and less competitive than the same products exported by neighbouring Ethiopia, which qualifies for duty-free status (Olander 2021).

For developing African countries, such as Nigeria, Kenya, Egypt and South Africa, which do not qualify for the DFQF scheme and do not have an FTA with China as Mauritius does, there are no trade concessions. What China has offered to them is improvements to its importing process through 'green lanes', but not preferential treatment. This is in sharp contrast to the preferential

Box 3.3: Kenya freezes up over avocado exports

In 2020, Kenya signed an SPS+ product-specific standard arrangement with China for avocado exports. The conditionalities include product sizing, freezing, and container shipping. Only 10 out of 100 export farms were allowed into the Chinese avocado market as exporters faced challenges in cold chain infrastructure. Kenya was only able to ship a single 20-foot container of ripe frozen avocados. Other developing countries like Vietnam export almost five million tonnes of avocados to China per year. During Foreign Minister Wang Yi's visit to Kenya in 2021, six MoUs were signed, including one that streamlines the export requirements to allow fresh avocados to enter China.

Sources: Anam (2021); Olander (2021).

schemes offered to African countries by the US, the EU, the UK, Canada and other OECD countries, which tend to include at least some offerings for both developing and least-developed African countries. On the other hand, not only do Asian LDCs benefit from China's DFQF scheme but almost all Asian non-LDCs have preferential access to the Chinese market.

In 2021, Mauritius signed an FTA with China. It is a reciprocal agreement that will cover 96 per cent of traded items when fully phased in. However, Mauritius already maintains a highly liberalised trade regime, with zero tariffs on almost all products (Ancharaz and Nathoo 2022). The agreement includes provisions to promote the development of a renminbi clearing and settlement facility in Mauritius, expand Mauritius's high-tech industries and financial services, and protect its fisheries. Crucially, it positions Mauritius as a future 'offshore' location for Chinese investments and firms interested in the African continent. Rules of origin exclude products that contain non-originating Mauritian materials that exceed 10 per cent. This is more restrictive than what is offered by the US under AGOA and its accommodative third-country fabric provision, which is of significant benefit to Mauritius's clothing and textile industry (Development Reimagined 2021a). Mauritius's liberalised trade regime is unlike most African countries. Others typically protect large sectors of their economy and demand long transition periods for trade liberalisation in agreements with partners, such as is the case with the EU and UK economic partnership agreements. The Mauritius example of an FTA with China is therefore not likely to be widely followed by other African countries.

What next for China–Africa trade

China's dual circulation policy to reduce capital outflows and rebalance growth towards domestic consumption, while also pursuing its geostrategic BRI objectives (PRC 2021), may appear contradictory (Garcia-Herrero 2021). But China will surely balance these imperatives while also dealing with immediate pressures including continuing to manage Covid-19, a construction sector bubble, global inflation, and the fallout from the Ukraine war. It is also well known that China's long-standing ambition is to achieve self-reliance in key high-technology sectors such as semiconductors and artificial intelligence and in more basic sectors like food and energy.

As the world's second largest economy, China remains an important trade and investment partner for Africa. A key outcome of the 2021 FOFAC was China's commitment to simplify customs processes for African agricultural exports. Although China is cutting back on financial commitments, its $200 billion investment in infrastructure projects in Africa between 2016 and 2020 (PRC 2021) is drawing in ambitious investment plans by other partners. Even where Chinese financing arrangements remain dubious and controversy lingers over the quality of some projects, connectivity across

Africa is improving, with significant spillovers for boosting trade (Fu and Eguegu 2021). Similarly, China's foray into manufacturing and the introduction of special economic zones (SEZs) in Africa exposed the diversity of 'geese' in its flock but also validated the central role of industrial development in economic transformation. Over 20 China-supported SEZs that provide infrastructure and logistical support for manufacturing are in operation or planned in almost as many African countries. Production in these SEZs is also aimed at the continent-wide market that is being created under the AfCFTA. The ubiquitous spread of China's digital hard- and software is unlocking new opportunities for e-commerce across sectors.

However, China's trade offer to Africa falls below expectations. While there is increasing uptake by African LDCs of China's DFQF market access, China is alone among the leading economies in not offering a generalised system of preferences or a comparable programme such as the US's AGOA (US–Africa trade is discussed and assessed in Chapter 4). This is an anomaly that needs to be fixed. It also highlights the need for coordination and prioritisation among African countries in dealing with China. To date, no African country has published a China strategy. There is more coherence in the Chinese approach towards African countries than there is within the African Union on China (Anam and Ryder 2021; Lisk 2017; Soulé 2021). Though there has been an African Union Office in China since 2018, and a long-standing and active African Ambassadors Group in Beijing, with 51 representatives out of 55 AU members, there remains little evidence of strategic coordination.

As China's relationship with Africa settles into a mature courtship, along with the withdrawal of the former's 'going out' policy and rebalancing of its priorities and interests, there is scope for African countries to ramp up their collaboration as China's preferred modality appears to be bilateral engagement with individual African countries (Mboya 2021). An AGOA-style preferential programme should be a key priority. This matters in the face of the competition Africa faces in the Chinese market from Asian countries that have better market access arrangements with China. The ambition announced at the 2021 FOFAC by President Xi to triple African non-oil exports to China within three years by 2024 provides a basis for coordinated initiatives on the African side to establish modalities for achieving this target. If achieved, the target will provide a major boost not only for Africa's exports to China but also for intra-African supply and value chains. The potential spillover for intra-African trade will require China to put a preferential scheme in place for Africa's non-LDCs to complement the DFQF scheme for African LDCs. As a collective forum that meets periodically, FOCAC does not itself provide an institutional framework for follow up and monitoring its outcomes. However, a coordinated approach on the African side to overcome the bottlenecks for exporting successfully to China is more likely to achieve the benefits of increased trade with China.

In relation to the framework for trade policy analysis outlined in Chapter 1, only relatively low grades can be given for openness and transparency, inclusive participation, and accountability since these have not been given much consideration on either side of the China–Africa trade relationship. Slightly higher grades can be given for efficiency and appropriateness in the light of China's response to African pressure to streamline customs procedures for imports from Africa. China's support for building manufacturing capacity and infrastructure development also deserves credit, although the evidence on development impact is mixed.

Summary

In reviewing and assessing Africa–EU and Africa–China trade arrangements, we can conclude that the trade offers of these partners fall short of Africa's development needs. If the EU has been zealous in devising multiple trade regimes for Africa, China on the other hand offers only a basic policy framework for guiding its trade with Africa. The harmonisation of trade rules between African countries is the rationale of the AfCFTA. This incentivises African countries to seek trade opportunities with each other across the continent and derive benefits from economies of scale. By ensuring the right sequencing for the AfCFTA to be implemented before Africa enters reciprocal trade deals, the risk of trade diversion is mitigated. Empirical evidence from economic modelling suggests that trade gains with advanced partners such as the EU and China would be preserved, while intra-African trade would expand significantly benefitting trade in industrial goods. This will help Africa to achieve its potential for strong and diversified growth in intra-African trade. With all but one AU member state to date, signatories to the AfCFTA, a trade offer to all AfCFTA parties by the EU and China that is modelled after the positive elements of the US's AGOA, such as non-reciprocity and uniformity, will overcome the divisions associated with the EU trade arrangements and enable China to extend preferential market access to African countries that are not LDCs. As was the case with AGOA, WTO backing can be sought for such an offer from the EU and China as a concession to the world's least-developed continent.

Note

1   The countries currently covered by the scheme in Africa are the 33 LDCs in Africa – namely: Angola, Benin, Burundi, Burkina Faso, Central African Republic, Chad, Comoros, the Democratic Republic of the Congo, Djibouti, Eritrea, Ethiopia, Gambia, Guinea, Guinea-Bissau, Lesotho, Liberia, Madagascar, Malawi, Mali, Mauritania, Mozambique, Niger, Rwanda, Sao Tome and Principe, Senegal, Sierra Leone, Somalia, South Sudan, Sudan, Tanzania, Togo, Uganda and Zambia.

Annex 1: List of key informants interviewed (KIIs)

Name	Organisation	Position
Carlos Oya	School of Oriental and African Studies (SOAS)	Professor of political economy of development; director of research, SOAS China Institute
Shirley Yu	London School of Economics and Political Science (LSE)	Director of the China-Africa Initiative at the LSE Firoz Lalji Institute
Patrick Anam	Development Reimagined	Trade policy analyst and consultant
Eric Olander	The China Africa Project (CAP)	Co-founder
Geoffrey Osoro	East African Community	Trade policy adviser
Gyude Moore	Center for Global Development	Senior policy fellow
Anzetse Were	Financial Sector Deepening Africa (FSD Africa)	Economist
Oluwatosin Adeshokan		Economist and journalist

References

Adeshokan, O. (2021) 'ATPR Key Informant Interview'.

African Union Commission (2015) 'Agenda 2063: The Africa We Want.' https://perma.cc/2LEY-23E9

African Union Commission (2018) 'Assembly of the Union: Thirty-First Ordinary Session', 1–2 July. https://perma.cc/UV3W-9VZQ

Anam, Patrick (2021) 'ATPR Key Informant Interview'.

Anam, Patrick and Ryder, Hannah (2021) 'Reimagining FOCAC Going Forwards', Development Reimagined. https://perma.cc/2LEY-23E9

Ancharaz, Vinaye and Rajiv Nathoo (2022) 'Mauritius' Free Trade Agreement with China: Lessons and Implications for Africa', South African Institute for International Affairs. https://perma.cc/UV3W-9VZQ

Bräutigam, Deborah; Xiaoyang, Tang; and Xia, Ying (2018) 'What Kinds of Chinese 'Geese' Are Flying to Africa? Evidence from Chinese Manufacturing Firms', *Journal of African Economies*, vol.27, no.1, pp.i29–i51. https://doi.org/10.1093/jae/ejy013

Bräutigam, Deborah (2021) 'Foreword', in Xiaoyang, Tang (ed.) *Coevolutionary Pragmatism: Approaches and Impacts of China-Africa Economic Cooperation*, Cambridge: Cambridge University Press.

Calabrese, Linda and Tang, Xiaoyang (2020) 'Africa's Economic Transformation: The Role of Chinese Investment', DEGRP. https://perma.cc/UUL3-A7Q5

Calabrese, Linda; Huang, Zhengli; and Nadin, Rebecca (2021) 'The Belt and Road and Chinese Enterprises in Ethiopia: Risks and Opportunities for Development', ODI: Think Change. https://perma.cc/9KSY-Y532

Concord (2021) 'CONCORDs reaction to the Communication Trade Policy Review – An Open, Sustainable and Assertive Trade Policy', Press Release, April.

Development Reimagined (2021a) 'From China-Africa to Africa-China: A Blueprint for a Green and Inclusive Continent-Wide African Strategy towards China'. https://perma.cc/VLR5-7AEA

Development Reimagined (2021b) 'Q&A: Kenya's Ambassador to China Reflects on the Current State of Ties With Beijing'. https://perma.cc/VKF5-W22U

European Commission (2019) 'The European Green Deal', Brussels: European Commission. https://perma.cc/H7L4-BP8U

European Commission (2021a) 'Trade Policy Review: An Open, Sustainable and Assertive Trade Policy', European Commission. https://perma.cc/AKE6-PQ25

European Commission (2021b) 'Joint Communication to the European Parliament, the Council, the European Economic : The Global Gateway', Brussels: European Commission. https://perma.cc/Z4GU-UXWM

European Commission (2021c) 'Global Gateway', European Commission. https://perma.cc/PA9E-ZGF4

European Parliament (2022) 'The Future of EU-Africa Trade Relations'. https://perma.cc/4A9V-8HP3

Fu, Yike and Eguegu, Ovigwe (2021) 'Mapping the Future of China–Africa Relations: How the Continent Can Benefit', SAIIA. https://saiia.org.za/research/mapping-the-future-of-china-africa-relations-how-the-continent-can-benefit

FOCAC (n.d.) 'Previous Focac Conferences.' https://perma.cc/SJ5M-LSH9

Garcia-Herrero, Alicia (2021) 'What Is Behind China's Dual Circulation Strategy?', Bruegel. https://perma.cc/SUK5-NPJY

Hwang, Jyhjong (2021) 'AfCFTA Context: External Interests and Finance,' Brussels: Rosa-Luxemburg-Stiftung lecture series.

Huld, Arendse (2021) 'China Stops Issuing GSP Licenses to 32 Countries: An Explainer', China Briefing, 17 November. https://perma.cc/T3YS-6G33

Ishmael, Len (2021) 'Insights into the EU-OACPS Negotiations 2018-2021', Brussels: The Multinational Development Policy Dialogue – KAS. https://perma.cc/5XPE-HQUP

Lisk, Franklyn (2017) 'Contextualising the China Development Model (CDM) in African Paradigms of Development: A Research Framework for Analysing China-Africa Relations in a Changing Global Order', Paper presented at the Hallsworth Conference on 'China and the Changing Global Order', University of Manchester, UK, 23–24 March.

Luke, David and Suominen, Heini (2019) 'Toward Rethinking the Economic Partnership Agreements,' in Bilal, San and Hoekman, Bernard (eds) *Perspectives of the Soft Power of EU Trade Policy*, CEPR Press. https://perma.cc/8PFS-EKQR

Luke, David; Mevel, Simon; and Desta, Melaku (2020) 'EU-Africa Trade Arrangements at a Crossroads: Securing Africa's External Frontier', SEF. https://perma.cc/XU33-SZLM

Luke, David; Mevel, Simon; and Desta, Melaku (2021) 'The European Union Is Undermining Prospects for a Free Trade Agreement with Africa', Africa at LSE, 14 December. https://perma.cc/D4T8 -X9K4

Mboya, Cliff (2021) 'Africa Should Negotiate Collectively with China at FOCAC, But That's Not Going to Happen', The Africa Report, 17 September. https://perma.cc/WSJ8-L5JY

Mevel, Simon; Valensisi, Giovanni; and Karinki, Stephen (2015) 'The Economic Partnership Agreements and Africa's integration and transformation agenda: the cases of West Africa and Eastern and Southern Africa regions', Conference Paper, 18th Annual Conference on Global Economic Analysis, Melbourne. https://www.gtap.agecon.purdue.edu/resources/res_display.asp? RecordID=4754

Moore, Gyude (2021) 'ATPR Key Informant Interview'.

Olander, Eric (2020) 'The Plunge in Chinese Overseas Lending Is a Big Deal. It's a REALLY Big Deal', The China Africa Project, 9 December. https://perma.cc/3LA5-RG5H

Olander, Eric (2021) 'ATPR Key Informant Interview'.

Olander, Eric (2022) 'China's Total Global Trade Passed $6 Trillion For the First Time Last Year With Africa's Share Set to Remain at Around 4%', The China Africa Project, 18 January. https://perma.cc/66CQ-5V82

Osoro, Geoffrey (2022) 'ATPR Key Informant Interview'.

Oya, Carlos (2021) 'ATPR Key Informant Interview'.

Soulé, Folashe (2021) 'Folashadé Soulé on West Africa's Priorities at FOCAC 8', The China Africa Project, 22 October. https://perma.cc/NP5J-TWG5

The State Council Information Office of the People's Republic of China (PRC) (2021) 'China and Africa in the New Era: A Partnership of Equals'. https://perma.cc/5CXJ-Q7EX

UNCTAD (2012) 'Handbook on Duty-Free Quota-Free (DFQF) and Rules of Origin', New York: United Nations. https://perma.cc/BGW6-GNMX

UNCTAD (2016) 'Handbook on the Special and Preferential Tariff Scheme of China for Least Developed Countries', New York: United Nations. https://perma.cc/NZW7-EPR7

UN Economic Commission for Africa (2021) 'Takeaways from the Expected Impact of the AfCFTA's Implementation', ATPC. https://perma.cc/A9YX-63EB

Were, Anzetse (2021) 'ATPR Key Informant Interview'.

Yu, Shirley (2022) 'ATPR Key Informant Interview'.

4. Africa's trade arrangements with the United States, the United Kingdom, and other prominent partners

Jamie MacLeod, David Luke and Jonathan Bashi

This book's metaphorical zoom lens scans out in this chapter to focus on the US, the UK and other selected trading partners. These are all significant but not dominating partners within Africa's trade, with each accounting for up to 5 per cent of Africa's trade. They are, however, countries with substantial and evolving trade policies with Africa. The US's importance to Africa's trade goes far beyond the modest level of trade flows. Not only does US trade policy shape its bilateral trade and investment relationship with African countries, it also influences the global trade policy environment in which African countries operate. The centrepiece of US–Africa trade policy is America's 2001 African Growth and Opportunity Act (AGOA). For all its shortcomings, it provides a model that could be emulated by other partners to allow the sequencing of trade reforms and building of productive sector capacities (including through implementation of the AfCFTA and other trade reforms) before Africa enters reciprocal trade deals.

For the UK, Brexit, or its withdrawal from the European Union on 31 January 2020, is the pivotal event that is driving its trade with Africa. While inside the EU, the UK was bound by the former's trade policy, the main pillars of which were discussed in Chapter 3. With Brexit, the UK can design its own trade policies and strategies. Disappointingly, the UK mainly replicated these agreements to which it had been a party in the EU to ensure continuity in its trading arrangements. Besides Africa's trade relations with the EU, China, the US and the UK, it is also worth highlighting some notable features in other bilateral trade relationships. India, Turkey, Japan, Russia and Brazil are considered in brief notes in this chapter.

4.1 US–Africa trade

US–Africa trade policy is in the mature phases of the trade policy cycle, with the cornerstone African Growth and Opportunity Act (AGOA) initiative having been in force for over 20 years. Yet with AGOA set to expire in 2025 change may be afoot. Despite this, the shape and contours of these changes remain unresolved, with significant implications for African trade policy and its coherence across the continent. This section presents US–Africa trade policy within the context of broader US foreign policy towards the continent. It explains the central role of AGOA in US–Africa trade arrangements and charts the ways in which the post-AGOA landscape is emerging, including with the discussions for bilateral negotiations between Kenya and the US.

Africa accounts for a relatively small share of US trade (1 per cent between 2018 and 2020). Accordingly, trade amounts to only a secondary part of overall US foreign policy towards Africa, which has instead long been dominated by issues of peace and security, counterterrorism, health, and support for democracy (such as through election monitoring). The US Strategy Toward Sub-Saharan Africa, launched in August 2022, reaffirms these priorities while introducing a greater emphasis on climate adaptation and a 'just energy transition', but largely overlooking trade engagement. Where trade most strongly comes out in that strategy, it is with regard to security of access to Africa's 'critical minerals'. Nevertheless, the US is an important part of Africa's foreign policy environment. That is clear from the 41 (out of 49 invited) African countries that attended at a heads of government level the December 2022 US–African Leaders' Summit. The US accounts for a relatively larger share of Africa's trade (5 per cent of both imports and exports), and the US is the second largest source of development assistance to the continent, after the EU. A substantial amount of this, amounting to $10 billion annually in recent years, can be classified as aid for trade. This includes investments in trade-related infrastructure and productive capacities, and support for technical assistance and economic adjustments to trade. Perhaps most importantly, however, the US also has an influential voice in shaping the multilateral financial, investment and trade frameworks that govern Africa's economic integration with the wider world. The influence of the US can directly affect Africa's trade relationships with third countries. To use just one example, the US pressured the EU in the WTO over the legitimacy of non-reciprocity in trade agreements offered by the EU to African countries (Simo 2018).

US trade policy towards Africa is curiously consistent. From the administrations of Bush, through Obama and Trump, to Biden, US trade policy towards Africa has changed little in substance (see Figure 4.1). Where it has changed, those changes have usually been retained across administrations. This consistency extends to trade-related development assistance, which has fluctuated little despite political pronouncements occasionally suggesting otherwise (von Soest 2021). The Biden administration has been expected to follow the traditions of US Africa policy with merely 'a different (more respectful) tone, but no major changes in policy' (Adegoke 2020).

Figure 4.1: US aid-for-trade disbursements to African countries, 2010–2019, US$ billions

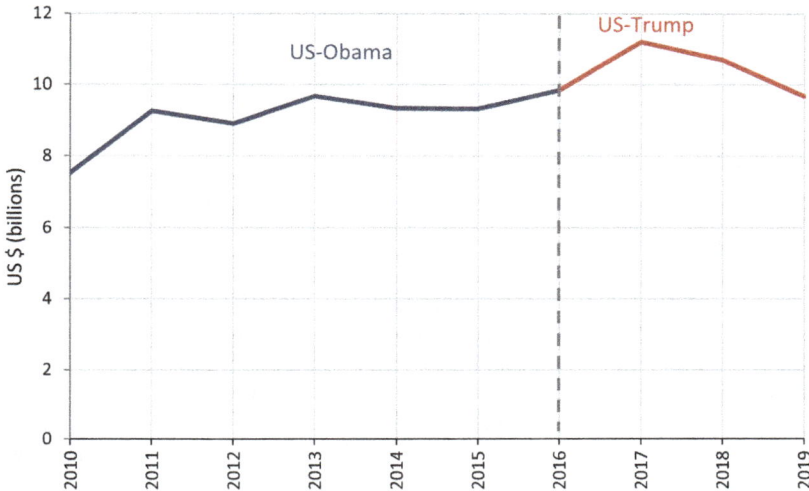

Source: Based on OECD (2022).

Looming large in the periphery of US trade policy towards Africa is of course China. So much so, in fact, that it might better be said that Africa is often more in the periphery of a US trade policy obsession with China. At the launch of 'A New Africa Strategy' in 2019, then US National Security Advisor John Bolton mentioned China over 20 times (Vaidyanathan 2022). It is no secret that the trick to engaging US policymakers on trade policy in Africa is to reframe core issues around a contestation with China, using narratives such as 'falling behind', 'catching up' or 'mak[ing] America greater than China … in Africa' (Signé and Olander 2019). Such a framing of Africa as merely a theatre of US geostrategic intervention has deep precedents, differing little from post-independence policy oriented around contesting Soviet influence (Schraeder 1991). Where US trade policy towards Africa has changed more notably, it is often merely in tone. The Trump administration's tone in this regard might best have been characterised as apathy. The then commerce secretary, Wilbur Ross, cancelled his attendance at the US–Africa Summit in Mozambique in 2019, an event attended by 11 African presidents, due to 'scheduling conflicts' (Paquette 2019) – leaving no cabinet-level US representation in attendance.

Since then, the Biden administration has shifted the tone of US engagement with Africa, ostensibly emphasising the importance of the continent while underlining messages of 'mutual respect and partnership' and downplaying its China rivalry (Sandner 2020). Biden chose to deliver his first speech at an international forum as US president at the 34th African Union summit (Rattner and Whitmore 2021), though it was just a video message. In his tour of three African countries at the end of 2021, Anthony Blinken, the US secretary of state under Biden, explicitly clarified that '[US] Africa policy is about Africa, not about China', but nevertheless retained oblique references to debt repayment and investment malpractices targeted at China (Hudson 2021). China was restated (alongside Russia) as representing strategic interests of 'contrast' in the continent in the 2022 US Strategy toward Sub-Saharan Africa.

The linchpin of US–Africa trade policy: AGOA

AGOA is the cornerstone of US–Africa trade policy for the sub-Saharan part of the continent. Beyond this, in North Africa the US has one trade agreement with Morocco (signed in 2004). In US trade parlance, AGOA is an Act of the US Congress that provides preferential – essentially duty-free – access to the US market for qualifying goods originating in eligible African countries south of the Sahara. Most notably, AGOA is *unilateral*, requiring no reciprocal trade openness from African countries. As a mature trade policy (having been in force since 2001), its impacts have been extensively monitored and evaluated, reviewed against their objectives, and its merits and failings analysed (Condon and Stern 2011; Cook and Jones 2015; Didia, Nica and Yu 2015; Tadesse and Fayissa 2008).

The empirical evidence on AGOA's impact is mixed. Most studies identify improvements in the volume and diversity of African exports to the US (Cook and Jones 2015; Didia, Nica and Yu 2015; Yeboah, Shaik and Musah 2021), but some find limited – or even negative – effects (Moyo, Nchake and Chiripanhura 2018). Some of those studies are frankly methodologically better than others; the higher-quality ones tend to find positive, though modest, results. In recent years, AGOA has supported on average $1.2 billion in qualifying annual automobile exports, mostly from South Africa, as well as $1.1 billion in qualifying annual textiles and apparel exports, and $0.3 billion in qualifying agriculture and food exports from the beneficiary African countries (Figure 4.2). While US imports from Africa fell precipitously under AGOA, that was mostly driven by falling mineral fuel imports that were replaced with US sources of shale oil from 2009 onwards. Many African countries have recorded product-specific successes in goods exported under AGOA to the US including textiles and apparel (from Kenya, Ethiopia, Mauritius, Lesotho and Madagascar); automobiles (from South Africa); plant roots and travel goods (Ghana); chocolate and basket-weaving materials (Mauritius); buckwheat, travel goods and musical instruments (Mali); sugar, nuts and tobacco (Mozambique); and wheat legumes and fruit juices (Togo) (Schneidman, McNulty and Dicharry 2021).

Beyond trade, AGOA was expected to promote investments in African countries. US investment in African countries did increase over the course of AGOA (Yeboah, Shaik and Musah 2021; Yeboah, Shaik and Wuaku 2021). However, and as indicated in Figures 4.3 and 4.4, these investments were disproportionally concentrated in a small number of countries and dominated

Figure 4.2: US imports from Africa, constant 2020 US$

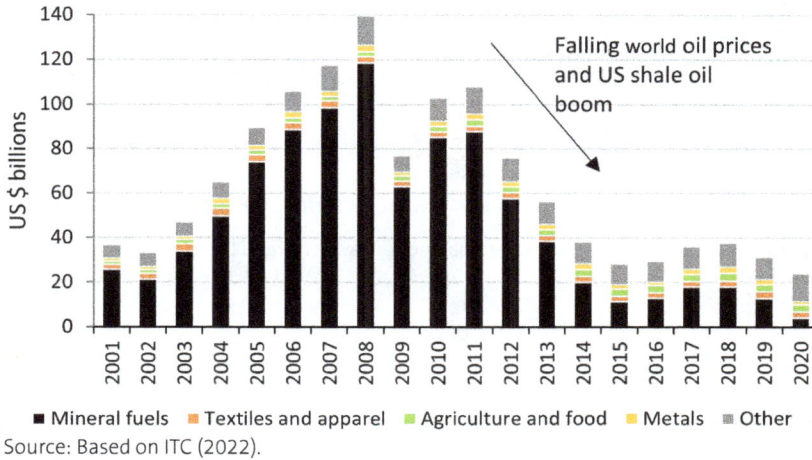

Source: Based on ITC (2022).

Figure 4.3: US direct investment positions in Africa, constant 2020 US$

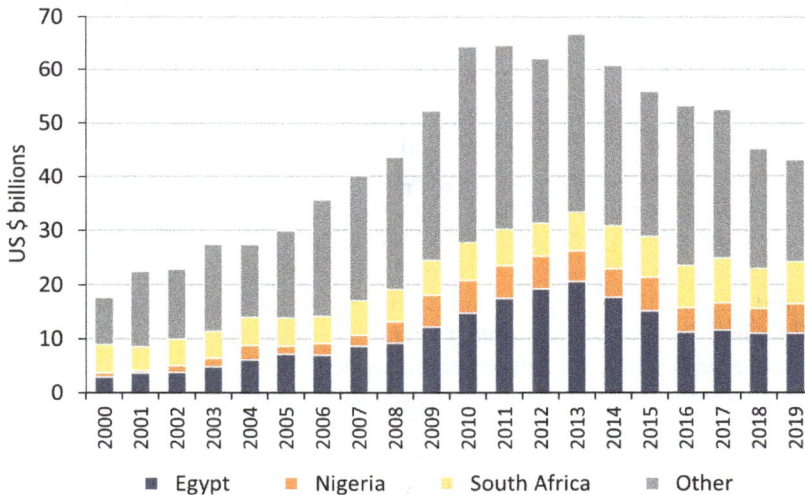

Source: Bureau of Economic Analysis, Balance of Payments and Direct Investment Position Data (2022).

by mining. Just 13 per cent of US FDI in Africa was in manufacturing, comparing unfavourably with EU investments, of which 41 per cent were in this sector (see Chapter 3). US FDI positions also fell following a decline in oil prices after 2014.

The most celebrated effect of AGOA has been the promotion of apparel exports from the subset of mostly lesser-developed African countries that

Figure 4.4: US direct investment positions in Africa, by industry, 2020

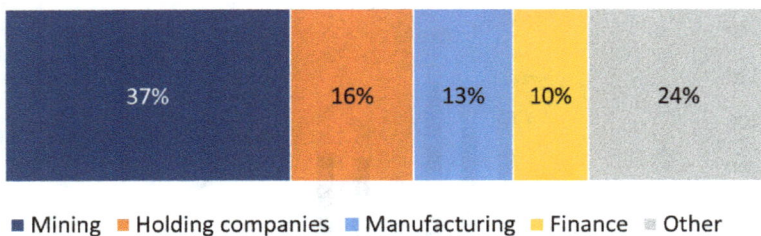

| 37% | 16% | 13% | 10% | 24% |

■ Mining ■ Holding companies ■ Manufacturing ■ Finance ▦ Other

Source: Bureau of Economic Analysis, Balance of Payments and Direct Investment Position Data (2022).

were granted more lenient rules of origin (known as the third-country fabric provision). These rules allowed qualifying countries to benefit from AGOA preferences on clothes made from imported fabrics (single-transformation rules of origin). In practice, this allowed them to import fabrics from the most competitive fabric producers, such as China, so that they could in turn be more competitive in downstream manufactures of clothing and apparel products. In most other US preferential arrangements, such as the US–Mexico–Canada Agreement (USMCA), the US requires countries to comply with the considerably more onerous requirement of using locally sourced fabric or even yarn (double-transformation or triple-transformation rules of origin). As Figure 4.5 indicates, the African countries that benefitted from the third-country fabric provision were able to better weather the expiry of the WTO Agreement on Textiles and Clothing in 2005, which increased competition in the sector by removing long-existing import quotas that had restrained imports from more competitive suppliers. The African countries that did not benefit from the third-country fabric provision conversely saw their textile and apparel exports to the US virtually disappear after 2005. Critics of the third-country fabric provision have, however, argued that it has nevertheless been insufficient to substantively transform textile and apparel production in these countries, with beneficiary countries remaining only in the downstream part of the value chain (Condon and Stern 2011). Nevertheless, the experience of African exporters under AGOA demonstrates the critical importance of technical parts of the regime, and particularly rules of origin, for its success.

The challenges confronting AGOA have been well evaluated. Understanding these helps to consider not just redesigns of the AGOA initiative but also comparable initiatives by other countries. These challenges with AGOA can be divided into four categories: issues with the AGOA regime itself, with US trade market requirements more broadly, and with the policy environment in African countries, and limitations in eligibility.

- **Issues with the AGOA regime.** Owing to the gradual lowering of US tariffs and the granting of preferential regimes to other countries (such as Africa's competitors in Central and Latin America), preference

Figure 4.5: Single- versus double-transformation rules of origin for AGOA-qualifying apparel exporters, constant 2020 US$

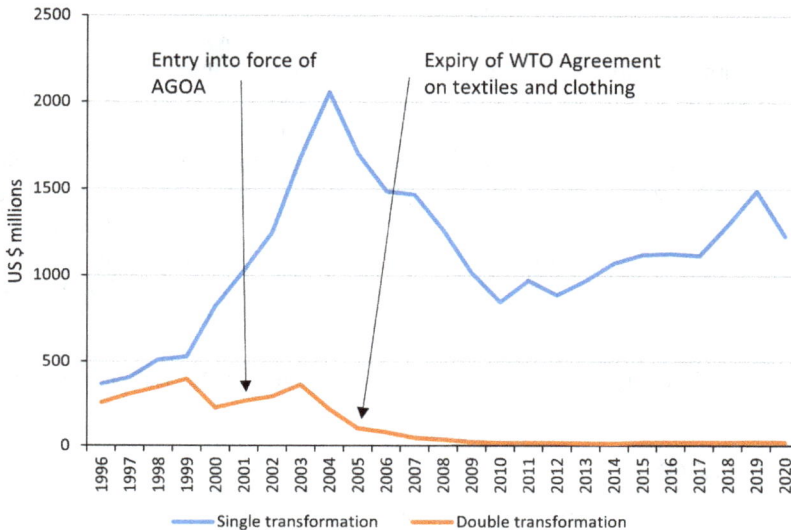

Source: UN Comtrade via WITS (2022).
Notes: Clothes and finished textiles comprise HS61–63 as well as HS57 (carpets, rugs etc.), but exclude HS6309 (worn clothes).

margins offered by AGOA were also relatively low to begin with. Important products are excluded, typically agricultural ones where tariffs remain high, and, except for the apparel sector, rules of origin are argued to be too strict for most least-developed countries (Condon and Stern 2011). The generosity of the preferential margins offered by AGOA have also been eroded by subsequent free trade arrangements created by the US for other countries.

- **Broader US trade requirements**. African businesses struggle to access the US market owing to many non-tariff barriers. Product standards, sanitary and phytosanitary measures, and technical standards, as well as challenges in attaining visas for African businesspeople, make it difficult for African businesses – and especially smaller businesses – to use AGOA (Simon, Munishi and Pastory 2022).
- **Policy environment in African countries**. The strength of the trade support environment in African countries has determined whether or not they have been able to take advantage of AGOA (Kassa and Coulibaly 2018; Owusu and Otiso 2021). Important determinants include the quality of trade infrastructure, trade facilitation efforts, institutional quality and the stability of the local macroeconomic environment (Kassa and Coulibaly 2018). Countries with AGOA utilisation strategies designed to take advantage of AGOA have performed better (notably Ethiopia, Kenya, Madagascar and Mauritius) (Davis 2017;

Schneidman, McNulty and Dicharry 2021). Such utilisation strategies were specifically called for in the act renewing AGOA in 2015 (Section 107 P.L. 114-27).

- **Limitation in eligibility**. Most obviously, AGOA is a regime that applies only to African countries south of the Sahara. As a unilateral preferential regime, rather than a free trade agreement, AGOA also permits the US to disqualify African countries whenever they are deemed to no longer meet a range of requirements related to the rule of law and political pluralism, through to health and labour practices (ITA n.d.). Ethiopia, Guinea, Burkina Faso and Mali, for example, were suspended from the scheme in January 2022 following the conflict in the Tigray region and military coups in the three West African countries. Such insecurity over country eligibility is argued to erode investor confidence and have significant impacts when eligibility is withdrawn (Hoekman 2005; Oxford Analytica 2022; Williams 2015).

Beyond AGOA

With AGOA set to expire in 2025, the United States has since the Obama administration considered the possibility of replacing the regime with reciprocal free trade agreements with interested African countries. The special interest is a perceived competitive scramble with China, which overtook the US as a supplier of Africa's imports in 2004, and the EU, which has reciprocal trade agreements of varying forms in place with 20 African countries (Pecquet 2021). Several African ministers of trade have pushed for a solution before AGOA expires. Alan Ganoo, Mauritian minister for foreign affairs, regional integration and international trade, remarked at the 2021 annual AGOA ministerial conference that 'both sides need to work together on a mutually acceptable solution before AGOA expires' (Pecquet 2021). The US thinking on post-2025 trade policy with African countries was first publicly outlined in the USTR's 'Beyond AGOA' report of 2016 and has persisted since then to guide the next steps in this policy area through the Trump administration. The report identified four main options (USTR 2016):

1. **Comprehensive US-style trade arrangements**: including substantial market access liberalisation and a wide range of behind-the-border issues.
2. **Asymmetrical EU-type agreements**: narrower in focus, dealing primarily with tariffs and matters directly related to trade in goods, and requiring less than full tariff product coverage and longer phase-down periods for tariff reductions on the African side, but argued to be unlikely to be offered by the US, which has 'no precedent' for such an approach.
3. **Stepping-stone arrangements**: collaborative arrangements for less capacitated countries involving work programmes towards minimum

trade facilitation standards and implementing labour laws, in return for specialised technical assistance and capacity-building. These already exist in the form of trade and investment framework agreements with several African countries, including South Africa, Ghana, Nigeria and the EAC and ECOWAS regions, and generally aim at the US securing market access openings and policies that go beyond what is obtainable at the WTO, including US priorities in the areas of labour, the environment and intellectual property rights (Simo 2018).

4. **Continued unilateral preferences**: for countries that are 'too fragile or resource-constrained' in the near term to fulfil the full suite of obligations that are traditionally part of US trade agreements.

In the final months of the Obama administration, the US pivoted towards launching negotiations 'with whichever country or countries and/or RECs that are ready to proceed to that kind of relationship, without having to wait for others' (USTR 2016). The explicit policy of seeking out these free trade agreements is set out in Section 108 of the act renewing AGOA in 2015.

Kenya–US FTA negotiations: first mover advantage?

The first post-AGOA negotiations were launched in February 2020 by the Trump administration's trade representative, Robert Lighthizer, and Kenya's cabinet secretary for trade, Betty Maina. In addressing the outgoing US ambassador, Kyle McCarter, in January 2021, the then Kenyan president, Kenyatta, remarked that 'We appreciate what has been achieved through AGOA, but it is time we moved to much closer trade arrangements that are mutually beneficial' and that '[Kenya] will not lose focus on concluding the FTA' (Mburu 2021). These negotiations were a priority for Kenya in early 2022, retaining policymaking attention – and indeed attracting funding for Kenya's lobbying efforts in the US – despite 2022 being a Kenyan election year in which political attention had other distractions.

Under the Biden administration, the Kenya–US negotiations did not progress beyond the pre-negotiations phase of the trade policy cycle. Both Kenya and the US initially embarked on an admirably open, transparent and relatively participative approach to the pre-negotiations, involving the publication of negotiating objectives (summarised in Table 4.1) and the solicitation of comments on those objectives, as well as through a public list of agreed common principles for the negotiations. The US Summary of Specific Negotiating Objectives was published in May 2020, while the Kenyan Negotiating Principles, Objectives and Scope was published in June 2020.

The Kenyan objectives revealed a general intent to seize a perceived 'first mover advantage' in being the first African country to engage in such negotiations with the US (MITED 2020). Kenya intended to retain, and expand upon, valuable preferential access into the US market after 2025. The interest for Kenya was clear: the US is an important destination for Kenyan products,

Table 4.1: Comparative analysis of US and Kenya FTA negotiating objectives

	United States	Kenya
General objectives	• Create a model for additional agreements across Africa • Support to regional integration • Promote good governance and the rule of law	• Reap a 'first mover advantage' among African trade agreement with the US • Create a framework for additional agreements across Africa • Compatibility with regional and continental integration • Safeguards and exceptions to protect 'nascent' sectors • Promote FDI inflows and Kenya's position as a transit hub for goods and services
Trade in goods	• Comprehensive liberalisation (targeting textiles and apparel, pharmaceutical and medical products, and agricultural goods) • Non-tariff barriers • Commitments on SPS, TBT and trade facilitation	• Comprehensive liberalisation (no specified target sectors) • Non-tariff barriers • Cooperation agreement on SPS, TBT and trade facilitation
Rules of origin	• Strong enforcement procedures • Production in the territory of the Parties	• Simple and easy to implement procedures • Asymmetry and cumulation to encourage regional value chains
Trade remedies	• Cooperation, transparency and scope for existing US trade laws	• New mechanism for resolving trade remedies within the agreement
Anti-corruption	• Rules on anti-corruption	• Information exchange and cooperation
Trade in services	• Horizontal liberalisation and specific commitments in telecommunications and financial services • Narrow exceptions	• Elimination of restrictions on high-interest sectors (none specified) • Asymmetricity

(Continued)

Table 4.1: (Continued)

	United States	**Kenya**
Data	• Free data flow commitments • Interoperability of data protection regimes • Prohibition on customs duties on digital products	• Facilitation of digital trade and cross-border data flows • Support to innovation, entrepreneurship and hubs for start-up incubation, acceleration and innovation
Investment	• Reduce investment barriers	• Investment protection, promotion, facilitation and liberalisation
Intellectual property rights	• Commitments on levels of protection, procedures, and enforcement	• Cooperation, capacity-building and technical assistance
State-owned enterprises	• Regulations on SOEs	• Asymmetry
Competition policy	• Rules on procedural fairness, transparency and limitations in competition law enforcement	• None
Labour	• Enforceable commitments	• Cooperation
Environment	• Enforceable commitments on environmental, wildlife and fishing standards	• Cooperation
Government procurement	• Rules on transparency and non-discrimination • Reciprocity	• Cooperation • Asymmetry

Source: Authors' elaboration based on USTR (2020) and MITED (2020).

amounting to Kenya's third most important export market after Uganda and Pakistan (Ogutu 2020). In recent years, Kenyan exports that have utilised the AGOA preferences have amounted to $500 million annually, predominantly in the apparel and accessories sector (AGOA.info 2020).

Kenya also sought, in its published negotiating objectives, to address non-tariff challenges in accessing the US market, targeting a cooperation agreement on sanitary and phytosanitary standards, technical barriers to trade and trade facilitation. Beyond this, Kenya expressed in its specific objectives an appetite for a substantial and deep agreement covering many behind-the-border regulatory issues such as intellectual property rights, investment, data governance, labour, the environment, and government procurement. Many of the Kenyan negotiating objectives were somewhat vague, however, and seem to amount to responses to US interests, rather than independent Kenyan priorities. It is curious, for instance, that the 'exchange of information on anti-corruption cases and initiatives' was among the negotiating objectives proposed by Kenya (MITED 2020). Their main objective was retaining US market access while diluting Kenyan commitments through aspects of asymmetry and special and differential treatment in which it would be held, as a less developed country, to lighter commitments than the US. In many areas of the negotiation menu, for instance, Kenya was more interested in provisions that would have established frameworks for cooperation, rather than binding rules.

The US objectives were considerable and deep. In addition to 'reciprocal' market access to the Kenyan market, the US objectives included substantial and hard behind-the-border reforms in the areas of intellectual property rights, digital trade and cross-border data flows, subsidies, competition policy, labour rights, the environment, anti-corruption, and government procurement. The US objectives also suggested a preference towards protectionist rules of origin, in line with US FTAs with other countries and regions (Erasmus 2020), and expressed little scope for the sorts of asymmetry or special and differential treatment desired by Kenya.

One of the greatest controversies with the Kenya–US negotiations was whether an agreement would undermine regional integration in the EAC or the AfCFTA. Though both Kenya and the US explicitly recognised the importance of Kenya's commitments to the EAC within their agreed negotiating principles, an agreement would have implied a deviation from the EAC's common external tariff. Such a deviation, though technically not impossible (Erasmus 2020), would have further undermined the longer-term aspirations towards the functioning of the EAC customs union by necessitating stronger checks on intra-EAC imports from Kenya to ensure that they did not amount to deflected US exports.

Conflict between the US–Kenya negotiations and the AfCFTA was less about technical feasibility than it was about prioritisation and eroding the value of Africa engaging as a coalition in trade policy. Part of the vision of the AU Agenda 2063 articulated in 2013 is for African countries to 'speak with one voice and act collectively to promote our common interests and positions in the international arena'. In the AU summit decision following the establishment of the AfCFTA in 2018, African heads of state 'Commit[ed] to engage external partners as one block speaking with one voice' and 'Urge[d] Member States to abstain from entering into bilateral trading arrangements until the entry into force of the Agreement establishing the AfCFTA' (African Union, Dec.692, 2018). In the subsequent summit of February 2019, this requirement was softened in a decision that stated that:

Member States wishing to enter into partnerships with Third Parties should inform the Assembly with assurance that those efforts will not undermine the African Union Vision of creating one African Market. (African Union, Dec.714, 2019)

Though there are clearly articulations of an ambition to negotiate as one and some seeds of effective coordination, the reality has included divergences that enabled the US–Kenya negotiations (Sunday and Wambu 2020). In bilateral negotiations with a large partner such as the US, Kenya would struggle to wield as much clout as would a united continental Africa. If the negotiations had progressed, Kenya would not have been as likely to achieve many of the asymmetricities and dilutions to the commitments it sought in the negotiations than could have been achieved by a united voice.

In early 2022, the US–Kenya negotiations were effectively suspended (Key Informant Interview 2022). The cessation of the negotiations came at the instigation of the US side: the Kenyan government and its private sector continued to exert diplomatic pressure and funded lobbying for the negotiations to resume (Key Informant Interview 2022). By 14 July 2022, the Kenya–US negotiations had been officially downgraded to merely the launch of a strategic trade and investment partnership (STIP). This is effectively, in the parlance of US economic engagements, a trade and investment framework agreement. The US has these in place with 13 other African countries and four African regional economic communities. Such agreements do not contain binding rules or rights but create a platform for further discussions that can evolve into commitments in a range of areas. The Kenya–US STIP is scheduled to involve discussions in eight areas: agriculture; anti-corruption; digital trade; environment and climate change; good regulatory practices; MSMEs; workers' rights and protections; and women, youth and others in trade. Notable, by their absence, are discussions on market access, which was the main negotiating objective of Kenya. Rather than attaining a 'first mover advantage', with the STIP, Kenya merely joined the groups of African countries that have collaboration frameworks in place with the US.

Introspection in US trade policy and 'Beyond AGOA' in flux

Four possibilities may have influenced the US in discontinuing FTA negotiations with Kenya and help to frame the likely shape of emerging US–Africa trade policy engagement. First, under President Biden, the US has become more focused on domestic priorities. Part of this relates to Biden's 'repeated call for America to lead by the power of our example', ahead of prioritising international trade engagements (Rattner and Whitmore 2021). The implication is a focus on the US first putting its own house in order and being less likely to strike trade agreements with any countries.

Second, in a reversal of the Trump approach, the US reprioritised multilateralism over bilateral foreign policy (May and Mold 2021). In November

2020, in her nomination acceptance speech to become the US ambassador to the UN, Linda Thomas-Greenfield declared 'America is back. Multilateralism is back' (Brodo and Opalo 2021). Markers of this renewed multilateralism include support to Nigeria's former finance minister Ngozi Okongo-Iweala as director-general of the World Trade Organization, rejoining the Paris climate agreement, and resuming funding for the WHO. Third, the trade and broader international policy attention of the Biden administration pivoted to Asia. The Biden administration prioritised a new Indo-Pacific Economic Framework, which was launched in May 2022 (Busch 2021).

Finally, and perhaps most importantly, the US became involved in a period of more general trade policy introspection. An ideological clash is resolving within US trade policymaking circles between the establishment narrative of laissez-faire market openness (see Chapter 5), which had dominated US trade policy preferences for decades, and new trade policy objectives revolving around a 'unionised worker-centric trade policy', and climate, environmental and security goals (Foroohar 2022; Oxford Analytica 2021). Specific regional or sectoral aspects of trade policy must derive from a large trade policy vision. Only once such overarching goals are agreed can the administration move along the trade policy cycle and articulate coherent policies and craft strategic trade deals – or otherwise focus on alternative trade policy instruments.

Until this introspective period has concluded, and a new unifying US trade policy is clarified, US trade policy towards Africa is unlikely to involve a step-wise shift in direction or large leaps forward. While the conclusion of full-scale free trade agreements is unlikely in the immediate term, little steps may be possible including the renewal of AGOA. The outcomes of the US–Africa Leaders' Summit, held in December 2022, are suggestive of this. The 2022 US–Africa Leaders' Summit resulted in an array of economic recommitments. This included the Prosper Africa programme, introduced by the Trump administration in June 2019 and described by some commentators as the new 'centerpiece of US economic and commercial engagement with Africa' (Nikkei Asia 2021). The summit also reaffirmed American commitment to the Power Africa and Partnership for Global Infrastructure and Investment programmes, though the latter is globally oriented rather than focused on Africa specifically. New announcements included the establishment of an Advisory Council on African Diaspora Engagement, to advise on a range of social and economic programmes and initiatives, and a Digital Transformation with Africa initiative. Such programmes are important for addressing supply-side constraints to trade, stimulating investment, and resolving business barriers that limit that capacity of African countries to take advantage of cornerstone trade policies such as AGOA. They have long featured as complements to the market access afforded by AGOA (Figure 4.6).

The latter Digital Transformation with Africa initiative is notable. It is focused on investments to expand the size of Africa's digital marketplace, build digital skills, and also influence the shape of Africa's 'digital enabling environment' with support to digital governance (White House 2022). That

Figure 4.6: Beside AGOA: trade policies and complementary programmes

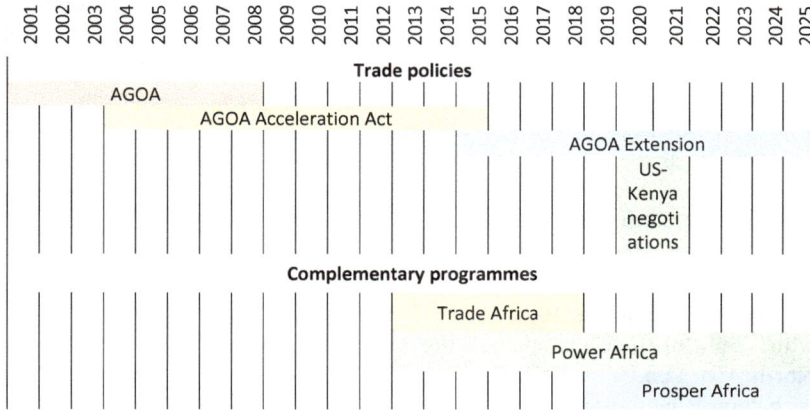

Source: Authors' elaboration.

cannot be viewed separately to the US seeking to encourage countries to come round to its vision of a relatively laissez-faire version of digital governance, as opposed to the more rights-based vision pushed by the EU, or authoritarian version offered by China (see Chapter 7). It may also involve 'advice' exerted against the imposition of digital services taxes levied by a number of African countries, including Kenya and Ghana.

The 2022 US–Africa Leaders' Summit also involved the signing of a memorandum of understanding between the US and the AfCFTA Secretariat. This will be the avenue for the US to follow through on its commitment to 'support the AfCFTA's implementation', announced in its August 2022 US Strategy Toward Sub-Saharan Africa. The memorandum of understanding contains limited substance beyond relatively soft, high-level commitments to cooperation activities such as information exchanges, best practice sharing, and dialogue. That is not surprising, and more details of the nature of the engagement will emerge once proposed technical working groups and an action plan have been developed. It is also commendably a publicly accessible document, unlike many other similar documents, which aids transparency and accountability. The identified areas of cooperation include digital trade, and presumably efforts to influence the AfCFTA Protocol on Digital Trade, industrial development and trade promotion, with an emphasis on sustainable development issues such as small and medium-sized enterprises and women in trade.

With regard to AGOA, and following the 2022 US–Africa Leaders Summit, the Biden administration sought to ask Congress to renew AGOA for 10 years. This followed successful lobbying efforts by African countries in 2022, such as the Lesotho Textile Exporters Association, which hired a Washington law firm, Ryberg and Smith, to help organise AGOA-focused meetings with US officials for Foreign Minister Matsepo Ramakoae during her visit to the

US for the UN General Assembly (Pecquet 2021). Efforts should now focus on ensuring that a renewed AGOA is even more effective than its previous iterations. Here the US seems to be receptive, with US Trade Representative Katherine Tai saying that '[AGOA] is no longer enough to boost [African countries'] development and a focus on improving investment is needed' and that AGOA needs an 'honest assessment' to 'increase utilisation rates', suggesting openness to its redesign in some form.

There are three categories of ways in which a better AGOA could be achieved. The first is through addressing problems with the programme itself, such as eliminating gaps in the product coverage of the AGOA programme and expanding the country coverage of AGOA to include North African countries. The latter may be possible if African countries can build a convincing case and link to the August 2022 US Strategy Toward Sub-Saharan Africa, which calls for the US to 'address the artificial bureaucratic division between North Africa and sub-Saharan Africa'. The second way to improve AGOA is with complementary measures, recognising that, for many of Africa's poorest countries, market access provisions in themselves are insufficient to motivate change. These complementary measures include the abovementioned programmes like Prosper Africa and Power Africa and support for the design and implementation of African countries' national AGOA utilisation strategies, as well as using trade and investment fairs and the US 'deal teams' within US embassies to boost practical trade and investment opportunities, alongside trade and investment facilitation services and trade capacity-building initiatives (Erasmus 2020). The final way in which AGOA could be improved is through linking it explicitly to Africa's regional integration initiatives and the AfCFTA, which is viewed favourably by the Biden administration. That would provide an opening for articulating a continental approach on trade that could link a beyond-AGOA deal to the AfCFTA (May and Mold 2021). That might also allow African countries more clout and influence in shaping the discussion than they could manage individually with such a large partner. Practical first steps would involve introducing supportive elements into AGOA, such as a cumulative rule of origin to encourage regional value chains across the continent.

Summary

AGOA is a generous offer, with positive elements such as non-reciprocity and uniform coverage among the eligible African countries. However, AGOA is limited to the countries south of the Sahara and, as a unilateral initiative, it comes with conditionalities that are determined by the US. As noted, the empirical evidence on the impact of AGOA is mixed. AGOA will expire in 2025. The US has been in an introspective phase on the role of trade in its foreign policy against the background of the Russia—Ukraine war and the geopolitical tensions associated with the rise of China. Various options are under consideration for a successor arrangement to AGOA. The signals suggest a lack of interest in the Biden administration in emulating the EU's EPAs and a reluctance in continuing the FTA negotiations with Kenya that were started by the Trump administration. It is also telling that Kenya's negotiation menu revealed a preference for trade and investment cooperation frameworks, rather than binding rules. The main Kenyan negotiating objective was to retain US market access while diluting Kenyan commitments through aspects of asymmetry and special and differential treatment, in which it would be held, as a less developed country, to lighter commitments than the US. Kenya's caution illustrates the unease of African countries in making reciprocal trade commitments at this stage of their development. The downgrading of the US–Kenya negotiations to a strategic trade and investment partnership allows Kenya to avoid difficult reciprocal commitments but also forgoes the Kenyan objective of securing continued US market access.

AGOA enjoys rare bipartisan support in the US Congress. As suggested, the US should use the opportunity for the renewal of AGOA to retain its positive features instead of replacing it with divisive bilateral agreements that would risk fracturing the continent and embryonic value chains. The US should establish a more conducive continent-to-continent arrangement. This would importantly include North Africa. For both the US and African countries, this would require greater vision and ambition. But, most significantly, it would require unity and consistency among African countries to work collectively and expeditiously. The African side should begin to lobby the US Congress, where Africa's small share of global trade flows is not seen as a threat and where 'trade not aid' is the basis of an already-broad consensus on the role that trade can and should play in Africa's development. They would need to show that such collective negotiations are possible, and beneficial. In AGOA, the generosity of the US's trade offer is unmatched by the EU, China, the UK and other partners. In the realm of geopolitics and geoeconomics, AGOA is surprisingly under-leveraged. A reformed AGOA along with a diversification of US investment flows would provide a model for the others to follow.

4.2 UK–Africa trade

Following its withdrawal from the European Union on 31 January 2020, or Brexit, the UK can design its own trade policies and strategies. However, to ensure continuity in its trading arrangements, the UK replicated the agreements to which it was a party in the EU. As seen in Chapter 3, these are the economic partnership agreements (EPAs), signed with selected African countries; the trade agreements with the North African countries; the Generalised System of Preferences (GSP), for low- and lower-middle-income countries; and the Everything But Arms (EBA) scheme, which provides duty-free and quota-free access to the EU market for countries classified by the UN as least developed (LDCs). In essence, these arrangements also reappeared in the UK's proposals for a Developing Country Trading Scheme (DCTS), which was launched for consultations in 2021. Along with the trade arrangements, the UK outlined a strategic vision of 'Global Britain' that centres on boosting trade and investment promotion to generate prosperity at home and abroad. As applied to Africa, the UK announced its intention to augment trade and business ties and become Africa's 'partner for prosperity' (DFID and DIT 2020; DIT and FCDO 2022). Notwithstanding the rhetoric, recent developments suggest both short-termism and opportunism as the guide to UK engagement with Africa (Brien and Loft 2021; Hadfield and Logie 2020). The merger of the Department for International Development (DFID) with the Foreign and Commonwealth Office (FCO), to become the Foreign, Commonwealth and Development Office (FCDO), resulted in a significant attrition of development expertise. A reversal in the UK commitment to contribute 0.7 per cent of GNI to a development assistance commitment of 0.5 per cent has eroded the financial heft behind UK development policy.

On the other hand, it is noteworthy that the UK emerged as a leading supporter of the COVAX initiative, which aimed to ensure fair global access to Covid-19 vaccines, pledging £548 million and 80 million Covid-19 vaccine doses (Gavi 2021; Loft 2022a; Loft 2022b). This contrasted with the UK government's decision to oppose the initiative at the WTO for a Trade-Related Intellectual Property Rights (TRIPs) waiver to boost vaccine production more widely (Loft 2022b; Yoon Kang et al. 2021; see Chapter 5).

However, in quite short order, the UK has reshaped its trade support institutions with the aim of making them nimbler and more responsive. Considering declining levels of UK–Africa trade flows as noted in Chapter 1, these were much-needed reforms, although they will take time to deliver. On 29 March 2022, the UK announced a £35 million programme to support AfCFTA implementation including customs and other trade facilitation reforms in collaboration with the Overseas Development Institute (ODI), AfCFTA state parties, the AfCFTA Secretariat, TradeMark Africa (TMA) and other regional partners (DIT and FCDO 2022). However, by December 2022 it had become clear that the proposed support will be substantially reduced as the UK struggled with fiscal consolidation.

This section outlines the main developments beginning with the UK–Africa trade arrangements that emerged after Brexit became effective and the UK's proposals for the DCTS; the efforts to promote the vision of prosperity through three African investment conferences in 2020, 2021 and 2022; and institutional arrangements that support trade and investment flows with Africa.

Continuity over disruption

In the lead-up to its withdrawal from the EU, British negotiators and their counterparts put considerable effort into roll-over arrangements to avoid a 'cliff edge' upon the UK's extrication from EU trading arrangements. Many of these, however, were finalised only after withdrawal in January 2020. Figure 4.7 shows the timeline for the UK's roll-over of the EU's trade agreements with African countries. The first to be signed was the East and

Figure 4.7: Timeline for the signature of UK EPAs with African countries

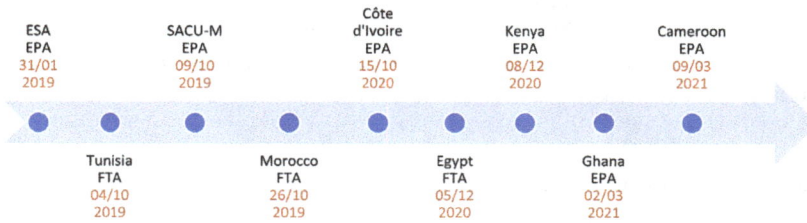

Source: Authors' elaboration.
Notes: ESA is Eastern and Southern Africa; SACU is the Southern Africa Customs Union.

Southern Africa (ESA) EPA with Comoros, Madagascar, Mauritius, Seychelles, Zambia and Zimbabwe. This was followed by an agreement with Tunisia, the Southern Africa Customs Union (comprising South Africa, Namibia, Botswana, Lesotho and Eswatini), and Mozambique. Morocco, Côte d'Ivoire, Egypt, Kenya, Ghana and Cameroon were next.

A reflection of the asymmetry between the UK and African economies, the agreements are of partial reciprocity. They provide for duty-free and quota-free access for most goods imported by the UK with a gradual and progressive reduction of duties on goods imported by the African countries along with limitations on services and public procurement in African markets. The agreements also include hortatory declarations, including to promote economic and development cooperation, build trade capacity, and support regional integration.

In replicating the EU's EPAs, the agreements carried over an anomaly that establishes a separate trade regime with the UK between African countries in the same customs union. This is in effect a hard border in the customs unions concerned. This is the case for Côte d'Ivoire and Ghana in ECOWAS, Kenya in the EAC and Cameroon in ECCAS. The trade deal with the UK incentivises these countries to abrogate customs union disciplines and puts the internal cohesion of these vehicles of economic integration under strain (Luke, Desta and Mevel 2021). A provision in the preamble of these agreements that accession of other countries in the same customs union remains open is the fig leaf that is used to cover up this anomaly.[1]

However, some African countries – Nigeria famously among them – remain wary of the EPAs. This is mainly because of economic asymmetries and aspirations to reduce dependence on imported manufactures. As these sensitivities were ignored, the House of Lords International Relations and Defence Committee felt compelled to call for a 'coherent strategy' for Africa (UK House of Lords 2020). This was echoed by President Buhari of Nigeria, who called for an Africa-wide trade agreement with the UK (Buhari 2022). However, like the EU, the UK government's ambition is to widen and deepen the EPAs by adding new chapters in such areas as services, investment, public procurement and sustainable development (DIT 2022). Rather than using its newfound trade policy independence to correct the mistakes of EU trade policy, the UK has merely replicated those policies and their errors. With regard to Africa, the UK's patchwork of trade agreements is no different to that which persisted while the UK was within the EU. Over the longer run, scope exists to improve upon these.

Developing Country Trading Scheme (DCTS)

In 2021, the UK published proposals on its concessional trade arrangements and launched consultations. The proposals, which mirror the EU's arrangements, embody measures for partial or full removal of customs duties on the UK's imports from developing countries. The government proposed three trade regimes for the DCTS (DIT 2021).

- A General Framework, for countries that are classified by international financial institutions as low-income and lower-middle-income countries.
- An Enhanced Framework with a wider range of product coverage for low and lower-middle-income countries with specific vulnerabilities such as small island states. This is like the EU's GSP+ scheme, and like its EU counterpart requires beneficiaries to adhere to certain conditionalities, such as implementation of international conventions on human and labour rights and the environment.
- The Least Developed Countries Framework, which provides for duty-free and quota-free access on all goods other than arms and ammunition, again mirroring the EU's EBA.

However, significant improvements to the EU's scheme were proposed by the government in the following areas.

- Tariffs: the government proposed to reduce or completely remove tariffs for goods in which low-income and lower-middle-income countries are competitive to stimulate trade with the UK.
- Rules of origin: the government proposed to introduce an updated list of product-specific rules for goods imported under the scheme and to expand the rules on cumulation for least-developed countries.
- Goods graduation: the government proposed to take a more targeted approach using UK trade data to graduate goods out of the scheme's preferential tariff rates.
- Conditionalities: the government proposed to simplify the conditions that could lead to a suspension or variation of preferences for any participating country and to simplify the reporting requirements for accessing preferences in the Enhanced Framework.

If introduced, these improvements will enhance the value of the scheme to the beneficiaries and better cater for the needs of vulnerable stakeholders, who are often overlooked when their country's concessions are withdrawn for violation of international conventions, sometimes causing long-term negative harm to them (te Velde and Mendez-Parra 2021). Scheduled to be launched in 2023, the proposed scheme is expected to cover 70 countries. According to the UK government, it will provide a 'simple, more generous and pro-growth approach to trading with developing countries' (Department for International Trade and Foreign, Commonwealth and Development Office 2021). Tables 4.2 and 4.3 provide an overview of what the UK's trade regime for African countries will look like following the introduction of the planned DCTS.

Table 4.2: African countries party to an FTA with the UK

North Africa free trade agreements (FTA)	– Egypt – Morocco – Tunisia
Economic partnership agreements (EPA)	– Cameroon – Côte d'Ivoire – Ghana – Kenya – ESA EPA: Comoros, Madagascar, Mauritius, Seychelles, Zimbabwe – SACU-M EPA: Botswana, Eswatini, Lesotho, Mozambique, Namibia, South Africa

Source: Authors' compilation.

Table 4.3: African countries that are beneficiaries of the UK's GSP

LDC Framework	Angola, Benin, Burkina Faso Burundi, Central African Republic, Chad, Comoros,* Congo DR, Djibouti, Eritrea, Ethiopia, Gambia, Guinea, Guinea-Bissau, Lesotho, Liberia, Madagascar,* Malawi, Mali, Mauritania, Mozambique,* Niger, Rwanda, Senegal, Sierra Leone, Somalia, South Sudan, Sudan, Tanzania, Togo, Uganda, Zambia
General Framework	Algeria, Congo, Nigeria
Enhanced Framework	Cabo Verde

Source: Authors' compilation.
Notes: *Comoros, Madagascar and Mozambique have also signed trade agreements with the UK (they are parties to the ESA EPA (Comoros and Madagascar) and SACU(M) EPA (Mozambique) and can trade under either the EPA or LDC framework regime (Key informant interview 2022a)).

The UK–Africa investment conferences

The Commonwealth provides the UK with a forum for regular meetings at the highest levels and other exchanges with the African member states. However, the UK has lacked a forum for engaging with Africa as a whole. The 'global Britain' ambition that was central to the vision of the 'leave campaign' during the Brexit debates, along with a nuanced view of a Britain that has shaken off its colonial past, required a new forum to engage Africa as a whole, not just the former British colonies. This was provided by the UK–Africa investment conferences, which have become institutionalised as an annual event for commercial diplomacy, mutual assessment of opportunities and exchange of ideas. Over 3,000 delegates from the UK and African countries attended each of the three events, held in 2020, 2021 and 2022.

The inaugural conference, held on 20 January 2020, was attended by several African heads of state including from countries outside the Commonwealth. It was envisioned by its organisers as an opportunity to facilitate business contacts. Among the announcements was an initiative to make $400 million available by the UK government-backed CDC Group (now British International Investment, BII) for a partnership with African regional banks for enterprise development (Reuters 2020). Twenty-seven deals were announced (Department for International Trade and Department for International Development 2020). But some commentators remained underwhelmed by the conference as a transformative initiative (Golubski and Schaeffer 2020; Yeates, Beardsworth and Murray-Evans 2020).

The second conference was held exactly a year later, on 20 January 2021. A new Africa Investors Group (a grouping of UK's largest investors in Africa) was unveiled, with a focus on four priority sectors – sustainable infrastructure, renewable energy, financial and professional services, agriculture and agri-tech (DIT, Duddridge and Grimstone 2020). A major theme was the government's roll out of a pro-business emphasis in its aid programmes. This followed the reversal of the commitment on ODA and the merging of the Department for International Development (DFID) with the Foreign and Commonwealth Office (FCO), effective from September 2020. The shift in focus was made clear in the government's Integrated Review of Security, Defence and Foreign Policy, published in March 2021:

> We will more effectively combine our diplomacy and aid with trade, working with our partners to adapt our offer. As governments become able to finance their own development priorities, we will gradually move towards providing UK expertise in place of grants using a variety of financing models to tackle regional challenges in our mutual interests. (UK Government 2021)

The UK, having hosted the UN Climate Change Conference in November 2021, focused on sustainable investment and green growth for the third event, in January 2022. A major announcement was £2.3 billion for the UK Export Finance Agency to facilitate UK–Africa business deals and the launch of the

Growth Gateway. This is a digital tool designed to provide information and practical advice to the UK and African business communities on investment and export opportunities. The Growth Gateway is the fourth instrument in a quartet of trade support institutions with key roles for boosting trade and investment with Africa (see Box 4.1).

Box 4.1: UK trade and investment support institutions

UK Export Finance (UKEF). UKEF is the government's export credit agency, operating under the Department for International Trade. Its main objective is to help exporters of UK goods and services to win business opportunities overseas by providing credit guarantees and insurance and reinsurance facilities. UKEF can also assist businesses that are not based in the UK with access to finance, loans and insurance for specific projects that rely on goods and services sourced from the UK (Tibke 2022). An example of a project funded through UKEF is £70.3 million for Contracta Construction UK to develop and modernise the Kumasi Central Market in Ghana (UKEF, DIT and Fox 2019).

British International Investment (BII, formerly Commonwealth Development Corporation – CDC). BII is the UK government's development finance institution, operating under the Foreign, Commonwealth and Development Office. Its mandate is to support the growth of businesses and jobs creation in Africa, Asia and the Caribbean (BII 2022). An example of its operations is a $100 million risk-sharing facility signed with the US bank Citigroup, aimed at expanding the latter's supply chain lending in Africa by boosting lending to small businesses across the continent by up to $400 million (Reuters 2022).

British Support for Infrastructure Projects (BSIP). Formerly the Developing Markets Infrastructure Programme, BSIP was revamped in early 2022 to support low- and lower-middle-income country governments to prepare, procure and finance development-focused, sovereign-backed sustainable infrastructure projects. Operating under the UK Foreign, Commonwealth and Development office with PricewaterhouseCoopers as the implementing partner, BSIP provides grants and technical assistance to enable governments to borrow at concessional rates for infrastructure projects where they are not able to do so commercially, or where they require concessional finance to support their national climate plans. It works collaboratively with UK Export Finance (FCDO 2022).

Growth Gateway. Operating under the Department for International Trade, the Growth Gateway is designed as a business support digital service that connects businesses in Africa and the UK to information and resources on trade, finance and investment opportunities. Very little information is currently (December 2022) publicly available on the Growth Gateway's operations.

Summary

In relation to the framework for analysing African trade policy outlined in Chapter 1, UK–Africa trade relations can be considered to be in the design stage at this early point of the UK's post-Brexit journey. Relatively low scores can be given for openness and transparency and inclusive participation since little attention has been given to these issues from both the UK and African perspectives. Some improvements in the DCTS were noted. But the scheme is essentially modelled after the EU's trade arrangements, which have a divisive effect on Africa's trade integration efforts. The priority has been efficiency. The UK and its partners in Africa strove for a roll-over of pre-existing EU regimes, like the EPAs, and the avoidance of a 'cliff edge' end to EU regimes to which the UK was a party. In imitating the EU's trade arrangements, the UK lost an opportunity to overcome the divisive implications of multiple trade regimes for Africa.

With the UK's investment in Africa highly concentrated in a few countries and sectors, the investment conferences highlighted new investment opportunities (Ottoway 2021). There is much that can be commended in the conceptual thought behind the design of the UK trade and investment support. But it is still too early to assess these initiatives for impact. However, it should be kept in perspective that through the 'invisible trade' of remittances it is the African diaspora in the UK that is the largest and most dynamic contributor to UK–Africa trade flows. This was estimated to be an annual $6.5 billion in 2015 (Westcott 2022), with scope for scale-up if transfer costs can be contained (FSD 2017; ODI 2022).

4.3 Recent developments in other bilateral trade relationships

While the EU, China, the US and the UK are Africa's most important trading partners, accounting for 48 per cent of Africa's exports, and intra-African trade accounts for another 18 per cent, a full 34 per cent of Africa's trade flows through other bilateral trading relationships. These are crucially important, if less individually significant, trading partners for the continent. Two aspects of Africa's trading relationships with these 'other' countries stand out. First, preferential trade arrangements are generally in place to incentivise trade growth. This is usually accompanied by significant trade promotion efforts supported by investment flows. Second, high-level summits are organised with periodic frequency to review and advocate for greater engagement in development and economic cooperation including trade and investment. One or both features are prominent in bilateral relations with India, Turkey, Japan, Russia and Brazil, which are considered in brief in this section. The actual trade flows with these countries are individually small, generally well under 3 per cent of Africa's total exports or imports (except for India, which accounts for about 6 per cent). In relation to the analytical framework outlined in Chapter 1, these relationships are mainly at the initial phases of trade policy design. But steps towards deeper trade arrangements have been taken through the negotiation of FTAs by India (with Mauritius) and Turkey (with North African countries).

India

Since the early years of the 21st century, Africa's trade with India has climbed steadily upwards, with exports rising from just over 2 per cent of total exports by value in 2001 to 7.6 per cent in 2021 (IMF 2022). Similarly, imports into Africa from India have increased from 1.8 per cent to 5.5 per cent by value of total imports. India has a trade preferential scheme in place for LDCs since 2008 that allows duty-free entry for up to 98 per cent of tariff lines. Exports from Uganda, Tanzania, Rwanda, Zambia and Mozambique have increased under the scheme (Afrexim Bank and India Exim Bank 2018). However, the structure of this trade follows the familiar pattern of Africa's exports consisting mainly of fuels, minerals and precious stones and imports of manufactures such as clothing, textiles, pharmaceuticals, cereals, chemicals and machinery. Services are a prominent feature of India's exports including health care and digital and agriculture services (Karingi and Naliaka 2022). The Indian diaspora in Africa plays a key role in forging economic ties. Three Africa–India summits were held between 2008 and 2015 and frequent meetings at the ministerial level promote further engagement.

Indian investment in Africa also shows an upward trajectory, with the stock of Indian FDI rising from $11.9 billion to $15.2 billion between 2010 and 2014 (Afrexim Bank and India Exim Bank 2018). Distribution is fairly diversified covering natural resources, oil and natural gas (Côte d'Ivoire, Libya, Mozambique, Libya, South Sudan and Sudan); coal (Mozambique and Zambia) and copper (Zambia); agriculture, including tea production (Uganda and Rwanda) and floriculture (Ethiopia and Kenya); services, such as telecommunications and health care (Kenya), information technology (Ethiopia and South Africa) banking (Botswana, Ghana, Kenya, Mauritius, South Africa, Uganda, Zambia and Mauritius); manufacturing (Ghana and Nigeria); and pharmaceuticals (Nigeria) (Afrexim Bank and India Exim Bank 2018).

In the other direction, between 2010 and 2014, the stock of African FDI in India increased from $57 billion to $73.3 billion. This is mainly from Mauritius, which is a widely used conduit for Indian inward and outward FDI, owing to its low tax rates. Eswatini, South Africa, Seychelles and Morocco are among the other largest African investors in India. Investments from South Africa include Tiger Brands, Airports Company South Africa & Bidvest, SAB Miller, FirstRand Bank, Standard Bank, Old Mutual, Balela Leisure, Anglo-American, Sasol and Nandos Group Holdings. Morocco has invested in the production of phosphates in India, with Zuari Maroc Phosphore holding a 74 per cent stake in the previously state-run Paradeep Phosphate Ltd (Afrexim Bank and India Exim Bank 2018).

However, Mauritius remains India's most important trade and investment partner in the African continent, a relationship that has been formalised in an FTA, the Comprehensive Economic Cooperation and Partnership Agreement (CECPA), which was signed on 22 February 2021 and entered into force on 1 April 2021. The CECPA covers both trade in goods and trade in services. The agreement provides preferential market access for 615 products from Mauritius, including frozen fish, speciality sugar, biscuits, fresh fruits, juices, mineral water, beer, alcoholic drinks, soaps, bags, medical and surgical equipment, and apparel. Some 310 export items from India benefit from preferential market access in Mauritius, including foodstuff and beverages, agricultural products, textile and textile articles, base metal, electricals and electronic items, plastics and chemicals, and wood. FTA negotiations between India and the SACU counties and COMESA are in progress (Chaudhury 2020). This raises the prospect that a hotchpotch of trade regimes between African countries and India may emerge and complicate trade policy coherence within Africa as trade and economic integration initiatives unfold (Goyal 2022).

Turkey

Turkey's engagement with Africa is a strategic objective of its foreign policy (Orakçi 2022). According to the Turkish Foreign Ministry:

> Developing our relations and cooperation with the African continent constitute one of the basic principles of our multi-dimensional foreign policy. It is expected that Africa will play a more active role in the international system as of the second half of the 21st century and assume an increasingly important role on the global stage. The economic and commercial potential and geopolitical weight of the rapidly developing continent in several areas have started to attract a vast number of countries and investors to Africa in recent years. (Turkey Ministry of Foreign Affairs 2022)

As a member of the EU's customs union, Turkey's trade arrangements with Africa reflect those of the EU. Accordingly, its EBA, GSP+, GSP, EPAs and FTAs with the North African countries are aligned to the EU's and awkwardly replicate the shortcomings of the EU's approach. Recent years have seen active engagement in Africa by Turkey. As in the case of Africa's trade with India, this century has seen an upward crawl in Africa's trade with Turkey, although the North African countries account for half of total trade, which grew from $2.2 billion in 2001 to $16.5 billion in 2020 (equivalent to 0.8 per cent of Africa's trade in 2001 and 1 per cent of its trade in 2021) (IMF 2022).

Turkey is also active in infrastructure projects and air transport services throughout the continent. The cumulative value of infrastructure projects in

Africa topped $71.1 billion in 2020. Turkish airlines maintain connections to 60 destinations in 39 African countries (Turkey Ministry of Foreign Affairs 2022). The importance Turkey attaches to cultivating economic ties with African countries is reflected in three summits that were held between 2008 and 2021. An outcome of the 2021 summit hosted by Turkey and attended by 16 African heads of state was a pledge to achieve $50 billion in two-way trade over five years, with manufacturing, agriculture, construction, textiles, and health care identified as priority sectors (Minney 2021).

Japan

Both preferential trade and high-level summits feature in Japan's trade relations with African countries. Japan offers duty-free, quota-free and GSP and concessions to African LDCs and developing countries, respectively, for qualified products. Rules of origin are moderate but cumulation that allows for sourcing inputs between African countries is restrictive, which is a disincentive for fostering supply chains. Japan's main interest in Africa follows a well-trodden path of importing strategic minerals (from South Africa and other countries) and petroleum (particularly from Algeria and Nigeria). This is driven by the need for Japan to diversify its energy sources in the wake of the Fukushima nuclear disaster (Pajon 2020; Pathirana 2021). Japanese exports are mainly chemicals, machinery, automobiles and other transport equipment. Japan accounted for 4 per cent of Africa's imports in 2001, falling to 1.8 per cent in 2021 (IMF 2022). Japan accounted for 1.6 per cent of Africa's exports in 2001, rising to 2.1 per cent in 2021 (IMF 2022).

Japan barely makes the list of top 10 overseas development assistance providers to Africa (ranking ninth, just ahead of the UAE), providing $1.5 billion in 2019 or 3 per cent of ODA disbursements, according to the OECD. However, Japan is active in some infrastructure projects such as upgrading the ports of Mombasa in Kenya and Nacala in Mozambique and connectivity along the corridors served by these ports (Pajon 2020). Since 1993, Japan has sponsored the Tokyo International Conference on African Development (TICAD) as a regular forum for dialogue on economic cooperation. These forums are co-organised with the African Union, UNDP and the World Bank to provide a high-level platform for Japan's multilateral development frameworks and norms. At TICAD VII in 2019, attended by 42 African heads of state, $20 billion was set as a target for Japanese private sector investment in the period up to 2022, with a strong emphasis placed on business and investment partnerships. This will build upon the activities of Japanese entities such as the Japan Oil, Gas and Metals National Corporation, whose investment ceiling in natural gas and energy projects has increased, and the Japan Bank for International Cooperation (JBIC), which has provided infrastructure financing and promoted Japanese commercial operations through loans, equity and investment guarantees.

Russia

Measured against Africa's relatively small bilateral trade flows, Africa's trade with Russia is even more modest, accounting for just 0.2 per cent of African exports and 1.8 per cent of African imports in 2021. Bilateral trade between the two parties has evolved over the past decades, from $1.4 billion in total goods trade in 2000 to $10.3 billion in 2021. Africa mainly exports horticultural and other agricultural produce, minerals and precious stones and imports arms and cereal grains. Wheat accounts for 95 per cent of formal imports (although less thoroughly recorded weapons trade is also large) from Russia, making it crucial for food security, as the Russia–Ukraine war has revealed. Egypt, Sudan, Nigeria, Tanzania, Algeria, Kenya and South Africa are the main importers (Agence Ecofin 2022). By comparison, the main importers of wheat from Ukraine are Libya, Morocco and Tunisia (Millecamps and Toulemonde 2022).

While the Soviet Union was active in Africa during the Cold War years, including through backing liberation movements and leftist regimes, its successor, the Russian Federation, reduced its engagement. However, parading as a significant player on the geopolitical stage, Russian interest in Africa has grown in recent years including through paramilitary interventions in conflict situations in the Central African Republic, Burkina Faso and Mali. On the diplomatic front, Russia convened the first Russia–Africa Summit, which took place in Sochi, from 23 to 24 October 2019 (Panara 2019). Attended by 43 heads of state and government, it was a diplomatic success, although concrete deliverables in the key areas identified for cooperation such as high-tech extraction and processing of mineral resources, agriculture, and infrastructure development are yet to materialise (Foy 2019; Roscongress 2021). With extensive economic sanctions imposed on Russia following its invasion of Ukraine in 2022 and with 28 out of 54 African countries supporting a UN resolution that condemned the invasion (with most of the rest abstaining), the prospects for economic cooperation as envisaged at the summit have diminished (White and Holtz 2022). A second summit that had been planned for 2022 did not materialise (Devonshire-Ellis 2021).

Brazil

The Lusophone African countries (Angola, Cabo Verde, Guinea-Bissau, Mozambique and Sao Tome and Principe) were traditionally the leading trading partners with Brazil, with which they share historical and cultural ties. From 2003, under President Lula da Silva, who pursued an active 'South–South' foreign policy, this expanded to new trading partners such as Nigeria, Ghana, Mali and the Southern Africa Customs Union (SACU) countries (Freitas 2016; Oloruntoba 2014). An FTA between the Common Market of the South (MERCOSUR), of which Brazil (along with Argentina, Paraguay and Uruguay) is a member, and SACU (which includes Botswana, Eswatini,

Lesotho, Namibia and South Africa) was signed on 15 December 2008 and entered into force on 1 April 2016 (Tralac 2016). Agricultural and industrial sectors are covered but the spread of the preferential margin is wide-ranging, between 100 and 10 per cent. The threshold for rules of origin is high, requiring that non-originating materials do not exceed 40 per cent of value. Although trade flows remain small, two-way trade between the parties appear to have been given a nudge by the agreement. South Africa, for example, was able to increase its exports to Brazil by 37 per cent, going from $483 million in 2017 to $663 million in 2018 (DTIC 2019). A joint administration committee of the parties provides an institutional framework for monitoring the agreement.

Summary

Trade flows between Africa and what might be considered its important, but 'second tier', trading partners are modest, with trade relations at a nascent stage of trade policy design. A few FTAs are in place. These are limited in geographical coverage and generally arise out of specific circumstances. This is the case of the India–Mauritius FTA, with close ties between the two countries combined with Mauritius's general openness to trade liberalisation (see Chapter 3, which covers the China–Mauritius FTA). Turkey's FTA with North African countries is mainly a result of its membership of the EU customs union, which requires alignment with the bloc's trade arrangements. The MERCOSUR–SACU FTA has been led by Brazil's efforts to engage African countries, driven by a 'South–South' foreign policy launched by Brazil in 2003.

India, Turkey, Japan and Russia offer duty-free, quota-free (DFQF) access to the African LDCs but each places restrictions on what can be exported from the African countries. For India, the exceptions are meat and dairy products, vegetables, coffee, tobacco, iron and steel products, and copper products. For Japan it is rice, sugar, fishery products and leather products. For Russia it is petroleum products, copper, iron ores, leather products, apparel and clothing. Indeed, Russia's DFQF scheme only covers 36.3 per cent of tariff lines, compared to most others, which are over 90 per cent (WTO 2015). Turkey has no significant restrictions except arms and ammunition, replicating the EU's Everything But Arms offer to LDCs. In all cases, market access is further restricted by rules of origin and sanitary and phytosanitary requirements.

The strategic and symbolic importance attached to engagement with Africa by the partners is reflected in the institutional arrangements in various formats to facilitate discussions with African countries on common approaches to development, trade and investment. Japan's TICAD and the comparable efforts of India, Turkey and Russia (see Table.4.4) provide a forum for mutual geopolitical diplomacy between African leaders and the partners. The results of these partnerships so far have been modest, with an overwhelming focus on short-term trade and investment issues and interests. A strategic vision on how these partnerships (and others not reviewed in this section) can be

Table 4.4: Partner summits with African countries

	Japan	India	Turkey	Russia
Forum	TICAD	India–Africa Forum Summit	Turkey–Africa Summit	Russia–Africa Summit
First edition	1993	2008	2008	2019
Frequency	Every five years	—	—	—
Latest edition	2019 (TICAD VII)	2015	2021	2019
Latest edition's attendance	42 African leaders	41 African leaders	16 African leaders	43 African leaders

Source: Authors' compilation.

leveraged to support long-term economic transformation in Africa is yet to emerge from either the African side or the partners.

Conclusions: what Africa needs from trading partners

The main takeaway from this chapter builds upon the conclusions that were reached in Chapter 3 on Africa's trade with the EU and China, its biggest trading partners, which argued that the trade offer of these partners falls short of Africa's development needs. The current trading arrangements offered to Africa by its partners have done too little to transform Africa's trade from its disproportionate concentration in raw commodities and fuels. A new trade deal is needed for the continent. This should incentivise and reward trade diversification, expanded productive capacities, interconnected supply chains, and sustainable growth. The empirical evidence suggests that for these goals to be met, two complementary measures are required: the right sequencing of trade policy that prioritises intra-African trade (which is already more diversified than Africa's external trade) and liberalised trade with harmonised trade rules between African countries, as offered by the AfCFTA initiative (Mevel et al 2015). In that regard partner countries would, like physicians hoping to help their patients, do well to 'first do no harm'. But that is not always the current practice. The evidence suggests that implementing the EU (and other advanced country) reciprocal agreements like the EPA ahead of Africa's AfCFTA would result in losses in trade – or trade diversion – between African countries (Mevel et al 2015). The problem is that such agreements force African countries to undertake divergent regulatory and trade reforms rather than first consolidating better regionally.

The ideal trade deal for Africa is one that requires a broader trade-support framework. Trade preferences alone are an important but insufficient part of the solution. The experience of trade under AGOA with the US, through the

EU's various regimes, and under China's DFQF regime, show that more is needed. African businesses struggle with non-tariff barriers, such as product standards, sanitary and phytosanitary measures and technical standards. African businesspeople sometimes face challenges in obtaining visas, making it difficult for them – and especially smaller businesses – to meet business partners and strike deals. The policy environment in African countries themselves is often not supportive either. Many African countries have sub-par trade infrastructure, trade facilitation efforts, institutional quality and unstable macroeconomics.

Africa's trade partners can help by buttressing their trade preferences to Africa with a set of complementary measures. First among these are deliberate efforts to boost investments in African countries, but also to improve the type of investment, diversifying away from that disproportionately concentrated in extractive resources to instead those in agriculture and industry. Second are initiatives to ease the ability of African businesses to overcome non-tariff barriers. China has shown the value of deliberate, value-chain specific, 'green lanes' to fast-track agricultural exports, for instance. Third is the alignment of development assistance with trade. In programmes such as the EU's Global Gateway, China's Belt and Road, the US's Prosper Africa and Power Africa, the UK's British International Investment and British Support for Infrastructure Projects, and the multi-partner Trade Mark Africa, Africa's advanced country partners have recognised the need for investments to help unlock supply side constraints in infrastructure, energy, transport, education, health, research, and digitalisation, among others. Yet Africa's deficits in these areas persist and more support is needed.

As a 'late developer', Africa requires efforts to level the playing field if it is ever to catch up and achieve key elements of economic convergence. With strategic sequencing that would offer unilateral preferential access for African exporters now, and deeper reciprocal trade deals only when African economies are better integrated and ready, the world can create the right trade environment for the continent. Buttressed with complementary support measures, Africa's development partners can help unlock trade as the tool it should be to African sustainable development. By following the right sequencing for AfCFTA implementation prior to reciprocal deals, Africa will be given the opportunity to build productive capacities and achieve its potential for strong and diverse growth in intra-African trade, with inclusive and transformational consequences.

Note

[1] See, for example, Article 3.1 of the Explanatory Memorandum on the Interim Agreement Establishing an Economic Partnership Agreement between the United Kingdom of Great Britain and Northern Ireland and the Republic of Cameroon.

References

Adegoke, Yinka (2020) 'How a Biden Administration Will Change US-Africa Relations', Quartz Africa, 1 February. https://perma.cc/ZZ2D-6R2X

Afrexim Bank and India Exim Bank (2018) 'Deepening South-South Collaboration: An Analysis of Africa and India's Trade and Investment', Cairo, Egypt: The African Export–Import Bank (Afreximbank) and the Export–Import Bank of India (Exim India).

African Business (2021) 'Third Turkey-Africa Partnership Summit Delivers "Win-Win" Agreements', African Business Trade and Investment, 18 December. https://perma.cc/FV5U-QHFV

African Union (2018) 'Assembly of the Union', Thirty-First Ordinary Session. 1 July. https://perma.cc/U7KU-ZF3E

African Union (2018) 'Assembly of the Union', Thirty Second Ordinary Session. 10–11 February 2019. https://perma.cc/PMD8-76W2

Agence Ecofin (2022) 'L'Afrique importe sept fois plus de produits qu'elle n'en exporte vers la Russie', Ecom News Afrique, 8 March. https://perma.cc/XR8M-F4YQ

AGOA.info (2020) 'The Proposed Kenya – USA Free Trade Agreement'. https://perma.cc/2U7V-AQS2

Brien, Philip and Loft, Philip (2021) 'Reducing the UK's Aid Spending in 2021', United Kingdom House of Commons Library Research Briefing, 5 November. https://perma.cc/QK27-6ZYA

Brodo, Mike and Opalo, Ken (2021) 'Multilateral Trade Agreements Should Constitute the Cornerstone of Biden's US-Africa Policy', Center for Global Development, 1 June. https://perma.cc/ZQA8-U2SN

Bureau of Economic Analysis US Department of Commerce (2022) 'U.S. Direct Investment Abroad: Balance of Payments and Direct Investment Position Data'. https://perma.cc/L3M2-FKZB

Buhari, Muhammadu (2022) 'A UK-Africa Trade Deal Would Create Jobs and Boost the Commonwealth: Post-BREXIT, It Is Now Possible', Daily Trust, 24 January. https://perma.cc/W62P-7RCY

Busch, Marc (2021) 'Biden's Muddled Trade Policy', The Hill, 24 December. https://perma.cc/K5J7-RK78

Chaudhury, Dipanjan Roy (2020) 'India Revives Initiative for Preferential Trade Agreement with S. African Customs Union', The Economic Times, 19 July. https://perma.cc/8V2K-9W6L

Condon, Niall and Stern, Matthew (2011) 'The Effectiveness of African Growth and Opportunity Act (AGOA) in Increasing Trade from

Least Developed Countries', London: EPPI Centre, Social Science Research Unit, Institute of Education, University of London. https://perma.cc/S8BM-L7EY

Cook, Nathaniel and Jones, Jason Cannon (2015) 'The African Growth and Opportunity Act (AGOA) and Export Diversification', *The Journal of International Trade & Economic Development*, vol.24, no.7, pp.947–67. https://doi.org/10.1080/09638199.2014.986663

Davis, William (2017) 'The African Growth and Opportunity Act and the African Continental Free Trade Area', *AJIL Unbound*, vol. 111, pp. 377–83. https://doi.org/10.1017/aju.2017.92

Department for International Development, Department for International Trade (2020) 'UK Aims to Be Africa's Partner of Choice for Trade and Investment', Press Release, 20 January. https://www.gov.uk/government/news/uk-aims-to-be-africas-partner -of-choice-for-trade-and-investment

Department for International Development, Prime Minister's Office, 10 Downing Street, Department for International Trade, Foreign and Commonwealth Office, The Rt Hon Boris Johnson MP and The Rt Hon Alok Sharma MP (2020) 'UK Government Statement on UK-Africa Investment Summit', 20 January. https://perma.cc/4PN4-2C9T

Department for International Trade (2020) 'Guidance: Trading with Developing Nations', 31 December. https://www.gov.uk/government/publications/trading-with -developing-nations

Department for International Trade (2022) 'Response to the House of Commons' International Trade Committee's Call for Evidence on the UK's Trade Approach towards Developing Countries', 28 February. https://perma.cc/KS55-RBLX

Department for International Trade and Department for International Development (2020) 'UK-AIS Commercial Deals: A Summary of 27 Commercial Deals Worth Over £6.5bn from Across the Africa Markets Invited to the UK-Africa Investment Summit', News Story, 20 January. https://www.gov.uk/government/news/uk-ais-commercial-deals

Department for International Trade and Foreign, Commonwealth and Development Office, Vicky Ford MP, and The Rt Hon Anne-Marie Trevelyan MP (2022) 'UK Backs Africa's Ambitious Continental Free Trade Initiative', Press Release, 29 March. https://www.gov.uk/government /news/uk-backs-africas-ambitious-continental-free-trade-initiative

Department for International Trade and the Foreign, Commonwealth, Development and Development Office (2021) 'New UK Scheme to

Drive Trade with Developing Countries', Press Release, 19 July. https://www.gov.uk/government/news/new-uk-scheme-to-drive-trade -with-developing-countries

Department for International Trade, James Duddridge MP and Lord Grimstone of Boscobel Kt (2020) 'UK to Host the Africa Investment Conference in the New Year', Press Release, 10 December. https://www.gov.uk/government/news/uk-to-host-the-africa-investment -conference-in-the-new-year

Devonshire-Ellis, Chris (2021) 'Russia Prepares for 2022 Africa Summit as Trade & Investment Increase', Russia Briefing, 2 December. https://perma.cc/324R-R5QU

Didia, Dal; Nica, Mihai; and Yu, Geungu (2015) 'The Gravity Model, African Growth and Opportunity Act (AGOA) and US Trade Relations with sub-Saharan Africa', *The Journal of International Trade & Economic Development*, vol.24, no.8, pp.1130–51. https://doi.org/10.1080/09638199.2014.1000942

Erasmus, Gerhard (2020) 'The Proposed US-Kenya Trade Deal: Context and Consequences', Tralac, 13 April. https://perma.cc/R9CY-FX7K

Foreign, Commonwealth, and Development Office (2022) 'Supporting Indian Trade and Investment for Africa', Development Tracker, 24 March. https://perma.cc/J33D-WXXA

Foroohar, Rana (2022) 'US Trade Policy Needs a Radical Redesign', *Financial Times*, 6 February. https://perma.cc/KW89-RXYQ

Foy, Henry (2019) 'Russia Turns On the Charm at First Africa Summit', *Financial Times*, 24 October. https://perma.cc/VS6G-ZE7W

Freitas, Marcus (2016) 'Brazil and Africa: Historic Relations and Future Opportunities', Policy Brief, OCP Policy Centre, 8 February. https://perma.cc/U3CV-2RWU

FSD Africa (2017) 'Reducing Costs and Scaling up UK to Africa Remittances through Technology', Report, June. https://perma.cc/975W-F6WQ

Gavi (2021) 'UK-Donated Covid-19 Vaccine Doses Reach African Countries', Gavi Newsletter, 13 August. https://perma.cc/83EP-BFV8

Golubski, Christina and Schaeffer, Anna (2020) 'Africa in the News: UK-Africa Investment Summit, Turkey's Increased Engagement, and Angola Fraud Scandal', Brookings Africa in Focus, 25 January. https://perma.cc/33VC-CFNS

Goyal, Tanu M. (2022) 'The African Continental Free Trade Area: Opportunities for India', ORF Occasional Paper, 7 February 2022. https://perma.cc/B6WY-6A6F

Hadfield, Amelia and Logie, Chris (2020) 'UK Development Ambitions: The Impact of the 2020 FCO-DFID Merger', Political Studies Association Blog, 28 October. https://perma.cc/ZFX4-9GBH

Hoekman, Bernard (2005) 'Operationalizing the Concept of Policy Space in the WTO: Beyond Special and Differential Treatment', Journal of International Economic Law, vol.8, no.2, pp.405–24. https://doi.org/10.1093/jielaw/jgi027

Hudson, John (2021) 'Blinken Lays Out U.S. Policy towards Africa and Deliberately Avoids Mentioning China', Washington Post, 19 November. https://perma.cc/8LS4-BMSX

IMF (2022) 'Direction of Trade Statistics', Database, accessed June 2022.

ITA (International Trade Administration) (n.d.) 'General Country Eligibility Provisions'. https://perma.cc/NKQ4-X8LF

ITC (International Trade Center) (2022) 'Trade Map', Database.

Karingi, Stephen and Naliaka, Laura (2022) 'The Future of India-Africa Relations: Opportunities Abound', Brookings Africa in Focus Blog, 25 February. https://perma.cc/7H9D-JT8J

Kassa, Woubet and Coulibaly, Souleymane (2018) 'Revisiting the Trade Impact of AGOA: A Synthetic Control Approach', Policy Research Working Paper, World Bank. https://perma.cc/NHZ6-77ZG

Key Informant Interview (2022) 'Updates on Kenya-US Negotiations and Lobbying'.

Key Informant Interview (2022a) 'Updates on the UK Developing Country Trading Scheme'.

Loft, Philip (2022a) 'COVAX and Global Access to Covid-19 Vaccines', United Kingdom House of Commons Library Research Briefing Number 9240, 11 January. https://perma.cc/H4UA-4BLD

Loft, Philip (2022b) 'Waiving Intellectual Property Rights for Covid-19 Vaccines', United Kingdom House of Commons Library Research Briefing Number 9417, 8 April. https://perma.cc/J3GS-MPHL

Luke, David; Desta, Melaku; and Mevel, Simon (2021) 'The European Union Is Undermining Prospects for a Free Trade Agreement with Africa', Africa at LSE Blog, 14 December. https://perma.cc/88VQ-SCQJ

May, Liz and Mold, Andrew (2021) 'Charting a New Course in US-Africa Relations: The Importance of Learning from Others' Mistakes', Brookings, 21 June. https://perma.cc/CW8W-WAEH

Mburu, Peter (2021) 'Kenya: Govt to Continue Pursuing Trade Deal With U.S. All Africa', All Africa, 19 January. https://perma.cc/89XQ-39RN

Millecamps, Matthieu and Toulemonde, Marie (2022) 'Ukraine-Russie: Quels sont les pays africains les plus exposés à la flambée des cours du blé?' Jeune Afrique, 25 February. https://perma.cc/PD7W-WLED

MITED (Ministry of Industrialization, Trade and Enterprise Development) (2020) 'Proposed Kenya – United States of America Free Trade Area Agreement: Negotiation Principles, Objectives, and Scope'. https://perma.cc/CLJ5-T25W

Moyo, Busani; Nchake, Mamello; and Chiripanhura, Blessing (2018) ' An Evaluation of the US African Growth and Opportunity Act (AGOA) Trade Arrangement with Sub-Saharan African Countries', PSL Quarterly Review, vol.71, no.287, pp.389–418. https://doi.org/10.13133/2037-3643/14251

OECD (2022) QWIDS (Query Wizard for International Development Statistics).

Ogutu, Moses (2020) 'Caught between Africa and the West: Kenya's Proposed US Free Trade Agreement', 19 June. https://perma.cc/9WLL-MPRV

Oloruntoba, Samuel (2014) 'Africa-Brazil Relations in the Context of Global Changes', Institute for Global Dialogue, Issue 109, July. https://perma.cc/7NN2-F32B

Orakçi, Serhat (2022) 'The Rise of Turkey in Africa', Aljazeera Centre for Studies, 9 January. https://perma.cc/9P3F-3ABJ

Ottoway, Richard (2021) 'UK-Africa: Britain Must Act Quickly to Boost Trade and Investment across the Continent', The Africa Report, 23 March. https://perma.cc/2NVG-MBBV

Owusu, Frances and Otiso, Kefa M. (2021) 'Twenty Years of the US African Growth and Opportunity Act (AGOA): Policy Lessons from Kenya's Experience', Kenya Studies Review, p.16. https://perma.cc/D7YN-C753

Oxford Analytica (2021) 'US Trade Policy Extends 'Trump's Themes but Adds Nuance', Expert Briefings. https://doi.org/10.1108/OXAN-DB263815

Oxford Analytica (2022) 'AGOA Exclusion Adds to Economic Pressure on Ethiopia', Expert Briefings. https://doi.org/10.1108/OXAN-DB266658

Pajon, Celine (2020) 'Japan's Economic Diplomacy in Africa: Between Strategic Priorities and Local Realities', Notes de l'Ifri, December. https://perma.cc/MB3M-B77D

Panara, Marlene (2019) 'Russie-Afrique: l'économie au coeur du nouveau partenariat', Le Point, 21 October. https://perma.cc/39T9-PKTB

Paquette, Danielle (2019) 'Trump Administration Unveils Its New Africa Strategy — with Wins and Snags', Washington Post, 19 June. https://perma.cc/F52M-YDTJ

Pathirana, Dilini (2021) 'Promoting Japanese Private Investments in Africa: A Clash of Interests', Afronomicslaw Blog, 20 August. https://perma.cc/CP8Y-6FTM

Pecquet, Julian (2021) 'US-Africa Trade Pact AGOA at Risk? African Leaders Raise Alarm', The Africa Report, 20 October. https://perma.cc/JND2-Q3NK

Rattner, Rebecca and Whitmore, Bjorn (2021) 'President Biden's Africa Policy', LSE Ideas, May. https://perma.cc/E3DA-WQAT

Reuters (2022) 'Citi, British International Investment Agree $100 Million Risk-Sharing Lending Deal for Africa', Reuters, 17 May. https://perma.cc/7DDW-642G

Roscongress (2021) 'Outcomes of the First Russia-Africa Summit and Economic Forum', 3 June. https://summitafrica.ru/en

Sandner, Philipp (2020) 'US-Africa Policy: Biden's New Africa-US Policy', DW, 29 April. https://perma.cc/YLM8-JDX4

Schneidman, Witney; McNulty, Kate; and Dicharry, Natale (2021) 'How the Biden Administration Can Make AGOA More Effective', Africa in Focus, Brookings blog. https://perma.cc/5LU6-EPA5

Schraeder, Peter J. (1991) 'Speaking with Many Voices: Continuity and Change in US Africa Policies', The Journal of Modern African Studies, Vol.29, No.3, pp.373–412. https://www.jstor.org/stable/160879

Signé, Landry and Olander, Eric (2019) 'Can Trump's Prosper Africa Make America Greater than China and Other Partners in Africa?', Brookings, Africa in Focus, 26 June. https://perma.cc/Y49P-BZRU

Simo, Regis (2018) 'The AGOA as Stepping Stone for USA–Africa Free Trade Agreements', Journal of International Trade Law and Policy, vol.13, no.7, p.115. https://perma.cc/8JAS-7B57

Simon, Edward; Munishi, Emmanuel; and Pastory, Dickson (2022) 'Local and International Factors Affecting Participation of Tanzanian Small and Medium Enterprises in Market Opportunity Brought by the African Growth and Opportunity Act (AGOA)', International Journal of Economics and Finance, vol.14, no.1. https://doi.org/10.5539/ijef.v14n1p68

South Africa's Department for Trade, Industry and Competition (DTIC) (2019) 'SACU/MERCOSUR Preferential Trade Agreement Leads to Exponential Increase of SA Exports to Brazil', Media Statement, 5 April. https://perma.cc/P52N-LUVX

Sunday, Frankline and Wambu, Wainaina (2020) 'Kenya Risks AU Wrath as It Seeks Solo Deal with America', Standard Media, 31 January. https://perma.cc/D29U-YNHV

Tadesse, Bedassa and Fayissa, Bichaka (2008) 'The Impact of African Growth and Opportunity Act (Agoa) on US Imports from Sub-Saharan

Africa (SSA)'. *Journal of International Development: The Journal of the Development Studies Association*, vol.20, no.7, pp.920–41. https://doi.org/10.1002/jid.1446

te Velde, Dirk Willem and Mendez-Parra, Maximiliano (2021) 'Importing for Development: Reforming the UK's Trade Preferences', ODI, 14 September. https://perma.cc/FSL7-932P

Tibke, Patrick (2022) 'UK Export Finance More Than Triples Its Investment in Africa to £2.3bn', Trade Finance Global, 21 January. https://perma.cc/6LU8-AFVZ

TRALAC (Trade Law Centre) (2016) 'Entry into Force of the Preferential Trade Agreement between MERCOSUR and SACU', 28 October. https://perma.cc/LM5U-SH5M

Turkey, Ministry of Foreign Affairs (2022) https://perma.cc/SFD8-STT8

Turkish Economic Relations Board (DEIK) (2017) 'New Agreement for Trade Enhancement Signed with Tunisia', Press Release, 24 July. https://perma.cc/69LL-9YJ6

Turkish Ministry of Foreign Trade, 'Free Trade Agreements'. https://perma.cc/9YRD-YJTX

UK Export Finance, Department for International Trade, The Rt Hon Liam Fox MP (2019) 'UKEF Supports UK Firms to Develop Critical Ghanaian Infrastructure', Press Release, 27 February. https://www.gov.uk/government/news/ukef-supports-uk-firms-to -develop-critical-ghanaian-infrastructure

UK Government (2021) 'Global Britain in a Competitive Age: The Integrated Review of Security, Development and Foreign Policy', March. https://perma.cc/9FVQ-UVFB

UN Comtrade (2022) Customs Trade Dataset.

UNCTAD (2017) 'Generalized System of Preferences: Handbook on the Scheme of Turkey', New York, and Geneva: United Nations. https://perma.cc/PJM6-63FA

UNCTAD (2017) 'Handbook on India's Duty-Free Tariff Preference Scheme for Least Developed Countries', New York and Geneva: United Nations. https://perma.cc/2SMV-BT3S

UNCTAD (2020) 'Handbook on the Preferential Tariff Scheme of the Republic of Korea in favour of Least Developed Countries', Geneva: United Nations. https://perma.cc/2CT8-PPNA

UNCTAD (2021) 'Generalized System of Preferences: Handbook on the Scheme of Japan', 7th edition, Geneva: United Nations. https://perma.cc/7F68-8GTP

UNCTAD (2021) 'Generalized System of Preferences: Handbook on the Scheme of Canada', 3rd edition, Geneva: United 'Nations. https://perma.cc/6BRK-KSH6

United Kingdom House of Lords (2020) 'The UK and Sub-Saharan Africa: Prosperity, Peace, and Development Co-operation', Select Committee on International Relations and Defence's 1st Report of Session 2019–21, 10 July. https://perma.cc/862D-L6S2

USTR (United States Trade Representative) (2016) 'Beyond AGOA: Looking to the Future of US-Africa Trade and Investment', Report, USTR. https://perma.cc/UE47-CMGM

USTR (United States Trade Representative) (2020) 'United States-Kenya Negotiations: Summary of Specific Negotiating Objectives'. https://perma.cc/5CPV-2DDR

Vaidyanathan, Veda (2022) 'What Could a Non-China-Centric US Africa Policy Look Like?', African Arguments, 22 February. https://perma.cc/YK85-S7NN

von Soest, Christian (2021) 'The End of Apathy: The New Africa Policy under Joe Biden'. German Institute for Global and Area Studies focus on Africa, No. 2. https://perma.cc/69SS-3F5L

Westcott, Nicholas (2022) 'Shared Fortunes: Why Britain, the European Union, and Africa Need One Another', European Council on Foreign Relations Policy Brief, April. https://perma.cc/7GZW-ZENN

White, Abraham and Holtz, Leo (2022) 'Figure of the Week: African Countries' Votes on the UN Resolution Condemning Russia's Invasion of Ukraine', Brookings Africa in Focus Blog, 9 March. https://perma.cc/K9TG-DQEP

White House (2022) 'Fact Sheet New Initiative on Digital Transformation with Africa', Press Release. https://perma.cc/H2NU-G298

Williams, Brock R. (2015) 'African Growth and Opportunity Act (AGOA): Background and Reauthorization', Washington, DC: Congressional Research Service. https://perma.cc/V2ZW-HPCF

WTO (2015) 'Duty-Free and Quota-Free Market Access for LDCs', Report by the Secretariat. https://docs.wto.org/WT/COMTD/W214.pdf

Yeates, Emily; Beardsworth, Nicole; and Murray-Evans, Peg (2020) 'What Happens Next for UK-Africa Relations Post-Brexit?', Africa at LSE Blog, 4 February. https://perma.cc/8WFZ-JU83

Yeboah, Osei; Shaik, Saleem; and Musah, Jamal (2021) 'Impact of AGOA on Agricultural Exports Growth of Member Countries: A Dynamic Shift-Share Analysis', Journal of Applied Business & Economics, vol.23, no.4, p.101. https://perma.cc/KN67-8PXW

Yeboah, Osei; Shaik, Saleem; and Wuaku, Michael (2021) 'AGOA: Economic and Political Effects on FDI Flows into Sub-Saharan Africa', *Journal of Applied Business & Economics*, vol.23, no.5, p.258. https://perma.cc/2F3F-DQ55

Yoon Kang, Hyo; McMahon, Aisling; Dutfield, Graham; McDonagh, Luke; and Thambisetty, Siva (2021) 'COVID-19 Vaccines: Wealthier Nations, Including the UK, Must Drop Their Opposition to the Proposed TRIPS Waiver at the WTO', LSE British Politics and Policy Blog, 14 July. https://perma.cc/6SHL-LG9T

5. Africa in the World Trade Organization

Colette van der Ven and David Luke

The multilateral trade regime, centred on the World Trade Organization (WTO), is the umbrella under which trade between its members is regulated, based on key principles including openness, predictability and non-discrimination. With over a quarter of the WTO's 164 country membership being African, it is important that the WTO works for and with Africa (African Business 2020). The appointment of Dr Ngozi Okonjo-Iweala in 2021 as the first African WTO director-general sent a strong signal that Africa, as a late-developing continent, has a vested interest in the WTO and its rules that help to shape development outcomes.

This chapter delves into the question of how African agency at the WTO is exercised to achieve pro-development results against the backdrop of geopolitical shifts, anti-globalisation sentiments, the re-emergence of nationalism, the digital revolution and an increasingly urgent climate crisis. The stalemate over the Doha Round that was launched in 2001 to respond to developing country concerns, coupled with the failure of the WTO to achieve consensus to enlarge its negotiating agenda to encompass new issues that have since emerged, have led many to question the organisation's continued relevance. Having walked away from the Doha Round, most developed countries are determined to press on with a new agenda on a plurilateral basis. This carries the risk of splintering the WTO into a two-tier operation. The collapse of the Appellate Body, the pinnacle of the WTO's dispute settlement process, has weakened its adjudicative function. While these issues remain to be substantively addressed, the WTO's 12th ministerial conference, in June 2022, saw progress regarding fishery subsidies, one of the outstanding issues in the Doha Round, and agreed on a partial waiver on certain TRIPS provisions for Covid-19 vaccine patents.

These developments form the backdrop against which the WTO must be examined in relation to the role it could play to enhance Africa's development prospects. This is not straightforward as it depends on one's narrative about the role of the WTO from a developmental perspective. For those who see the

How to cite this book chapter:

van der Ven, Colette and Luke, David (2023) 'Africa in the World Trade Organization', in: Luke, David (ed) *How Africa Trades*, London: LSE Press, pp. 117–140. https://doi.org/10.31389/lsepress.hat.e License: CC-BY-NC 4.0

WTO trade regime as 'the tide that lifts all boats', the key principles comprising the multilateral trade system, including discrimination, enhanced transparency and lower trade barriers, are believed to generate strong development outcomes. This may also be described as the neo-liberal or 'establishment' narrative. Conversely, those who consider WTO rules to be inherently unfair and constraining, limiting opportunities for agricultural development, industrialisation and catch-up growth, will emphasise the importance of securing flexibilities and exemptions from existing rules. This may be described as the 'principled' narrative.

At the risk of oversimplification, the current gridlock at the WTO can be seen as a stand-off between these two narratives, with developed countries predominantly pointing to trade's development benefits, while developing and least-developed countries highlight the system's constrains. But it is also possible to draw upon elements from these two perspectives – some of which are intertwined – to construct a third narrative as a strategy for action. This may be labelled the 'pragmatic' narrative. A pragmatic narrative would focus on results over principles and procedural niceties, technical analysis over ideological positioning, and would be future-oriented.

This chapter addresses two main themes. The first two sections outline the main elements in the two narratives to set the scene for the second half of the chapter, which assesses African member states' record of engagement with the WTO. The assessment is conducted from three perspectives: in relation to the deliberative bodies that oversee the WTO regime; negotiations that establish the rules of the regime; and in the settlement of disputes that arise in the application of the rules. African agency has in a few areas been effective in pursuing African interests. In other areas, Africa has failed to obtain desired results. Moreover, in relation to the analytical framework for assessing the trade policy cycle outlined in Chapter 1, African engagement at the WTO presents a mixed record given the gaps with respect to openness, transparency, inclusive participation, accountability and efficiency. But Africa's capacity and resource limitations must also be recognised. These issues are taken up in the concluding section of the chapter. Inspired by the framework established in *Six Faces of Globalization* (Roberts and Lamp 2021), a deconstruction of the narratives that dominate discussions about the WTO helps to explain diverging views about how African countries can maximise the benefit of WTO membership. It also enables an approach to the question of African engagement at the WTO from an analytical as opposed to an ideological perspective. The merits of the 'establishment' and 'principled' narratives are now considered.

5.1 The establishment narrative

The establishment narrative has dominated Western thinking in the post-World War II international economic order, with antecedents that go back even further. Free trade is the starting point. Specifically, free trade has enabled countries to specialise, allowing economic actors to focus on their comparative advantage and to exchange products (and services) that they are good and efficient at making with products (and services) in which other countries have a comparative advantage. By creating new markets, free trade has also led to advances in technology and productivity. With respect to development, the economist Paul Krugman, for example, argued that:

> the raw fact is that every successful example of economic development this past century – every case of a poor nation that worked itself up to a more or less decent, or least dramatically better, standard of living—has taken place via globalization; that is, by producing for the world market rather than trying for self-sufficiency. (Krugman 1999, cited in Roberts and Lamp 2021)

This establishment narrative underlies the thinking of the 'the guardians' of the international economic order, including the WTO Secretariat. In assessing the role of the WTO in Africa's development, official WTO publications consistently tout the benefits of free trade. For example, a 2021 report under the title 'Strengthening Africa's Capacity for Trade' noted that:

> [A] stable, multilateral trading system and access to international markets has had positive effects on the development of industrialization in Africa, and efforts to build capacity, to enable African countries to take fuller advantage of the benefits that trade brings. (WTO Africa Report 2021)

It further notes that:

> Trade has allowed many developing countries to benefit from the opportunities created by emerging new markets by enabling them to integrate into the world market through global value chains. Moreover, the unbiased, predictable and non-discriminatory regime maintained by the multilateral trading system places all economies – developing and developed, small and large – on an equal footing.

More explanation is provided in the 2021 WTO Annual Report that:

> The system's overriding purpose is to help trade flow as freely as possible – provided that there are no undesirable effects – because this stimulates economic growth and employment and supports the integration of developing countries into the international trading system. (WTO, 2021 Annual Report)

Similarly, a joint World Bank and WTO report celebrated:

> [A] dramatic increase in developing country participation in trade has coincided with an equally sharp decline in extreme poverty worldwide. Developing countries now constitute 48 percent of world trade, up from 33 percent in 2000, and the number of people living in extreme poverty has been cut in half since 1990, to just under one billion people. (World Bank 2015; WTO 2015)

Another prong of the establishment narrative is the focus on technical assistance. Here the WTO recognises the role of technical assistance to help developing countries build capacity. In this sense, capacity-building is itself part of the narrative that the WTO is working for Africa. For example, the 2021 WTO report 'Strengthening Africa's Capacity for Trade' claimed that '[t]hrough technical assistance programs and support for economic diversification and industrialization on the African continent, the WTO has played a role in fostering economic transformation'. The same report highlighted that 'the WTO has supported trade and development in Africa through its leadership on Aid for Trade'.

5.2 The principled narrative

The principled narrative focuses on the system's inherent biases and unfairness. Reflecting neo-colonial perspectives, proponents of this narrative consider that international economic rules have evolved primarily to advance the interests of developed countries, at the expense of developing countries and LDCs. According to this narrative, 'developed countries have used international law and international institutions to perpetuate quasi-colonial domination of developing countries in the spheres of international trade, investment and finance' (Roberts and Lamp 2021). While the principled narrative acknowledges that open trade can be beneficial, it considers that countries at dissimilar stages of development should be treated differently to benefit from trade liberalisation. This view is aptly captured by the economist Ha-Joon Chang, who explains that the WTO rules are 'kicking away the ladder' (2002) that was used by now-developed countries to climb up to where they are now. While proponents of the establishment narrative emphasise the positive contribution of the multilateral system to industrialisation, the principled narrative points to the constraining nature of the WTO rules on policy space to achieve industrialisation and economic transformation.

The principled narrative also focuses on the hypocrisy of developed members' negotiating positions. While touting the benefits of trade liberalisation, developed countries ensured that high trade barriers were maintained in sectors of particular interest, notably agriculture, where the rules they constructed allowed a subset of developed countries to continue to subsidise agricultural production. These rules have distorted global agriculture including incentives for greenfield investments in countries where subsidies are not available thereby undermining their competitiveness (African Business 2020). As set out in Annex 1, various statements have been submitted by developing countries and least-developed countries to reform agricultural domestic subsidies – including with respect to cotton, which stands out as an egregious example of global market distortion. These countries have also sought a right to public stockholding for food security purposes, which likewise has market distorting implications.

Over the years, the submissions to WTO deliberative bodies by the Africa Group, the Africa, Caribbean and Pacific (ACP) Group and the LDC Group have repeatedly stressed the importance of policy space to promote economic development. For example, a 2022 Africa Group submission emphasised 'the need to ensure that S&DT is strengthened in all WTO agreements to provide the necessary flexibilities and policy space that African countries need to achieve their economic development objectives'. (African Group 2022). Similarly, a statement submitted by South Africa and others to the WTO General Council focused on the need for the WTO to ensure that its rules enable, and do not inhibit, developing and least-developed countries from pursing policies to achieve industrialisation, structural transformation, and diversification of their economies (WTO 2019b).

The view that WTO rules are unfair as they limit the policy space necessary to develop translates into a position that seeks deeper, longer and greater exemptions from these rules. Indeed, as further detailed in Annex 1, statements submitted by the Africa Group, the Least Developed Country (LDC) group and the G90 all focus on deepening special and differential treatment (SDT) provisions. Some of these provisions establish explicit derogations from rules to create policy space. A focus on capacity constraints, as well as the concern that future rules would result in unfair outcomes for African countries, has translated into calls for technical assistance. The link between narrative and position is further set out in Table 5.1. Procedural rectitude (i.e. the view that a set of negotiations that was previously agreed, e.g. the Doha Round, must be satisfactorily concluded before new issues are addressed) has translated into continued adherence to the decisions and ministerial directives that were adopted as part of the Doha Round. Geneva-based African ambassadors interviewed as part of the research for this chapter emphasised the continued reluctance of African governments to engage in new issues, given that these do not reflect the priorities which were set out in the Doha Round.

The principled narrative is evolving to include the concept of common but differentiated responsibilities as regards issues at the intersection of trade, climate and sustainability. The view here is that decades of overconsumption by developed countries, which have generated various planetary emergencies, should not take away a right to economic development. These concerns have appeared most prominently in the context of the fisheries negotiations. For

Table 5.1: Connecting the principled narrative to positions of African countries

Narrative	Position
Process is unfair due to unfinished Doha Round which sought to rebalance the outcome of the Uruguay Round	Principled opposition to any new negotiations; emphasis to adhere to Doha Decisions and Ministerial Declarations
Rules selectively applied to areas in which industrialised countries have comparative advantage; protectionism prevails in other areas (agriculture)	Amend rules (e.g. domestic support in agriculture)
Rules limit policy space, thereby limiting industrialisation opportunities	Seek exemptions from rules; extend transition phases; do not make new commitments
Difficult to comply with rules because of capacity constraints	Seek exemptions, provide technical assistance, capacity-building; make compliance contingent on provision of technical assistance
Future rules could prevent countries from taking advantage of economic opportunities that were available to other countries (e.g. fisheries subsidies negotiations)	Seek exemption from the rules; ensure rules apply only to a targeted group of WTO members

Source: Authors' compilation.

example, the LDC Ministerial Declaration for the WTO's 12th Ministerial Conference (MC 12) called for an agreement on fishery disciplines that are 'balanced and proportionate to the responsibility of Members' and notes that 'LDCs are not the contributors to overfishing and overcapacity and therefore should be exempted from such subsidy disciplines' (LDC Group 2021). Environmental concerns will increasingly feature in WTO initiatives and climate-justice arguments can be expected to become more prominent in the principled narrative.

Having outlined the narratives that define the current impasse at the WTO, the focus now shifts to the record of African agency at the WTO in securing results that are in its interest. Three specific areas of WTO operations are assessed: the deliberative bodies that oversee the WTO regime; negotiations that establish the rules of the regime; and the settlement of disputes that arise in the application of the rules.

5.3 Participation in deliberative bodies

Governance of the multilateral trading system is carried out through an inter-governmental committee system devoted to the myriad of issues under the

WTO's purview. The WTO operates on a consensus basis, which means that each member state technically has a veto. There is provision for voting, but this is rarely utilised as consensus decision-making is the practice. This is important as the WTO has few means of pressing unwilling governments to obey its decisions (Hoekman and Kostecki 2009). As a member-driven organisation, the deliberative bodies administer the WTO's rules and disciplines, with the Secretariat providing back-office support and technical advice.

Except for key bodies that are of obvious strategic interest, African members' attendance and participation in WTO deliberations are generally low. This reflects both capacity constraints and the high cost of maintaining diplomatic missions in Geneva. Typically, African diplomatic missions are understaffed, with concurrent responsibility for covering deliberations at other international organisations in Geneva like the UN Human Rights Council, the World Intellectual Property Organization (WIPO), the World Health Organization (WHO) and the International Labour Organization (ILO). This, in turn, necessitates prioritisation. Participation in WTO committees is not always at the top of the list (van der Ven 2018a).

However, with the African diplomatic missions stretched thin, the Africa Group at the WTO – which comprises African countries that are WTO members and observers – provides a forum for coordinating African participation in the committees and for aligning negotiating positions. The Africa Group typically assigns a member to follow specific issues and report back. This helps with keeping abreast of the latest developments. The same can be said for other groupings that operate at the WTO, in which African countries participate such as the Least Developed Country (LDC) Group, the Africa, Caribbean and Pacific (ACP) Group and the G90.

Aside from the General Council, which is the WTO's main forum for decision-making between ministerial summits, where African attendance and participation are high, the deliberative bodies that attract the highest level of African participation are the Committee on Trade and Development (CTD) and the Trade-Related Intellectual Property Rights (TRIPS) Council. The former is responsible for oversight of development matters that impact WTO rules and trade capacity development initiatives, among other concerns. The latter deals with the sensitive issue of intellectual property rights. At the CTD, for example, African members in coalition with other developing countries continue to press the question of fair rules and a level playing field including through provisions for SDT. The Aid for Trade initiative that provides a framework for development partners' accountability for support to trade development is monitored by the CTD with strong backing from African members. At the TRIPS Council, African members helped to put through an amendment to the TRIPS Agreement that entered into force in 2017. This secured a legal pathway for developing countries to obtain access to generic medicines. African members led by South Africa have been instrumental in pressing for a waiver from certain provisions of the TRIPS Agreement to facilitate access to vaccines and medicines for the prevention, containment and treatment of Covid-19.

On the other hand, African participation in most other WTO deliberative bodies is less substantial. This is a missed opportunity to engage in the strategic use of trade policy instruments to advance national commercial interests, including in areas of importance to African countries, such as sanitary, phytosanitary and other technical standards (Low, Osakwe and Oshikawa 2016).

5.4 Participation in negotiations

Since the WTO's establishment in 1995, it has failed to conclude a major round of negotiations. As earlier noted, the Doha Round, launched in 2001, aimed at an ambitious programme of reform in agriculture, tariffs on industrial goods, and to provide developing countries with flexibilities and policy space. WTO members are divided over the merits of further pursuing the Round (Okonjo-Iweala 2020; World Trade Organization 2015). Developed country members have effectively turned their back on it. Moreover, WTO members have negotiated few new agreements, apart from the 2015 decision to eliminate all forms of agricultural export subsidies (not to be confused with domestic subsidies, which remain) and the Trade Facilitation Agreement (TFA), which entered into force in 2017.

Meanwhile, in response to a changing world – geopolitically, economically and socially – several initiatives and negotiations have been launched with enthusiastic promotion by developed country members. These include joint statement initiatives (JSIs) on e-commerce, investment facilitation, services domestic regulation, trade and environmental sustainability, plastics pollution and environmentally sustainable plastics trade, and micro, small and medium-sized enterprises (MSMEs) in trade. Gender equality in trade has also featured as a new area of interest. Africa's participation in these negotiations and discussions is characterised by either low levels of engagement and/or an overwhelming focus on re-emphasising the issues in the unfinished Doha Round.

As set out in Table 5.2, 25 out of 44 African WTO members are participating in at least one JSI. Participation between the different JSIs is not equally spread, reflecting, in part, the distinct set of draft provisions set out in each of the JSIs. For example, the draft JSI on e-commerce includes market access provisions and other measures on cross-border data flows and data localisation requirements that will have implications on a country's regulatory approaches to e-commerce and data governance. African members remain wary of making commitments in these areas. The JSIs on services domestic regulation and investment facilitation do not cover market access but envisage binding commitments. The JSIs on MSMEs, plastic pollution, and trade and environmental sustainability reflect mostly best endeavour provisions focused on regulatory cooperation. Investment facilitation is the JSI with the highest level of African participation.[1] This reflects not only African prioritisation of investment mobilisation but also the fact that the draft proposals

Table 5.2: Overview of African countries that have signed on to the JSIs (April 2022)

E-commerce (as of January 2021)	Investment Facilitation for Development (as of December 2021)	MSMEs (as of January 2022)	Services Domestic Regulation (as of December 2021)	Trade and Environmental Sustainability (as of 17 November 2020)	Plastics Pollution and Sustainable Plastics Trade (as of November 2021)	Joint Ministerial Declaration on the Advancement of Gender Equality
Benin	Benin	Côte d'Ivoire	Mauritius	Cabo Verde	Cabo Verde	Angola
Burkina Faso	Burundi	Gambia	Nigeria	Chad	Cameroon	Botswana
Cameroon	Cabo Verde	Kenya		Gambia	Central African Republic	Burundi
Côte d'Ivoire	Central African Republic	Nigeria		Senegal	Chad	Chad
Kenya	Chad				Gambia	Côte d'Ivoire
Nigeria	Congo				Morocco	Democratic Republic of the Congo
	Djibouti					Eswatini
	Gambia					Gabon
	Guinea					Gambia
	Guinea-Bissau					Lesotho
	Liberia					Liberia
	Mauritania					Madagascar
	Mauritius					Malawi
	Morocco					Mauritius
	Nigeria					Namibia
	Sierra Leone					Niger
	Togo					Nigeria
	Uganda					Rwanda
	Zambia					Senegal
	Zimbabwe					Sierra Leone
						Togo
						Uganda
						Zambia
6	20	4	2	4	6	23

Source: Authors' own compilation

do not cover controversial matters such as market access but focus on facilitating investment through rules on streamlining bureaucratic requirements and processes.

Several factors explain the general lack of engagement in most of the JSIs that address so-called 'new issues', such as e-commerce or services domestic regulation, which are meant to update the WTO rulebook. These include a lack of trust in that agreeing to an additional set of rules would further limit developing countries' policy space; the perception that the new initiatives favour the interests of the developed economies at the expense of developing countries and LDCs; the disincentive provided by the WTOs most favoured nation (MFN) provision, envisioned to be included in some JSIs, which would enable African countries to 'free ride' on the benefits without having to make concessions; and questions about whether the WTO is the right institution to engage in some of the issues (e.g. e-commerce and MSMEs). In addition, on grounds of both principle and procedural rectitude, most African members are reluctant to engage fully in the JSIs and other new issues until the core subjects of the Doha Round are addressed.

Even so, African countries registered some consequential results at the MC 12 that took place in June 2022. For example, led by South Africa, African members obtained a waiver to the TRIPS Agreement to override patents and produce vaccines to combat the Covid-19 pandemic. A multilateral agreement on fishery subsidies, one of the major outcomes the ministerial conference, also includes some gains for African members. Table 5.3 summarises key outcomes of the ministerial conference, and highlights how this relates to known positions of the Africa Group, LDCs and/or ACP Group. These outcomes demonstrate that negotiating breakthroughs, technical solutions and results that are development-friendly are possible even in a systemically biased and polarised WTO.

5.5 Participation in dispute settlement

As was earlier mentioned, the WTO is grappling with an ongoing disputes settlement crisis. The absence of a functioning Appellate Body allows for panel reports to be appealed 'into the void', thereby leaving disputes unresolved (Lester 2022). This makes it difficult to enforce WTO obligations when members are in violation of these (Lester 2022). While some members have set up an alternative arbitration arrangement, the Multi-Party Interim Appeal Arbitration Arrangement (MPIA), this will be at best a partial solution given that membership is optional and contributes to the risk of a splintered WTO. The Africa Group addressed the Appellate Body crisis in a June 2019 communication, noting the importance of the dispute settlement system as a 'central element in providing security and predictability to the multilateral trading system'. The Africa Group further highlighted the importance of the disputes settlement system as a legitimate forum where members have equal

Table 5.3: Outcome of the 2022 WTO Ministerial Conference

Issue/topic/outcome	Known position of Africa Group/LDCs/ACP Group	Comments
Fisheries: Multilateral Agreement on Fishery Subsidies		
Prohibition of subsidies to illegal, unreported and unregulated (IUU) fishing	Strong support for the elimination of harmful fish subsidies that lead to IUU fishing	A gain for African countries
Prohibition of subsidies to fishing overfished stocks	Disciplines on harmful subsidies that contribute to overfishing and overcapacity	A gain for African countries
LDC exemption and technical assistance and capacity provision	Need for common but differentiated responsibility in the negotiations and their outcomes, and the need for SDT for developing countries in order to ensure food security, protect the livelihoods of coastal communities and provide policy space to strengthen their fisheries industries and capacities for economic and social development	Specific exceptions were granted only for LDCs, while technical assistance and capacity-building provision was included. Subsidies for disaster relief were excused (the latter was requested by the ACP Group, WT/MIN (22)/3)
Transitional period was granted to developing countries with respect to implementing disciplines on IUU and overfished stocks subsidies	An appropriate *de minimis* threshold and sufficient transitionary periods to accommodate the development objectives of African countries. Further exclusion of small artisanal/small-scale fishing	No *de minimis* rule was introduced. Still, developing countries have a period of two years to grant or maintain such subsidies. No exemption for small artisanal/small-scale fishing was granted
Ministerial Declaration on the WTO Response to the Covid-19 Pandemic and Preparedness for Future Pandemics/Ministerial Decision on the TRIPS Agreement		
Partial waiver on certain TRIPS provisions relating to grant of compulsory licences and patents over Covid-19 vaccines	African countries supported the India–South Africa submission seeking a TRIPS waiver for copyrights, industrial designs, patents and protection of undisclosed information with regard to vaccines, diagnostics and therapeutics on Covid-19	Only a part of what was requested in the India–South Africa draft waiver, which was co-sponsored by many African countries, was included in the declaration, namely compulsory licences and patents

(Continued)

Table 5.3: (Continued)

Issue/topic/outcome	Known position of Africa Group/LDCs/ACP Group	Comments
Ministerial Declaration on the Emergency Response to Food Insecurity		
Ministerial Declaration on the Emergency Response to Food Insecurity	African countries supported the draft Ministerial Decision on Food Insecurity in net food importing developing countries (NFIDCs) and LDCs to respond to immediate and urgent challenges of food insecurity and loss of livelihoods	A gain for African countries
Agriculture		
Domestic support	Call for a substantial reduction of trade-distorting domestic support	No agreement was reached. Generally, agriculture subsidies were not properly addressed
Ministerial Decision on World Food Programme (WFP) Food Purchases Exemptions from Export Prohibitions or Restrictions	Support for the Ministerial Decision on WFP Food Purchases Exemptions	A gain for African countries
Public Stockholding for Food Security Purposes	Adoption of a Draft Ministerial Decision on Public Stockholding for Food Security Purposes for Developing Country Members. This would include reference to adequate agricultural food security tools, including through the establishment of a permanent solution on public stockholding that caters for the needs of all developing and least-developed countries and through adopting a meaningful special safeguard mechanism	No agreement was reached
Sanitary and Phytosanitary Declaration on Modern Challenges		
Sanitary and Phytosanitary Declaration for the 12th WTO Ministerial Conference: Responding to Modern SPS Challenges	Support for the Ministerial Declaration on SPS	A gain for African countries

Issue/topic/outcome	Known position of Africa Group/LDCs/ACP Group	Comments
Special and differential treatment		
Special and differential treatment	African countries supported additional special and differential treatment rules, especially with respect to agricultural trade disciplines, services and TRIPS	Aside from certain aspects in the TRIPS waiver and the fishery subsidies agreement, no additional provisions were agreed
Aid for Trade and Enhanced Integrated Framework		
Aid for Trade	African countries sought to strengthen and improve Aid for Trade and ensure that it contributes towards achieving trade-related capacity-building objectives, including removing supply-side constraints, developing infrastructure and facilitating the integration of developing economies, particularly LDCs, in regional and global trade	No new provisions were agreed
Ministerial Decision on the E-commerce Moratorium and Work Programme (extension of moratorium)		
Moratorium on not imposing customs duties on electronic transmissions was extended until MC13	South Africa, along with India and Indonesia, considered adopting positions against the extension of the moratorium, highlighting the deep digital and technological divide between developing and least-developed countries	African countries are divided on this issue
Services		
Special and differential treatment for LDCs	Implementation of the 2015 Ministerial Decision on Preferential Treatment to Services and Service Suppliers of Least Developed Countries	No new provisions were agreed
Ministerial Declaration on the WTO Response to the Covid-19 Pandemic and Preparedness for Future Pandemics	African countries sought to address the impact of the Covid-19 pandemic and services challenges and opportunities, especially in the travel, tourism, hospitality, air freight, maritime and land transport sectors to developing countries	The ministerial declaration contained only minor references to these issues, and did not identify any particular commitment or action plan

opportunity to enforce their rights (African Group 2019). It further emphasised that any dispute settlement reform should seek to enhance the participation of African countries in the dispute settlement system. The latter concern refers to low levels of African participation in the WTO's dispute settlement system. Here again, key factors limiting participation are the expense involved in litigation, technical and capacity constraints at the African diplomatic missions in Geneva and at home in the capitals, fear of retaliation by donor countries in some situations, and the reality that most African countries mainly trade under preferential schemes.

Systemically, low-income countries have less economic heft to back up settlements. The benefits to low-income country complainants for filing a case

Figure 5.1: Number of disputes participated in as a complainant, by country

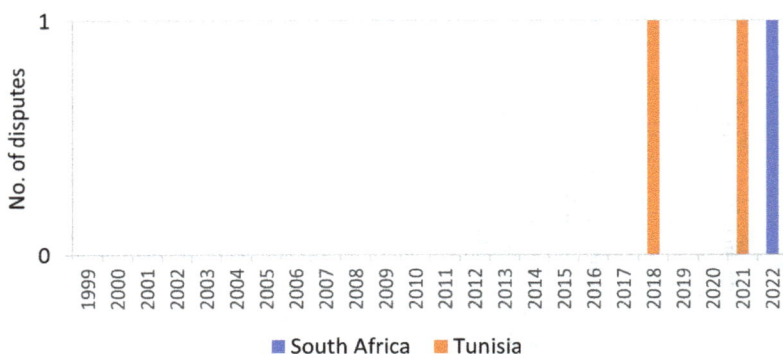

Source: Authors' calculations.

Figure 5.2: Number of disputes participated in as a respondent, by country

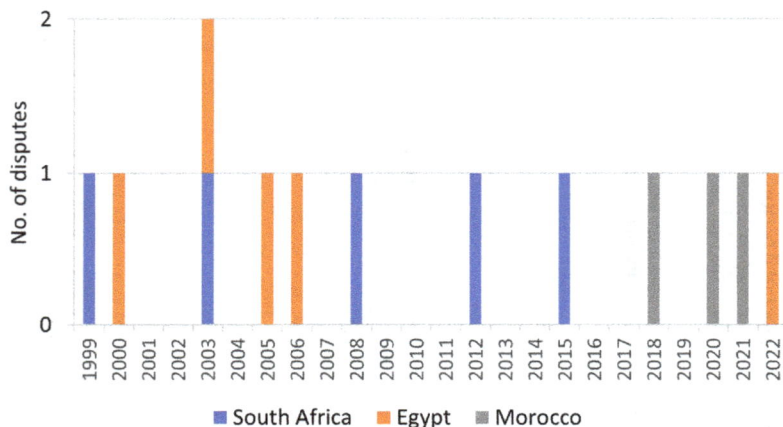

Source: Authors' calculations.

are limited by their imports comprising only a small share of the respondent's total exports. Given that retaliation rights must be equivalent to the cost of damage, retaliation might not present a sufficiently strong incentive for the respondent to bring its measures into compliance if this is the outcome of the adjudication (Bartels 2013). As underlined in the Africa Group communication, systemic biases like these must be addressed in dispute settlement reform procedures.

Until 2022, Tunisia was the only African country ever to have filed a dispute as a complainant (Figure 5.1). This concerned a case against Morocco on anti-dumping measures on school exercise books. In July 2022, South Africa filed a complaint against EU phytosanitary requirements on its fruit exports. On the respondent side, only three African countries (Egypt, Morocco and South Africa) have been sued, being subject to a total of 13 disputes (Figure 5.2). Most of these disputes concerned anti-dumping claims and were resolved in the consultation phase. Two disputes advanced to the panel stage and, in one, Morocco filed an appeal that it later withdrew. Unsurprisingly, the three African countries that have been subject to disputes are among the largest economies on the continent.

With respect to third-party participation, a total of 19 African countries had reserved their rights to participate as third parties in various disputes by the end of 2020 (Figure 5.3). These countries participated as third parties 104 times, out of a total of 3,311 participating third parties. Since African countries comprise over a quarter of WTO membership, this is relatively low. The African countries concerned had a direct commercial or strategic interests in the cases, which included sugar and cotton subsidies, bananas, tobacco advertisement laws, trade remedies, and trade and environmental issues in relation to extraterritoriality.

Another indicator of African participation in the WTO dispute settlement concerns the appointment of African panellists. These are the assessors who review complaints. As illustrated in Figure 5.4, African panellists' participation is low and concentrated in a handful of countries. Prior to 2010, African panellists originated exclusively from three countries: South Africa, Egypt and Morocco. Since 2011, however, this list has expanded to include Botswana, Kenya, Zimbabwe, Zambia and Tunisia. This reflects a long-standing practice of drawing panellists from traditional regional pools. This could be remedied by concerted effort to enhance diversity in the composition of panels (Apecu 2013). Overall, African participation in the WTO's dispute settlement processes has mainly been as third parties in cases of interest. But, even here, African countries account for less than 5 per cent of participation as third parties.

Low levels of participation in the core functions of the WTO suggests that African members are not sufficiently linking development priorities to their rights and obligations under the WTO framework. It also reflects systemic biases against small economies, such as in dispute settlement, and severe capacity constraints. With respect to negotiations, low levels of participation

Figure 5.3: Number of disputes participated in as a third party, by country

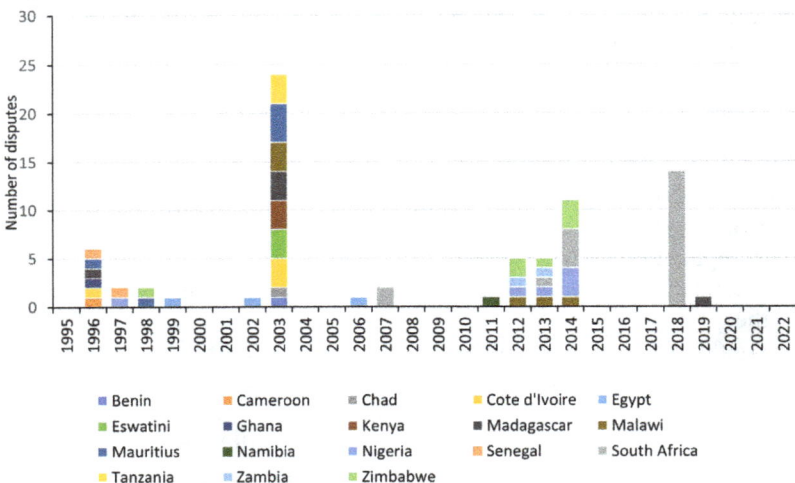

Source: Authors' calculations.

Figure 5.4: Number of disputes participated in as a panellist, by country

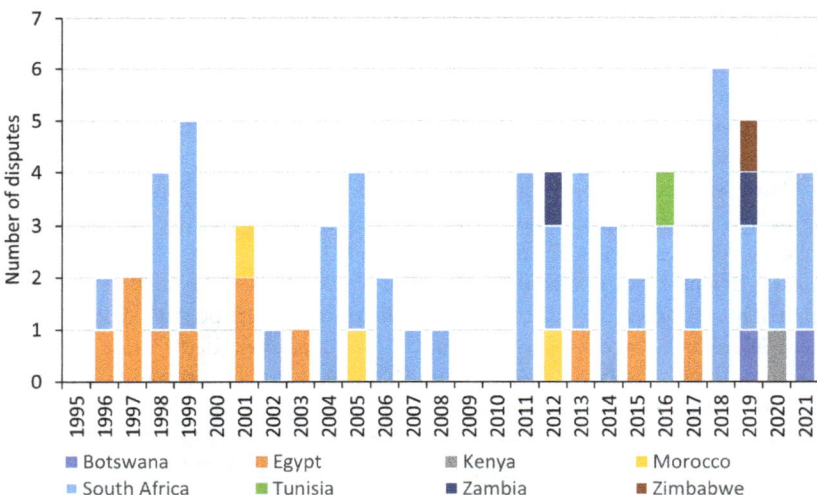

Source: Authors' calculations.

reflect adherence to the Doha Round procedural rectitude and the belief that signing up to additional rules and commitments will be detrimental to Africa's development. At the same time, where major interests are perceived to be at stake, African agency has been exerted in pursuing them in the deliberative bodies and negotiations – including through coalitions such as the Africa Group and the LDC Group – and in dispute settlement.

Summary

The main conclusion from this examination of African agency at the WTO must be that overall performance is mixed as measured against the steps of the trade policy cycle outlined in Chapter 1. Results have been meagre but significant. With limited resources and capacity constraints in Geneva and the capitals, African members have worked in coalitions, including the Africa Group, but also with other developing or least-developed countries. This achieves both a pooling of resources and an amalgamation of economic clout and influence. However, the downside of coalitions involving both African and other developing countries' groups is that this does not allow for sufficient differentiation of Africa's specific needs. On some SDT issues, for example, emerging economies or higher-income developing countries that have already acquired substantial market share in some sectors are unlikely to be granted policy space flexibilities, having already climbed some distance 'up the ladder'. Here, it should be noted that China and other emerging economies still claim developing country status at the WTO. Refusal of advanced countries to accept this is another driver of paralysis at the WTO. As the region with the smallest (and declining – see Chapter 1) share of world trade, and having seen that technical solutions are possible, African members can differentiate their needs better and pinpoint with finer clarity where SDT is required to support their growth (Bacchus and Manak 2021).

The red lines that were established by African countries have been clear and consistent in the two decades since the Doha Round was launched, despite pressure from other parties. They have balanced offensive and defensive interests by sticking to their red lines. But procedural rectitude and ideological positioning have limited their engagement in the JSIs that address 'new issues' to update the WTO rulebook in a changing global economy. Here ideology trumped pragmatism. The latter would have entailed reliance on empirical evidence and analysis for guidance on how JSI proposals are likely to impact development concerns and formulating negotiation priorities and strategies accordingly.

All the same, African countries have registered some results, for example in securing the first ever substantive amendment of a WTO agreement. The amendment to the TRIPS Agreement concerned new disciplines to secure access to medicines to combat the HIV/AIDS epidemic. The experience from this episode emboldened the African members led by South Africa to pursue a waiver to the TRIPS Agreement to override patents and produce vaccines to combat the Covid-19 pandemic as was noted.

Capacity and resource constraints being a perennial challenge, however, implementation of WTO obligations has not always been straightforward, though still commendable in some areas. As regards implementation of obligations related to the Trade Facilitation Agreement (TFA), for example, all except for three African members have to date ratified the TFA and fulfilled notification obligations employing the novel SDT provisions of this agreement (van der Ven 2018a).

The analytical framework that was set out in Chapter 1 further outlined good governance principles for trade policymaking. Assessed against these principles, African engagement at the WTO has been mixed. In terms of efficiency and appropriateness, gaps were noted in African members' attendance and participation across the deliberative bodies – although they have been effective at prioritising where to engage. However, compelling evidence is yet to emerge that African governments and their representatives in Geneva are actively pursuing openness and transparency, inclusive participation, and accountability with their publics in their engagement with the WTO. Some African ambassadors who were interviewed for this chapter complained about the lack of sufficient input based on national-level consultation from their capitals, especially on issues that are not within the domain of the trade ministries to which they report on WTO matters. Among examples cited were digital trade and environmental issues such as trade-related aspects of plastics pollution, which fall under the responsibility of communications and environmental ministries, respectively.

A final takeaway is the urgent need to address deficits in the technical capacities of African missions in Geneva. Here, the African Union, which maintains a representative office that monitors deliberations at the Geneva-based international organisations, could play a key role. It should strengthen its establishment to pool expertise and provide technical services to the Africa Group, including in drafting proposals and preparing responses to proposals from interlocutors. Some African ambassadors who were interviewed identified the dearth of drafting skills as a priority to be remedied and the need to surmount over-reliance on a few Geneva-based development-friendly think tanks. To enhance the role of the African Union in Geneva, it is essential that it is given observer status at the WTO, which it is currently denied. More broadly, the fact that there is no think tank on the African continent that is devoted to WTO issues is also a matter that needs to be urgently addressed by the African Union. India's Centre for WTO Studies in India, now in its 23rd year, is the powerhouse behind the country's formidable WTO performance.

Note

1 The Ministerial Declaration on Gender has the highest number of participating African countries, but this does not have the status of a JSI.

Annex 1

Table 5A.1: Linking the principled narrative to statements made by the LDC, Africa Group and G90

Narrative	Position	LDC proposal for MC12	G90 Declaration on SDT (G90, 2021)	Africa Group Job/Ag/204 12 July (TWN, 2021)	African Declaration on WTO Issues 8 Jan 2019
Process is unfair due to unfinished Doha Round which sought to rebalance the outcome of the Uruguay Round	Principled opposition to any new negotiations	Urge members to find pragmatic solutions to unfinished business of 20 years ago			Recall and reaffirm importance of implementing WTO ministerial, General Council decisions and declarations adopted since Doha in 2001; reiterate commitment to SDT in para 44 of Doha
Rules selectively applied to areas in which industrialised countries have comparative advantage; protectionism prevails in other areas (agriculture)	Amend rules (e.g. domestic support in agriculture)	Need for reform of the Agreement on Agriculture; ensure that MC12 negotiations result in substantial cuts in trade-distorting support and reduce existing asymmetries; eliminate domestic support on cotton; develop permanent solution to public stockholding		Detailed overview of perceived imbalances in WTO's Agreement on Agriculture concerning conditions attached to public stockholding for food security and flawed calculations; highlight need for permanent outcome on public food stockholding programmes	Reaffirmation of positions on outcomes to trade-distorting domestic support, cotton, public stockholding for food security, special safeguard mechanism, and SDT

(Continued)

Table 5A.1: (Continued)

Narrative	Position	LDC proposal for MC12	G90 Declaration on SDT (G90, 2021)	Africa Group Job/ Ag/204 12 July (TWN, 2021)	African Declaration on WTO Issues 8 Jan 2019
Rules limit policy space, thereby limiting industrialisation opportunities	Seek exemptions from rules; extent transition phases; do not make new commitments	Reaffirmation of the importance of SDT for LDCs to achieve structural economic transformation and take full advantage of international trade	'WTO rules must give space for economic actors to grow local production capacities, thereby energizing local, domestic, and regional markets and economies, and improving the quality of employment and living standards.'		Reaffirm SDT, to address development needs in line with Africa's industrial development priorities as set out in Agenda 2063 on structural transformation and industrialisation; various reiterations of importance of SDT
			Ensure 'sufficient flexibility and policy space in tariff structure' to 'grant the tariff protection required for infant industries.'		
			Flexibilities are required with respect to local content requirements in the ASCM Agreement to promote resuscitation of ailing industries, upgrade and modernise domestic manufacturing capabilities, employment generation, support SMEs and promote exports		

Narrative	Position	LDC proposal for MC12	G90 Declaration on SDT (G90, 2021)	Africa Group Job/ Ag/204 12 July (TWN, 2021)	African Declaration on WTO Issues 8 Jan 2019
Difficult to comply with rules because of capacity constraints	Seek exemptions, provide technical assistance, capacity-building; make compliance contingent on provision of technical assistance	Notes of appreciation for EIF and the importance of Aid for Trade; calls for extension of LDC-specific exemptions after LDC graduation	WTO members should always undertake commitments commensurate with their level of development in recognition of differences in capabilities, capacities and resources	Reaffirm importance that Aid for Trade contributes to meeting objectives related to capacity-building, overcoming supply-side constraints, infrastructure development, facilitating integration of developing economies. Calls for strengthening and improving of Aid for Trade and 'avoid conditioning implementation to the participation on negotiation new issues in the WTO'	
Future rules could **prevent countries from taking advantage of economic opportunities that were available to other countries (e.g. fisheries subsidies negotiations)**	Seek exemption from the rules; ensure rules apply only to a targeted group of WTO members	Ensure that fishery disciplines are 'balanced proportionate to the responsibility of Members'; exempt LDCs from overfishing and overcapacity disciplines		Reaffirm importance of negotiations on fisheries subsidies and need for SDT for Africa to 'guarantee policy space necessary to strengthen fishing industries and capacities necessary for economic and social development'	

References

African Business (2020) 'Opinion: Making the WTO Work for Africa', African Business, 23 September. https://perma.cc/B37J-D8S3

African Group (2019) 'Appellate Body Impasse: Communication from the African Group', World Trade Organization, 26 June. https://perma.cc/H6F6-J7JP

African Group (2022) 'African Ministers of Trade Declaration on WTO Issues', World Trade Organization, 11 June. https://perma.cc/B5M9-QA43

Apecu, Joan (2013) 'The Level of African Engagement at the World Trade Organization from 1995 to 2010', *Revue internationale de politique de développement*, vol.4, no.2, pp.29–67. https://doi.org/10.4000/poldev.1492

Bacchus, James and Manak, Inu (2021) *The Development Dimension: Special and Differential Treatment in Trade*, London: Routledge.

Bartels, Lorand (2013) 'Making WTO Dispute Settlement Work for African Countries: An Evaluation of Current Proposals for Reforming the DSU.' *Law and Development*. http://dx.doi.org/10.1515/ldr-2013-0020

Chang, Ha-Joon (2002) *Kicking Away the Ladder: Development Strategy in Historical Perspective*, London: Anthem Press.

G90 Declaration on Special and Differential Treatment, WT/GC/234. 15 July 2021. https://perma.cc/HHE9-4T53

Hoekman, Bernard and Kostecki, Michael (2009) *The Political Economy of the World Trading System, From GATT to the WTO*, 2nd edition. Oxford: Oxford University Press.

International Monetary Fund (n.d.) 'Direction of Trade Statistics (DOTS)' https://data.imf.org/?sk=9D6028D4-F14A-464C-A2F2-59B2CD424B85&sId=1390030341854.

Krugman, Paul (1999) 'Enemies of the WTO', *Slate*, 24 November. https://perma.cc/6QZG-ETCY

LDC Group (2021) 'LDC Ministerial Declaration'. https://perma.cc/H4CU-JNV7

Lester, Simon (2022) 'Ending the WTO Dispute Settlement Crisis: Where to from Here?' International Institute for Sustainable Development, 2 March. https://perma.cc/5BJ4-BNUL

Low, Patrick; Osakwe, Chiedu; and Oshikawa, Maika (2016) *African Perspectives on Trade and the WTO: Domestic Reforms, Structural Transformation and Global Economic Integration*, Cambridge: Cambridge University Press.

Okonjo-Iweala, Ngozi (2020) 'Reviving the WTO', Brookings, 22 June. https://perma.cc/8WGK-5JN7

Roberts, Anthea and Lamp, Nicolas (2021) *Six Faces of Globalization*, Cambridge, MA: Harvard University Press.

Third World Network (2021) 'African Group Calls for Robust Deal on Public Stockholding at MC12', Third World Network, 13 July. https://perma.cc/9L4B-QSF5

van der Ven, Colette (2018a) 'Special and Differential Treatment in the Context of the Digital Era'. CUTS International, Geneva. https://perma.cc/ZZT2-U85V

van der Ven, Colette (2018b) 'Trade, Development and Industrial Policy in Africa: The Case for a Pragmatic Approach to Optimizing Policy Coherence between Industrial Policy and the WTO Policy Space', *Law and Development Review*, vol.10, no.1, pp.29–80. https://perma.cc/K32K-EBTE

World Bank (2017) 'The Role of Trade in Ending Poverty'. https://perma.cc/BX58-DFDZ

World Trade Law (n.d.). 'Dispute Settlement Statistics' https://perma.cc/SR8H-Y3WW

World Trade Organization (2012) 'The WTO Can … Stimulate Economic Growth and Employment'. https://perma.cc/6N6A-WAN8

World Trade Organization (2015) 'Nairobi Ministerial Declaration'. World Trade Organization, 19 December. https://perma.cc/AW7C-2WLK

World Trade Organization (2017) 'Fisheries Subsidies Disciplines: Submission by Guyana on Behalf of the ACP Group', World Trade Organization, 17 July. https://perma.cc/GT57-ST36

World Trade Organization (2019a) 'Joint Statement on Electronic Commerce: Communication from Côte d'Ivoire', World Trade Organization, 16 December. https://perma.cc/ZRZ6-TFY4

World Trade Organization (2019b) 'Strengthening the WTO to Promote Development and Inclusivity: Communication from Plurinational State of Bolivia, Cuba, Ecuador, India, Malawi, Oman, South Africa, Tunisia, Uganda and Zimbabwe', World Trade Organization, 13 December. https://perma.cc/C8G9-8JX6

World Trade Organization (2019c) 'The WTO Can … Help Countries Develop', World Trade Organization. https://perma.cc/KK2A-92FT

World Trade Organization (2020) 'Statement by Ambassador Amina Mohammed Cabinet Secretary for Sports, Culture and Heritage', World Trade Organization, 12 February. https://perma.cc/HMW2-HLGP

World Trade Organization (2021a) 'AfCFTA Secretary-General Delivers First Lecture in Series Dedicated to Ambassador Osakwe', World Trade Organization, 22 September. https://perma.cc/U9HC-JLBE

World Trade Organization (2021b) 'G90 Declaration on Special and Differential Treatment', World Trade Organization, 15 July. https://perma.cc/4TZK-WXR4

World Trade Organization (2021c) 'Statement of Director-General Elect Dr. Ngozi Okonjo-Iweala to the Special Session of the WTO General Council', World Trade Organization, 13 February. https://perma.cc/H3UN-VX74

World Trade Organization (2021d) 'Strengthening Africa's Capacity to Trade', World Trade Organization. https://perma.cc/NQ4N-L7V7

World Trade Organization (2021e) 'The Legal Status of "Joint Statement Initiatives" and Their Negotiated Outcomes', World Trade Organization, 19 February. https://perma.cc/N6FC-85TD

World Trade Organization (2021f) 'WTO Annual Report 2021', World Trade Organization. https://perma.cc/LKZ7-LG3H

6. How the Covid-19 crisis affected formal trade

Jamie MacLeod and Geoffroy Guepie

The word 'crisis' comes from the Greek 'to separate, to decide', marking a point at which a choice must be determined at a highly consequential turning point between continued or unchecked decline on the one hand, or recovery on the other. Implicit in this is that crises create powerful inflection points. This chapter sets out what actually happened to trade in Africa over the course of the Covid-19 crisis, focusing on three stories concerning Africa's *formal* trade. First, African countries' overall trade continued to be dominated by fluctuations in commodities and tourism, where volatility in prices and the collapse of travel strongly shaped trade performance. However, this meant nuanced and differentiated consequences across different parts of the continent. Second, manufacturing trade faced a potential turning point with whether Covid-19 would help to 'localise' production within the continent. Finally, did Covid-19 change trade policymaking itself in Africa, especially with the AfCFTA negotiations?

An overarching issue in any such period of intense disruption is to gauge the 'sticking power' of these changes. Which policies affected by Covid-19 will persist, and which will wither, as trade in Africa slowly re-establishes a new normal? We seek to assess the 'sticking power' of changes imposed by Covid-19 and in doing so to challenge the prevailing (sometimes lazy) narratives about Covid-19 in Africa, showing that realities were often more nuanced and complex. Commodity prices collapsed but also surged, and at different times and across different products, affecting countries across the continent differentially. While some manufacturing value chains did seem to localise, there is evidence that this was often merely transitory. The chapter highlights aspects of Africa's commodities and manufacturing trade that remain entrenched, despite the tumult of the Covid-19 pandemic. It also, however, demonstrates resiliency in African policymaking. The cumulative story is one of – in general – determined African trade policymaking.[1]

How to cite this book chapter:

MacLeod, Jamie and Guepie, Geoffroy (2023) 'How the Covid-19 crisis affected formal trade', in: Luke, David (ed) *How Africa Trades*, London: LSE Press, pp. 141–176. https://doi.org/10.31389/lsepress.hat.f License: CC-BY-NC 4.0

6.1 Commodity prices, lockdowns and supply disruptions

Africa's formal trade in goods was affected during the pandemic through three major impact channels: how it affected the prices of Africa's main export commodities, how lockdowns strained cross-border trade, and the disruptions created through global supply chains. These impact channels in turn help to explain how Covid-19 affected Africa's trade in the course of the pandemic.

Africa's exports are severely concentrated in a relatively small basket of products (as detailed in Chapter 1). Across the continent, petroleum oils, metals and ores account for almost 60 per cent of Africa's total exports (Figure 6.1).[2] Africa's exports, foreign exchange earnings and tax revenues are tied to the prices of these products and Covid-19 had a rollercoaster impact on these prices. After initially plummeting at the onset of the crisis, metal prices surged, recovering strongly and exceeding their pre-pandemic prices by July 2020 (Figure 6.2). The same was true for other agricultural commodity prices, such as cotton and food products, which had recovered to exceed their pre-pandemic prices by late 2020. The price recovery was driven by a faster-than-expected rebound in economic activity in China. Because modern China accounts for around half of global consumption of metals and a third of apparel exports, it helped to fuel a rebound many of these critical African exports.

The rebound was then further shouldered by economic stimulus measures in advanced countries and supply disruptions in several producer countries, which pushed prices higher still (Baffes and Nagle 2020; World Bank 2021a). An additional price surge in early February 2022, particularly in petroleum oils, was caused by the Russian invasion of Ukraine. The prices of gold, another key export from Africa, on the other hand, reacted counter-cyclically. Gold hit its highest ever price on 6 August 2020, before falling to still elevated levels throughout the remainder of 2020 and 2021. The cumulative effect of these swirling price fluctuations created differentiated impacts across the continent. In the first year of the crisis, major oil-producing countries struggled, while gold exporters benefitted. In the second (and third) years of the

Figure 6.1: Composition of Africa's exports

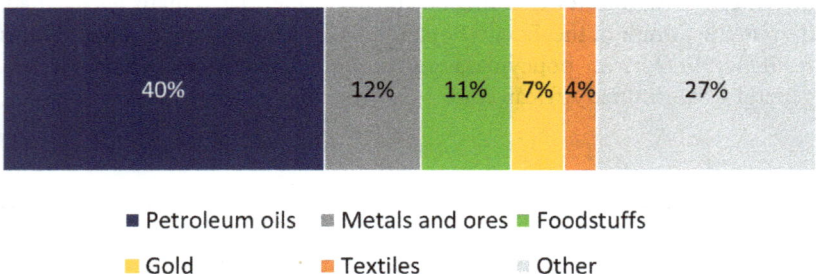

| 40% | 12% | 11% | 7% 4% | 27% |

■ Petroleum oils   ■ Metals and ores   ■ Foodstuffs
■ Gold   ■ Textiles   ▥ Other

Sources: Based on ITC TradeMap Data, FAO and Trading Economics, May 2022.
Notes: Composition of Africa's exports based on three-year average from 2016 to 2018.

Figure 6.2: Price developments for Africa's top exports through Covid-19 (Dec 2019 =100)

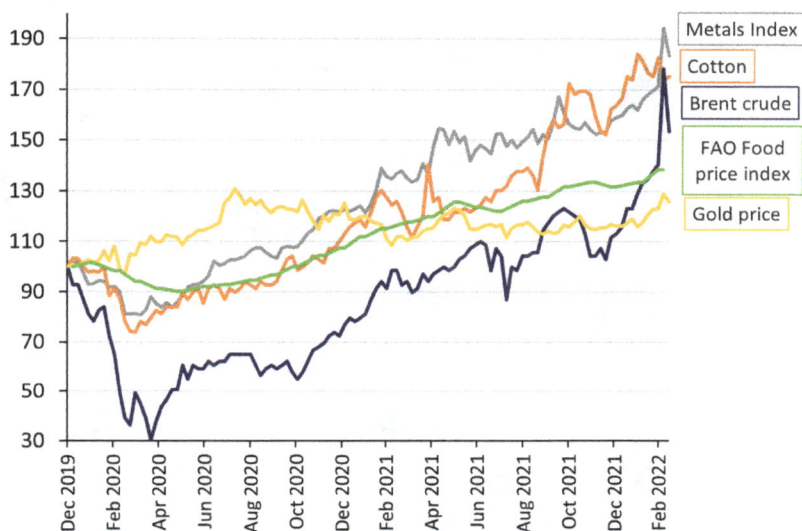

Sources: Based on ITC TradeMap Data, FAO and Trading Economics, May 2022.
Notes: Metals Index is the LME Index. Cotton prices are included as a (very) rough indicative proxy for textile prices.

pandemic, most African countries benefitted from elevated prices for their major commodity exports. Though such volatility may seem to 'balance out' over a longer time horizon, it exacerbates budgetary planning and investment (World Bank 2021a). It also erodes policymaking interest in fixing the pervading challenges of commodity dependency.

The second major disruptor impacting Africa's trade over the course of the pandemic was the lockdowns induced by Covid-19. As elsewhere in the world, these lockdowns severely – by design – restricted internal mobility, reduced economic activity, and closed borders to varying degrees. Figure 6.3 highlights the specific aspect of international travel closures that formed the most trade-relevant part of lockdowns. It shows how these varied across African countries and over time. Most African countries introduced, and then strengthened, lockdown restrictions beginning in late March 2020 and into early April 2020, as the extent of the Covid-19 pandemic became apparent. Lockdown restrictions then tended to gradually ease across Africa before stabilising between November 2020 and June 2021 (with some country idiosyncrasy). Travel closures were most prevalent and strict in the months of April to July 2020.

At that point, most major ports throughout the continent experienced delays and congestion as port authorities and maritime shippers reacted to additional health screening measures and port congestion (UNECA 2020a). Passenger

Figure 6.3: Africa's international travel closures: scale of 0 to 4 (white to blue), January 2020 to March 2022

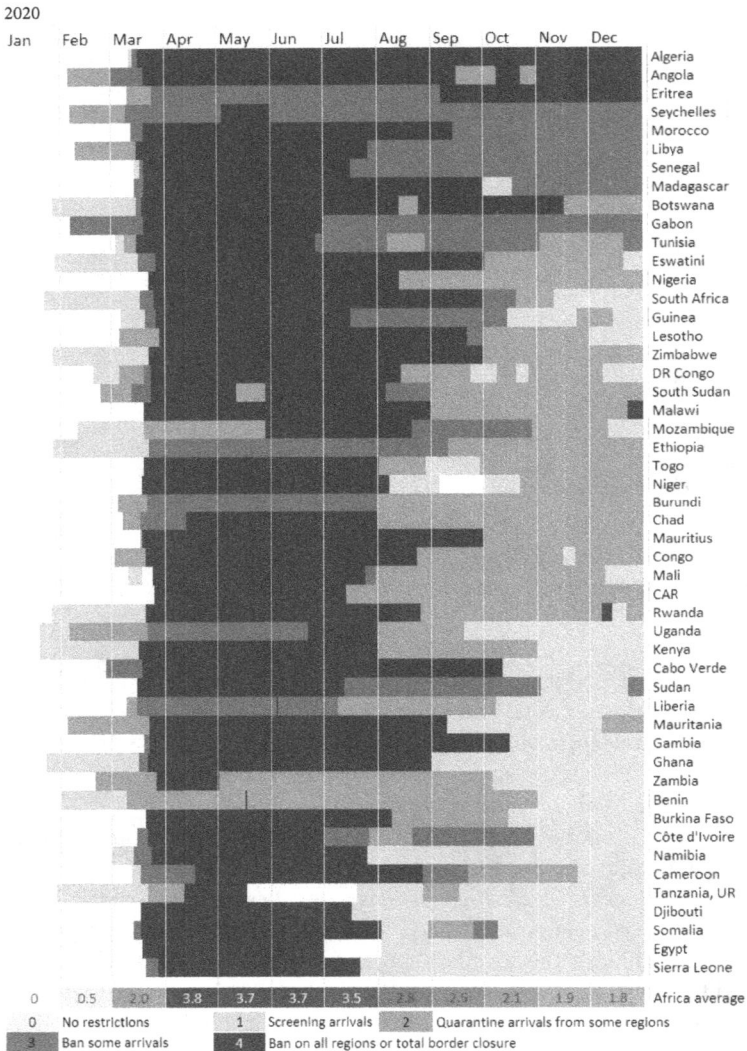

flights, which usually carry commercial cargo in their holds, declined precipitously in number and were wholly banned from many countries. Land borders became congested due to mandatory testing, the sanitisation of trucks and limits on crew numbers, and in some cases were completely closed between neighbouring countries (UNECA 2020a). As these measures were introduced

Figure 6.3: (continued)

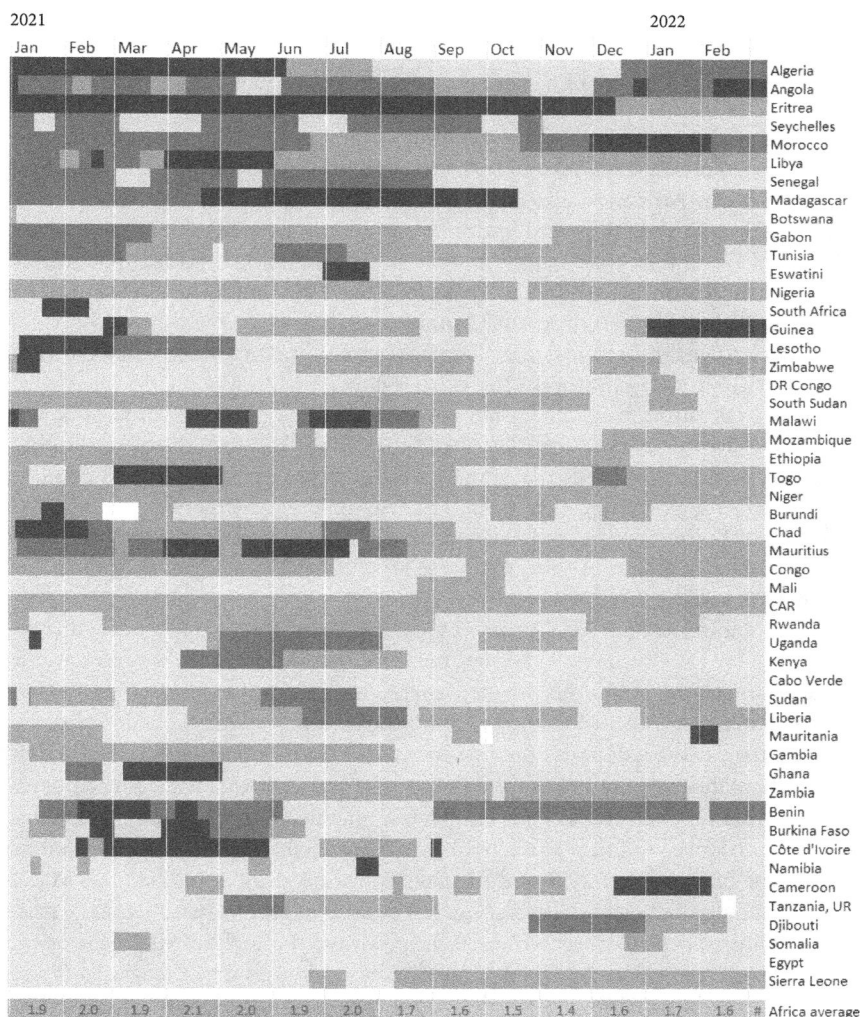

Source: Authors' calculations, based on Oxford Covid-19 Government Response Tracker.
Notes: Data was unavailable for Comoros, Sao Tome and Principe, Equatorial Guinea and Guinea-Bissau.

quickly in response to emergency conditions, there was initially little coherence or harmonisation in their introduction dates, coverage or stringency. As the pandemic persisted, two changes eased the restrictiveness of Africa's lockdowns on trade. First, the stringency of lockdowns gradually eased in general as countries refined the targeting of their lockdown interventions (UNECA

2020b). Second, countries and regional economic communities introduced and then harmonised cross-border 'safe trade' measures to facilitate trade and goods transit between their member countries. Regional guidelines were first introduced during 2020 on 6 April in SADC, 24 April in the EAC, 15 May in COMESA and 17 June in ECOWAS (UNECA 2020c). These guidelines varied, but generally aligned with international sector-specific practices on issues such as border health screening, testing and certification, truck crew sizes, digitalised trade procedures, electronic cargo tracking and information sharing. An African Union protocol was supposed to be under development in 2021 to further align and harmonise measures between RECs but had not – as of December 2022 – been issued. That belatedness represented a missed opportunity for the continental body to show leadership, while developments at the regional level moved ahead more nimbly.

Lockdowns did not just affect Africa's economies, of course, but also those of Africa's trading partners. The third major impact of Covid-19 on Africa's trade was through international supply chain disruptions (something discussed further in Section 6.2). Covid-19 caused the first long-term supply chain crisis in decades, disrupting patterns of production that had come to rely on lean global outsourcing and a crisis-free management mentality (Ivanov 2021). In an ECA and IEC business survey, 56 per cent of a sample of businesses in Africa in July 2020 were reported to be facing supply shortages (UNECA and IEC 2020).

As demonstrated in Figures 6.4 and 6.5 together, supply-side disruptions first hit China as lockdown measures were imposed there as early as late January in 2020. This affected a large number of companies, given China's extensive integration into global production systems. Lockdown measures then cascaded across the rest of Africa's trading partners in late March. As the pandemic continued, the stringency of lockdowns was fairly idiosyncratic to the specificities of each import-supplying country – rising and falling in accordance with different Covid-19 waves, such as the Alpha wave that hit Europe in December 2020 and the Delta wave affecting in India in late March 2021. China persistently had some of the strictest lockdown measures since their introduction in March 2020. In contrast, the lockdowns in European countries, the US and African countries eased more rapidly, eager to return to relative 'normality'.

The logistics component of supply chains confronted acute challenges through Covid-19. Border closures at the start of the crisis resulted in dramatic disruptions to the movement, and allocation of, shipping crewpeople as well as delays in complying with new port health and quarantine requirements. These caused spillover disruptions with shortages of equipment and containers, and less reliable services, as well as shipping turnaround delays. A strong rebound in global demand for goods in the second half of 2020, driven by an economic rebound in China and stimulus in Western economies, then created a surge in shipping prices as demand outstripped available supply capacities.

Figure 6.4: Composition of Africa's imports by supplier

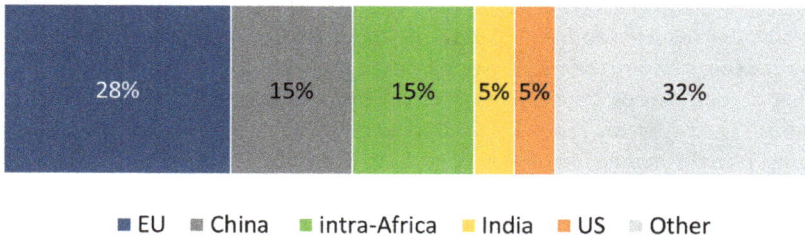

Source: Authors' calculations, based on IMF Direction of Trade Statistics 2022.
Notes: Composition of Africa's import suppliers is based on three-year average from 2016 to 2018.

Figure 6.5: Stringency of lockdowns in Africa's import partners, January 2020 to March 2022

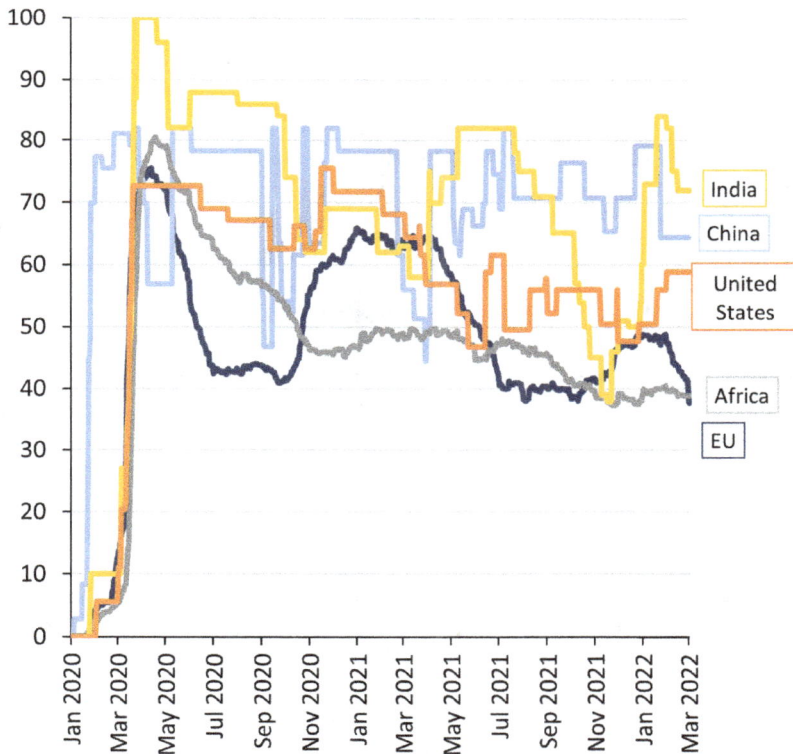

Source: Authors' calculations, based on Oxford Covid-19 Government Response Tracker 2022.

Supply chain management processes strengthened in the course of the pandemic, however. Businesses increasingly adopted supply chain visibility tools to better understand their supply chains, improved oversight of emerging constraints among suppliers, and began to more proactively model supply chain risks and costs (El Baz and Ruel 2021; Ivanov 2021). Supply chain resiliency was reported to have risen to the top of business priorities in a survey by Gartner of more than 1,300 supply chain professionals, which also revealed that 87 per cent of respondents planned to invest in supply chain resiliency within the two years following 2020 (Gartner 2020). These improvements to supply chain management practices, alongside the better targeting of lockdown measures, help to explain why the stringency of lockdowns declined as an indicator of negative quarterly economic growth after the second quarter of 2020 (König and Winkler 2021). Stringent lockdown measures increasingly had a more muted impact on economic activity. Supply chains – following an initial shock in March 2021 – were increasingly more resilient to further Covid-19 related disruptions.

Impacts on trade in goods

As the economic consequences of the Covid-19 pandemic unravelled across the world, there was no shortage of letter-based descriptors of recovery. Commentators wondered whether the global economy would rebound in a sharp V-shape, a slower U-shape or a double-dip W-shape. Inspired by this nomenclature, the impact on Africa's formal exports in merchandise goods might be described as 'J-shaped'. A sharp negative shock in April and May 2020, at the start of the crisis, gradually gave way to a strong rebound and growth in 2021. Though the value of Africa's total exports to the world was 11 per cent lower in 2020 than in 2019, by 2021 it was 19 per cent higher than in 2019. That this 'J-shape' replicates the prices of Brent crude oil (recall Figure 6.2 and see Figure 6.6) over this period is an important reminder that too much African trade continues to be concentrated in petroleum oils (40 per cent, in recent years). The impact of Covid-19 is, however, more complex, with prices of other African commodities reaching unprecedented heights by as early as mid-2020 and supply chain disruptions, including historical highs in container freight rates, weighing on relatively more complex value chains, such as manufactures.

The pattern with intra-African trade is a similar, if less smoothly rendered, 'J-shape', to Africa's total trade with all partners (Figure 6.7). Intra-African trade also fell precipitously in April and May 2020, before remaining muted throughout the remainder of 2020 and recovering well in 2021. In total, intra-African trade was only a little more resilient to the economic shock of Covid-19 than Africa's exports outside the continent. Unlike the global financial crisis of 2008 to 2009, when Africa's internal trade remained much more buoyant than its external exports, the Covid-19 crisis imposed a direct shock on intra-African trade through lockdowns and particularly border closures affecting contiguous countries, which account for most intra-African trade.

Figure 6.6: Africa's exports to the world, compared to equivalent month in 2019, percentage change

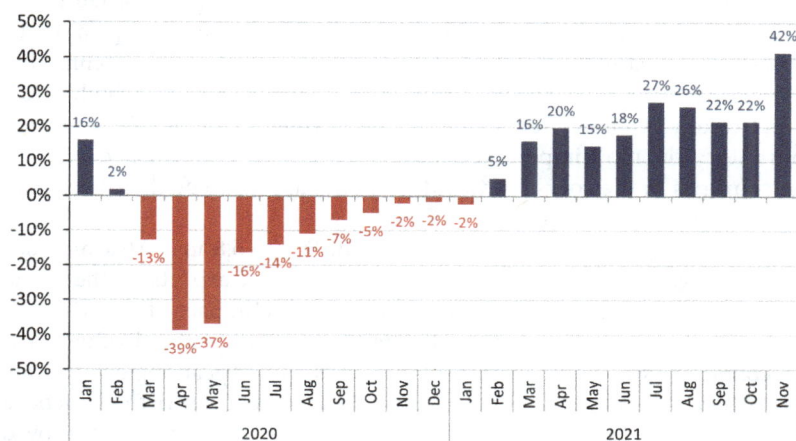

Source: Authors' calculations, based on IMF Direction of Trade Statistics 2022.

Figure 6.7: Intra-African exports, compared to equivalent month in 2019, percentage change

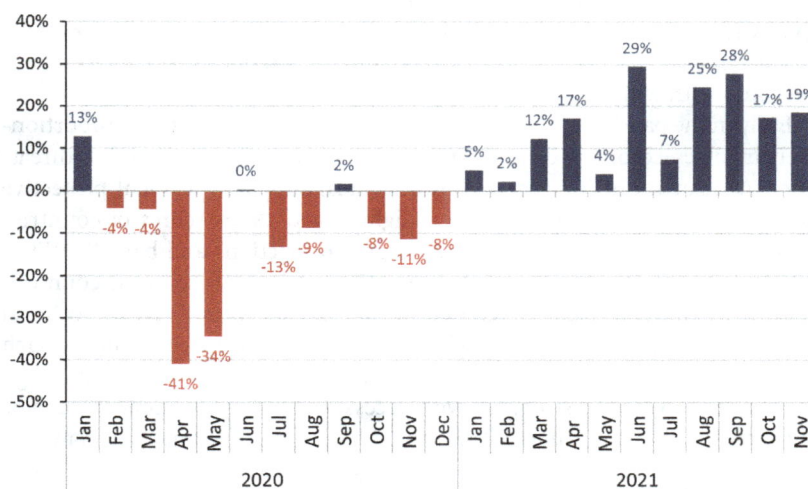

Source: Authors' calculations, based on IMF Direction of Trade Statistics 2022.

Nevertheless, the most significant indicator of the experience of African countries throughout the throes of Covid-19 in 2020 was whether or not they were major exporters of either petroleum oil or gold. We classify African countries as major petroleum exporters if petroleum oils account for at least

35 per cent of their total exports, and gold exporters if gold accounts for at least 35 per cent of their total exports (Figure 6.8). The former group of African petroleum oil-exporting countries suffered a net 34 per cent fall in the value of their exports in 2020, while the latter gold exporting group enjoyed a 20 per cent increase. This bifurcated response is clearly driven by commodity prices, with major gold exporters benefitting from exceptionally high prices as petroleum exporters suffered from price troughs. Though it is not the entire story, the most important determinant of trade performance for African countries in the course of Covid-19 would appear to be their particular commodity dependencies.

Figure 6.9 aggregates the data presented in Figure 6.8 into African country groupings while showing the difference between exports to the world and intra-African exports. It is again clear that the impact of Covid-19 on exports is driven, to a large extent, by the commodities that individual African countries export. The West, Central and North African regions that are host to most of Africa's major petroleum oil-exporting countries experienced the poorest export performance in 2020. While intra-African exports proved marginally more resilient than exports to the world in total, there was variance across African regions.

So far, the data presented has considered only exports. As Figure 6.10 shows, Africa's imports also fell in 2020 before rising in 2021 as compared to 2019. The impact of Covid-19 on Africa's imports has been broadly in line with the impact on exports – following the same 'J-shaped' curve. Imports into African countries were similarly constrained by the Covid-19 restrictions to movements, disruptions to supply chains, and reduced foreign exchange revenues with which to fund imports.

Early in the pandemic crisis, Africa's trade structure – which disproportionately involves exporting commodities and importing finished goods – threatened African countries' access to the medical supplies, personal protective equipment and medicines needed to fight Covid-19, as scores of countries that produced these goods instituted export restrictions and bans (UNECA 2020a; UNECA 2020b). As concern over the pandemic rose, some countries imposed additional bans or restrictions on food exports. Fortunately, local solutions emerged to address supply gaps in the case of simple products, such as disinfectants, facemasks and personal protective equipment, although African countries still struggled with access to complex equipment, such as ventilators (*Financial Times* 2020). The African Medical Supplies Platform, championed by South African President Cyril Ramaphosa and developed by the African Union, Africa CDC, Afreximbank and UNECA, further provided a pan-African solution, allowing for pooled government procurement of Covid-19 medical supplies across African countries.

Impacts on trade in services

The sectoral impact of the Covid-19 crisis on Africa's services exports is perhaps unsurprising. Transport and travel services plummeted during the

Figure 6.8: Individual African countries, change in annual exports, 2020 as compared to 2019, percentage change

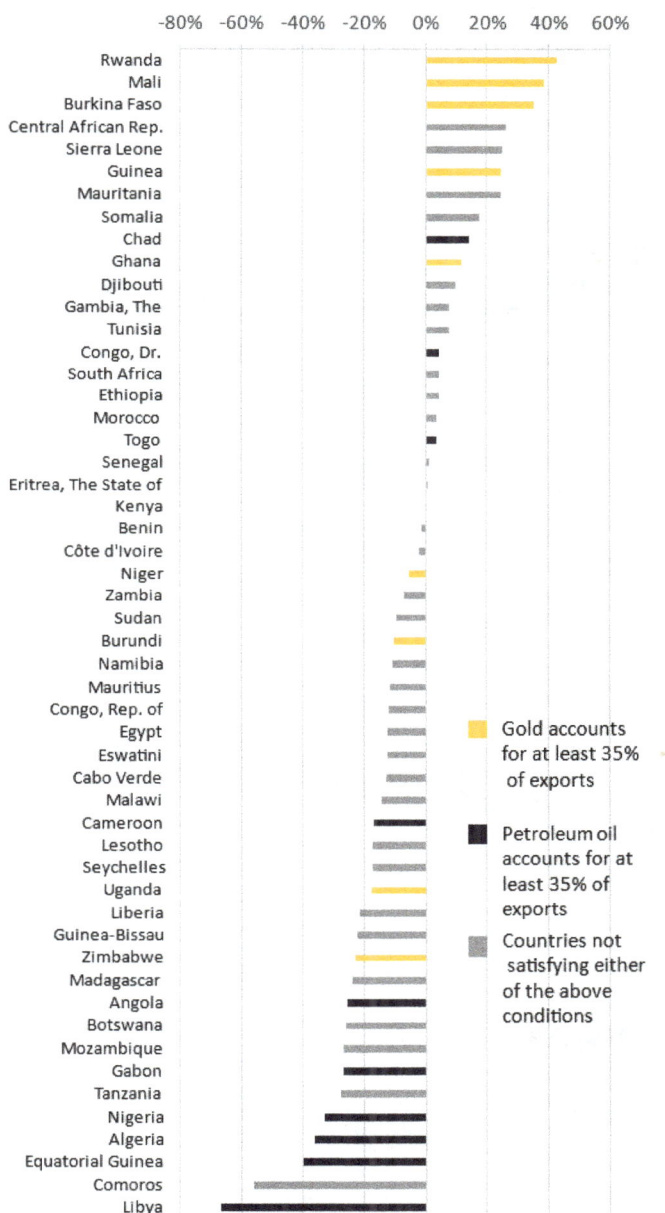

Source: Authors' calculations, based on IMF Direction of Trade Statistics 2022.
Notes: Gold and petroleum oil concentration categorisations calculated using CEPI BACI reconciled trade flows data for 2018. Countries that do not satisfy either condition are left grey.

Figure 6.9: African country groupings, annual change in exports, 2020 and 2021 as compared to 2019, percentage change

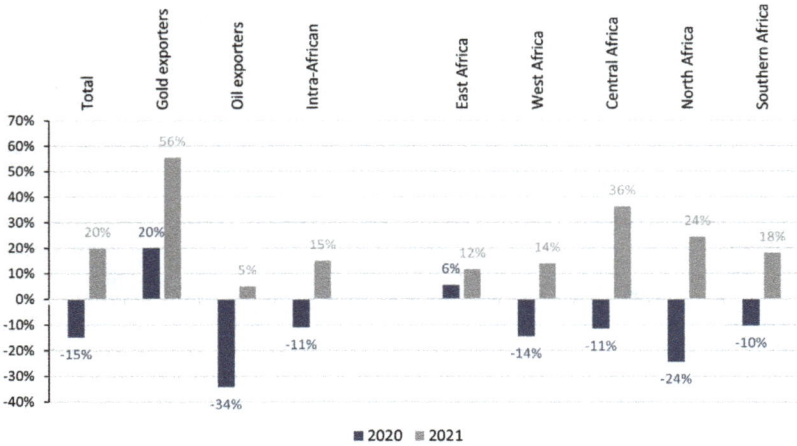

Source: Authors' calculations, based on IMF Direction of Trade Statistics 2022.

Figure 6.10: Africa's imports, compared to equivalent month in 2019, percentage change

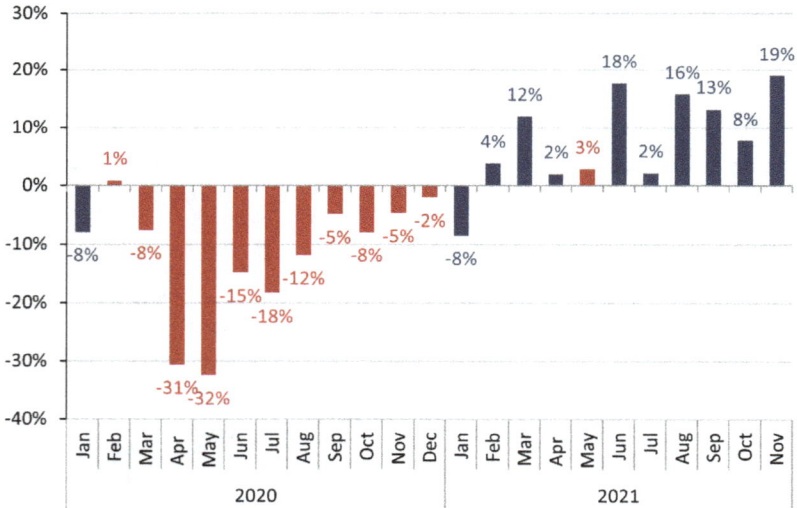

Source: Authors' calculations, based on IMF Direction of Trade Statistics 2022.

pandemic as can be seen in Figure 6.12, which shows service sector export indices quarterly between 2019 and 2021. These two sectors are, furthermore, the most important service exports for the continent in terms of value (Figure 6.11). The extent of the collapse in travel services was dramatic, falling

Figure 6.11: Contribution of BPM6 sectors to total African trade in services exports, 2019

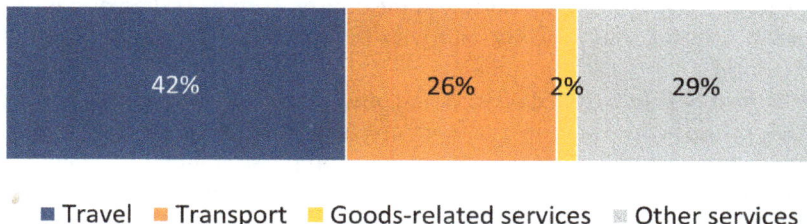

| 42% | 26% | 2% | 29% |

■ Travel ■ Transport ■ Goods-related services ▩ Other services

Source: Authors' calculations based on UNCTAD Stat, accessed September 2021.
Notes: Africa services trade data is patchy. The above indices are calculated on the basis only of countries for which sector services exports data was available for Q4 2019 through to Q3 2020, and only give a rough estimate for the continent more broadly.

Figure 6.12: Africa's services exports, sector indices, Q4 2019 = 100

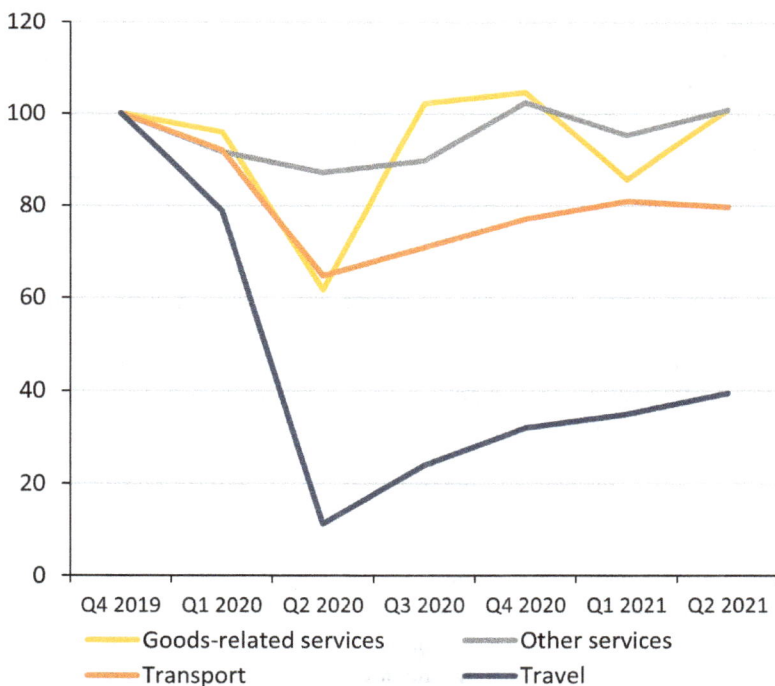

Source: Authors' calculations based on UNCTAD Stat, accessed September 2021.
Notes: Africa services trade data is patchy. The above indices are calculated on the basis only of countries for which sector services exports data was available for Q4 2019 through to Q3 2020, and only give a rough estimate for the continent more broadly.

89 per cent by the second quarter of 2020 as compared to the last quarter of 2019. Only a small rebound was experienced by the second quarter of 2020, the most recent data point available at the time of writing. As dramatic as this was, it was not wildly inconsistent with the experience in other regions of the world.

Exports of goods-related services and other services held up more strongly, likely owing to their lower dependency on cross-border movements of people. The former includes manufacturing services on physical inputs belonging to other countries and maintenance and repair services, but accounts for only about 2 per cent of total African services exports. The latter – 'other services' – in the African context includes primarily 'Other business services', such as research and development services, professional and management consulting services, and technical, trade-related and other business services, but also telecommunications services and government services. Clearly these are more resilient to border closures than services such as travel and tourism. These remained relatively more stable in the course of 2020, with telecommunications services, in fact, actually growing by about 11 per cent.

In normal years, tourism and travel account for about 42 per cent of African service exports, 6.9 per cent of Africa's GDP (equivalent to about $173 billion) and 6.5 per cent of total Africa's employment. It is also an important employer of women (UNWTC 2019; WTTC 2021). While tourism is a significant foreign exchange earner for large African economies, such as South Africa (where it accounts for one in 10 jobs), Kenya, Egypt and Morocco, it is most important for Africa's small island economies, notably the Seychelles and Cabo Verde, where tourism accounts for an estimated 26 per cent and 18 per cent of total GDP, respectively (World Bank 2021b; WTTC 2021). The crisis exposed Africa's dependency on foreign travellers for tourism. With fewer domestic tourists to absorb local tourism services, the impact on this sector was more pronounced than in other places, such as Europe or the US, where domestic tourism was able to replace international travellers to a certain extent. Domestic tourism as a share of total tourism is lower in Africa than any other region, accounting for around 55 per cent of travel and tourism spending in Africa, as compared to 83 per cent in North America, 64 per cent in Europe and 74 per cent in the Asia-Pacific (WTTC 2017). This has been particularly pronounced in Eastern and Southern Africa, with tourism offerings like safaris more oriented towards European, American and Asian visitors. Yet policy changes may be underfoot: Kenya launch a Domestic Tourism Recovery Strategy in 2020, focusing on, among others, marketing, infrastructure, and product diversification with their domestic market.

Both transport and tourism are included in the five priority sectors for services liberalisation under the AfCFTA. This creates an opportunity for promoting intra-African investments as African countries begin to recover from Covid-19 to accompany increased intra-African trade flows. In the words of Wayne Godwin, senior vice-president of JLL Hotels & Hospitality Group for Sub-Saharan Africa, the free-trade agreement is an absolute game changer for travel. If 97 percent of commodities and goods are tariff-free, that's going to do a lot for regional trade. And when there's regional trade, travel will follow. (Monnier 2021)

Doing so could be the catalyst African countries need to follow the successes of more developed countries like China, which, with an emerging middle class armed with increasing disposable incomes, experienced a fourfold increase in domestic travel and tourism spending in a decade, from $208 billion in 2008 to $836 billion by 2019 (see Box 6.1; WTTC 2017; WTTC 2021).

Box 6.1: Lessons from the rise of domestic tourism in China

When we think of China's growth miracle, most think of manufacturing. Yet domestic tourism has been one of the fastest-growing sectors of the Chinese economy, with spending quadrupling from $208 billion in 2008 to $836 billion in 2019, overtaking the United States to become the largest domestic tourism market in the world, despite China still being a developing country. Tourism in 2019 accounted for 11.6 per cent of the total Chinese economy (above the world average of 10.4 per cent). It was also the source of about 30 million jobs in China, equivalent to about 10 per cent of total employment. Though now a much wealthier region than Africa, lessons can be drawn from the tools used to promote domestic tourism in China.

A specific focus on domestic tourism has been present in China's national economic and social development plans since 1993, a time at which China's GDP per capita was much lower than that of most African countries today. National holidays have been an important tool. 'Tourism Golden Week' – a series of separate national holidays implemented in 2000 – were useful in stimulating demand. A developed rail network and air infrastructure – including low-cost carriers in second- and third-tier cities – have helped to make movement, a prerequisite for tourism, possible. An 'Internet + Tourism' strategy has improved information and awareness of tourism opportunities. Policy has also involved transposing the notion of 'industrial parks' to the tourism sector, with tourism bases focused on the theme of film and television in Hengdian and Song City, of history and culture in the ancient city of Xi'an and Luoyang, and of sports tourism in Chongqing. More recently, a focus on the preservation of cultural heritage and environmental sustainability have been introduced to promote a healthy local identity alongside tourism attractiveness.

Sources: Zhao and Liu (2020); WTTC (2017); WTTC (2021); Giorgi, Cattaneo and Enríquez Alatriste (2020).

However, despite being launched in 2018, the AfCFTA protocol on trade in services is yet – as of December 2022 – to be implemented. Technical components of this part of the agreement are being worked on by trade negotiators, with much work still needing to be done. Negotiators are involved in reviewing and making requests upon service sector liberalisation offers from other countries. Even once negotiations on these technical components are completed, implementation will take time before substantial impacts are realised. When eventually concluded, the AfCFTA services offers will include provisions that enable service providers from AfCFTA state parties better access in other African countries. This can involve, for example, lifting limitations on the participation of foreign capital in terms of maximum percentage limits on foreign shareholding, limitations on the total number of foreign employees, or limitations on the total value of service transactions or assets. Beyond liberalisation, the AfCFTA negotiators are also in the process of negotiating regulatory frameworks. These seek to improve regulatory convergence and harmonisation in different service sectors, to make it easier for services operators to expand operations across African countries.

Comparative perspectives

Covid-19 hit African trade harder than most other regions. Using January 2020 as a baseline, Africa's exports fell by 46 per cent by April 2020 – a fall that was more severe than any other region, with the exception of the Middle East and Central Asia, exports from which also fell by 46 per cent by May 2020 (see Figure 6.13). All of these regions are notable petroleum oil producers and struggled with the sharp decline in oil prices throughout 2020,

Figure 6.13: Africa's exports relative to selected regions through Covid-19: exports indexed to January 2020

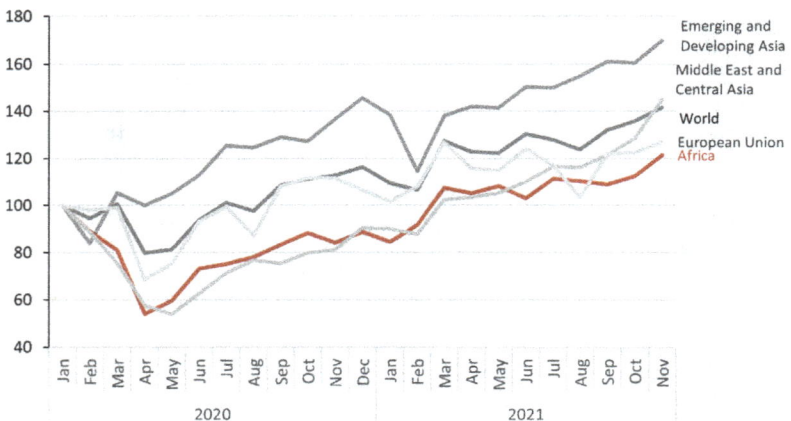

Source: Authors' calculations, based on IMF Direction of Trade Statistics 2022.

before recovering in 2021. However, exports from the Middle East and Central Asia recovered much more strongly than those from Africa in the second half of 2021. A sharp contrast is drawn with the Emerging and Developing Asia region, which, after an initial contraction in February 2020, recovered strongly from the pandemic crisis – with the East Asia region even managing to record GDP growth of 0.9 percentage points in 2020, and among the fastest growth in 2021 too. This recovery was led by impressive control of the virus in many Asian economies in 2020, such as China and Vietnam, which rode the subsequent wave of rising world demand to boost manufacturing exports.

The economic crisis surrounding Covid-19 marks only the most recent in a succession of global crises that have undermined development in African countries. Falling export receipts followed the global financial crisis of 2008 and 2009 and the East Asia crisis in 1997 and 1998, as well as a commodity prices recession in 1984 to 1986. In each of these instances, African trade was weighed down by crumbling commodity prices. The Covid-19 crisis in its impact on Africa's exports is notable for its brevity, compared to those preceding crises (see Figure 6.14). Despite comprising one of the greatest economic upsets in recent history, and imposing a particularly sharp drop in Africa's exports, it was characterised by a notably swift recovery. Africa's exports had returned to their January 2020 level just 14 months later, before then growing substantially as commodity prices continued to rise. It was an unusually rapid recovery for African exports, in comparison to other major economic troughs of recent decades. However, this recovery cannot be considered to have been delivered by much more than the commodity price rebound, which saw

Figure 6.14: Covid-19 relative to other economic crises: impact on Africa's exports, by month into crisis

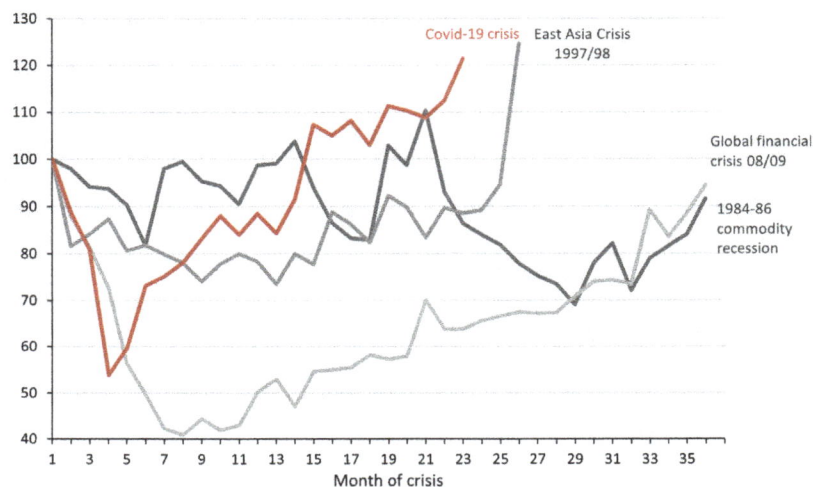

Source: Authors' calculations, based on IMF Direction of Trade Statistics 2022.

prices for most of Africa's traditional commodities soar. The African economy, in aggregate, remains structurally unchanged from its overconcentration in metals, ores and petroleum oils.

Great crises create moments in which entrenched outcomes within political economies can be revisited and changed. The risk of Africa's rapid trade recovery from Covid-19 is that it removes the incentives and impetus to structurally change African trade, leaving it persisting in its dependence on too few commodity products and their prices. High prices may help buoy government finances and foreign exchange reserves, for the African countries that export them, but will undermine the type of trade transformation that would better create jobs and sustainable development over the longer term. With commodity prices having recovered, Africa's export structure seems likely to continue in its persisting over-concentration in fuels and metals unless trade policy changes.

6.2 Did supply chains localise and bring production to Africa?

The Covid-19 pandemic sparked much interest over whether supply chain disruptions would lead to a great 'rebalancing' of global supply chains. This was particularly prevalent at the start of the crisis as countries scrambled to ignite domestic production of personal protective equipment and medical supplies in the face of excess global demand, disrupted supply chains, and export prohibitions. There were initial worries, too, over imported food supplies, as a small number of countries imposed export bans on strategic food crops including rice and wheat,[3] both important imports for Western and Northern African countries, respectively (UNECA 2020a).

In May 2020, the Institute of Management Development issued an article anticipating the re-emergence of logistics hubs at the regional level 'to eliminate single-source dependencies [and that] suppliers will source, assemble and deliver from their own backyards' (Cordon 2020). The consultancy firm McKinsey cautioned businesses in a 6 August 2020 report on exposure to over-extended supply chains designed for 'efficiency … but not necessarily for transparency or resilience', while projecting that $2.9 trillion to $4.6 trillion worth of exports could shift to 'domestic production, nearshoring, or new rounds of offshoring to new locations' as a result (Jayaram et al. 2020). As early as April 2020, policymakers in Northern economies seemed keen to actively court such a 'rebalancing'. The then EU trade commissioner Phil Hogan announced that the EU would seek to 'reduce [its] trade dependencies' after the pandemic. Japan unveiled a $2.2 billion fund to tempt Japanese manufacturers out from China. The then US director of the United States' National Economic Council, Larry Ludlow, pushed for US policy to help assist American manufacturing firms in relocating back from China.

However, as the pandemic progressed, 'early expectations of a spontaneous rapid shift in supply chains have been downgraded' (*Financial Times* 2020).

Manufacturing value chains continued to concentrate in Asia following the region's more rapid and early recovery from the Covid-19 crisis (Cable and Kihara 2020). An AmCham Shanghai survey of 346 American companies operating in China in 2020 found that American companies remained committed to the China market, with 79 per cent reporting no change in investment allocations (a larger share than in 2019) (AmCham 2020). A relatively short-lived supply chain rebalancing might be expected in Africa, too. While 56 per cent of an ECA and IEC survey of businesses reported in July 2020 to have switched suppliers in which they prioritised domestic and other African suppliers, 87 per cent of these firms also reported that they would switch back to original suppliers, mostly due to better prices (UNECA and IEC 2020).[4] Covid-19 may yet catalyse supply chain relocations, particularly in strategic sectors such as medical equipment and drugs (UNCTAD 2020), but at this point the extent and duration of these supply adjustments remain uncertain. For African countries, the opportunity to capture some of the localised supply chains would be beneficial to longer-term industrialisation goals. Particular value would derive from developing localised pharmaceutical industries, a sector of acute import dependency in Africa (Banga, MacLeod and Mendez-Parra 2021).

Did the crisis catalyse long-term changes or merely short-term adjustments in supply chain localisation? The measures taken to tackle the Covid-19 pandemic (lockdowns, movement restrictions, social distancing, border closures) had multiple impacts on global economies. One area in which this was most prevalent was the production of manufactured goods. Manufactures typically depend on more disaggregated and complex logistical supply chains comprising many parts produced at different locations. Comparing the second quarter of 2019 with the second quarter of 2020, global output growth in manufacturing industries declined by about 15 per cent, 12 per cent and 11 per cent for low-technology, medium-technology and technology-intensive industries, respectively (UNIDO 2022). In the first half of 2020, there was a significant decline in global vessel port calls, with the largest drop (nearly 21 per cent) occurring between mid-May and mid-June (Committee for the Coordination of Statistical Analysis 2021).

In general, the crisis highlighted the crucial role of supply and value chains at the global level, but also in Africa. For the African continent, it also highlighted opportunities. Indeed, following the crisis, the halt in the production in China of intermediate products necessary for the activity of various global industries (textiles, chemicals, pharmaceuticals etc.) raised the question of the relocation of industries in diverse countries, calling into question the fragmentation of production processes, the essence of globalisation. One of the conclusions of the Covid-19 crisis, but also of the crisis in Ukraine, is necessarily the fact that states and companies aim to diversify their source of supply in order not to depend only on a given country. Related to this, there may be new incentives for Africa to develop its manufacturing sector and have a resilient supply chain to deal with future crises.

At the peak of the pandemic, the United Nations Economic Commission for Africa conducted three surveys to understand the response and outlook of African businesses to the crisis. The surveys revealed that the crisis had affected businesses differently depending on their size. Large firms had lost between 50 per cent and 60 per cent of their production capacity, while small firms had lost between 30 per cent and 40 per cent of their production capacity. The impact was greater for larger companies because of their more significant dependency on global supply chains. Surprisingly, however, micro and small firms were also more dependent on the international market than the continental market for inputs to their production (ECA and IEC 2020). Indeed, most imports of intermediate goods into Africa come from the rest of the world. Only 16 per cent[5] of imported intermediate goods come from within the continent. The EU is the leading exporter of intermediate goods to Africa. It accounts for 26 per cent of total imports of intermediate goods, followed by China (15 per cent), the US (7 per cent), Saudi Arabia (4 per cent) and India (3 per cent). By focusing on these main import partners and comparing the periods before and during the Covid-19 crisis, Figure 6.15 provides a first glimpse of how the manufacturing industry, using intermediate goods as inputs, may have been affected by the crisis.

Trade in intermediate goods with each of the main importing partners declined during Covid-19. However, the declines were not overly substantial. For some partners, such as China and India, the decline was surprisingly small

Figure 6.15: African imports of intermediary goods from main partners (average 2018–2019 and 2020–2021)

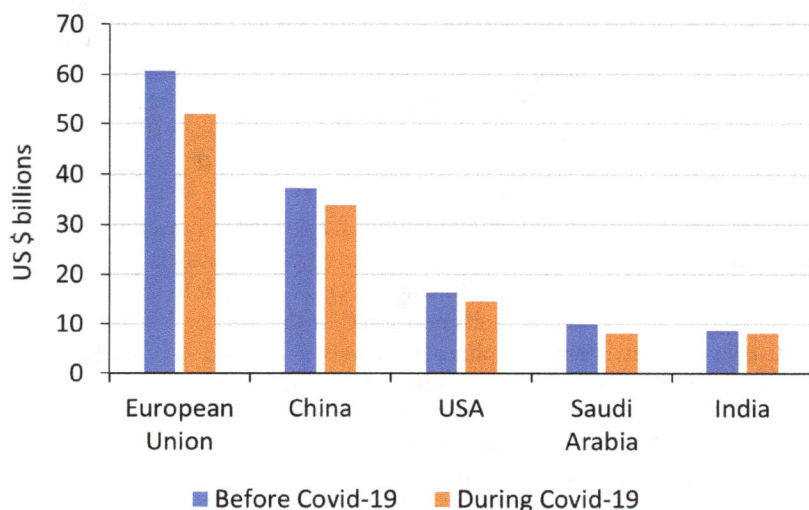

Source: Authors calculations based on UN Comtrade database and the System of National Accounts (SNA) classifications of goods.

despite these countries facing severe Covid-19 crises. However, looking at these figures alongside manufactured value added changes the perspective. Manufacturing value-added growth[6] in sub-Saharan Africa remains very low and in fact declined between 2010 and 2019, from 4.8 per cent to 3 per cent. With Covid-19 reducing the supply of industrial inputs, the average growth rate of manufacturing value added on the continent plummeted to −4.5 per cent in 2020. One driver of this decline was disrupted supply of intermediate products.

The phenomenon of declining manufacturing value added was not universal across the continent. Some African countries, such as the Central African Republic, Ethiopia, Mauritania, Benin, Niger, Burkina Faso and Cameroon, observed positive manufacturing value-added growth in 2020. While this seems to imply that the manufacturing sector in these countries has been more resilient than in other African countries, it does not mean that the manufacturing value added of these countries was entirely unaffected.[7] Nevertheless, many of these economies continue to be less integrated into global supply chains. Figure 6.16 clearly illustrates the relationship between integration into the world economy and manufacturing value-added growth. Many of the African countries that import the least experienced positive growth in manufacturing value added in 2020. But the countries most open to the rest of the world (except for Egypt) experienced negative growth in manufacturing value added. The manufacturing sectors in these countries suffered relatively more when their more globally integrated supply chains were disrupted by the Covid-19 pandemic.

Figure 6.16: African countries manufactured value-added growth and total imports in 2020

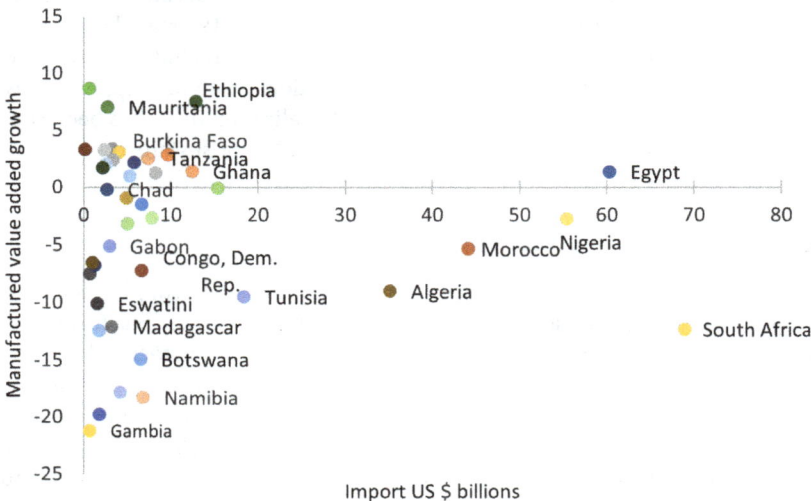

Source: Authors calculations, based on world development indicators and UNTACD annual trade data.

The Covid-19 crisis raised awareness of the value of regional production chains to reduce the dependence of African countries on the rest of the world in critical goods, such as medicines. In the pharmaceutical sector, African countries lobbied hard with investors to host mRNA vaccine production units. Egypt, Kenya, Nigeria, Rwanda, Senegal, South Africa and Tunisia were chosen to host such production facilities. Pharmaceutical investment and production deals were signed between Rwanda and BioNTech and between South Africa and Johnson & Johnson. In other sectors, such as machinery and equipment manufacturing, experts additionally argued for a greater weight of Africa in manufacturing (Martin 2020). However, efforts to support the localisation of pharmaceuticals production within the continent have not been without their challenges. As discussed in Chapter 5, the TRIPS waiver at the WTO, led by South Africa and India aiming to make licensing of Covid-19 vaccines and medicines easier, faced blockages from developed countries. Since investments were made in African countries, initial production efforts risked being undermined for a lack of orders as a result of free Covid-19 vaccine doses donated by high-income countries (Adepoju 2022).

If regional production chains in manufacturing can be developed, it could contribute to reinforcing Africa's industrialisation. A long-term relocation of firms to the continent could help reinforce a virtuous cycle of GDP per capita and manufacturing value-added growth. To do this, it would be necessary to incentivise policies for firms on the continent so that the cost of an input available on the continent is cheaper than when that same input comes from the rest of the world. This is a major challenge as the health crisis, which has favoured sourcing from the continent, does not appear to have turned this demand diversion into a long-term adjustment. As UN surveys reveal, firms say they want to return to their original suppliers mainly because of the price of inputs on the continent (ECA and IEC 2020). Covid-19 created a renewed policy and business interest in localising value chains, including within the continent. This was often necessitated by disruptions to global supply chains. However, there is yet little to suggest that this localisation drive has been substantial – beyond a few sectors like pharmaceuticals – or sustained.

Challenges for further localising supply chains in Africa

Digitisation is a vector for strengthening but also managing supplier relationships as well as logistics and shipping processes by companies (Baker McKenzie 2022). To better manage supply chains and identify associated risks, a good combination of the benefits of digitalisation through data accessibility and artificial intelligence can help African countries to shape a resilient supply chain. The continent can improve its traditional supply chain management methods by implementing tracking systems, digitised information flows, and automation to insert itself into the global value chain and attract a relocation of global industry to the continent. Such a 'revolution' should benefit trade on the continent, as digitisation will allow for efficient interconnection between ports.

Digitisation can also help to bridge the information gap within and outside of the continent. For example, the continent has the lowest internet penetration (standing at around 30 per cent), far below the global average, which was twice as high in 2020. Digital tools such as digital platforms can also be used to leverage human capital productivity in logistics activities. Indeed, one of the biggest challenges facing logistics managers and professionals is the level of competence and professionalism of their workers (Kuteyi and Winkler 2022). To benefit from the diversification of supply chains and to locate them on the continent, African countries should invest in infrastructure and logistics. For example, the expected gain from supply chain digitisation will not happen if the continent is not able to be supplied with electricity. Investment in energy supply in sub-Saharan Africa has fallen by more than 30 per cent since 2011, leaving an estimated 600 million people without access to electricity on the continent and needs to increase two and a half times through 2040 (IEA 2019). African countries face many logistical challenges that need to be addressed to increase trade and encourage regional companies to localise production and eventually enter the export market. These challenges include inefficient gateways and transport facilitation, among others (see Table 6.1).

The regulatory environment should evolve to better support the industrial sector to stimulate the regional supply chain. A weak regulatory environ-

Table 6.1: Logistic challenges in sub-Saharan Africa

Inefficiency	Examples
Gateway inefficiencies	• Cheaper demurrage than warehouse storage costs encourage longer dwell times at ports • Cumbersome custom clearance process and lack of single window • Poor GPS tracking systems
Trucking inefficiencies	• Low market transparency and excessive wait times • Poor inland road quality • 'Black box' pricing models with mostly fixed costs and limited variable costs due to powerful transporter unions • Old fleet operated by poorly qualified truckers • Current incentives are to strip containers and overload trucks • Scarce backload due to more imports than exports • More demand for transport of high-value products than supply which is readily available during most of the year
Trade and transport facilitation inefficiencies	• High shipping line and port handling charges • Weak information sharing and communication infrastructure • Unstable internet connectivity for efficient clearing processes • Excessive checkpoints, informal payments, and corruption • Low professionalism and expertise among freight forwarders

Source: Kuteyi and Winkler (2022).

ment can discourage companies from locating in the continent. In this context, the African Continental Free Trade Area can play a role in harmonising rules and then developing and implementing continental business and supply chain standards. This will give African companies a major role in global supply chains. The continent's particularity lies in the flexibility and an often non-existent regulatory environment, which allows for different forms of innovation in some respects. This phenomenon, referred to as 'reverse innovation' by Oke, Boso and Marfo (2022), is illustrated by the example of businesses like Zipline drone technology, in Rwanda. This company took advantage of the relative paucity of regulation in Rwanda, compared to more developed markets in Europe or the US, to develop and reach a critical size before starting its activities in the United States. In conclusion, when it comes to regulation, African governments should make a trade-off between the establishment of clear rules governing supply chains and the flexible nature of regulation so as not to harm innovation and then the value chain on the continent.

6.3 Negotiating the AfCFTA throughout Covid-19

Covid-19 changed trade in Africa, but it also changed the process of designing and formulating trade policy. With policymakers in many cases unable to meet physically to negotiate complex trade policy instruments, and with policymaking and business attention rediverted to the emerging health and economic emergencies thrown up by the crises, previously set pathways for policy development were disrupted. This section delves into how Covid-19 changed the negotiations for the AfCFTA.

AfCFTA negotiations involve the physical assembly of a large group of delegates, experts, interpreters and support staff. In just one example, the sixth negotiating forum, held in Niamey in June 2017, involved 246 delegates including representatives of negotiating states, their regional economic commissions, supporting international organisations, and staff of the African Union Commission, which was at that time the Secretariat for the negotiations.[8] The impact of Covid-19 caused a clear cessation of negotiating meetings in the first half of 2020 (Figure 6.17). With negotiating forums cancelled, these disruptions undermined a deadline set by the African Union summit to commence trading under the AfCFTA by July 2020.

As the longevity of the crisis became clearer and an adjustment to a 'new normal' resolved, negotiators were forced to identify a mechanism for virtual negotiations. This process mirrored efforts internationally, where negotiations such as those at the OECD over tax reform (OECD 2020), EU–UK over Brexit (BBC 2020) and the UN Human Rights Council continued through virtual or hybrid platforms. Secure online platforms for the AfCFTA were put in place by mid-2020. A flurry of negotiating meetings – including seven at the chief negotiator, senior trade official and ministerial levels – were then held in the second half of 2020 in a push to conclude the AfCFTA negotiations and

Figure 6.17: AfCFTA negotiation meetings, by subject and seniority level, October 2019 to November 2021

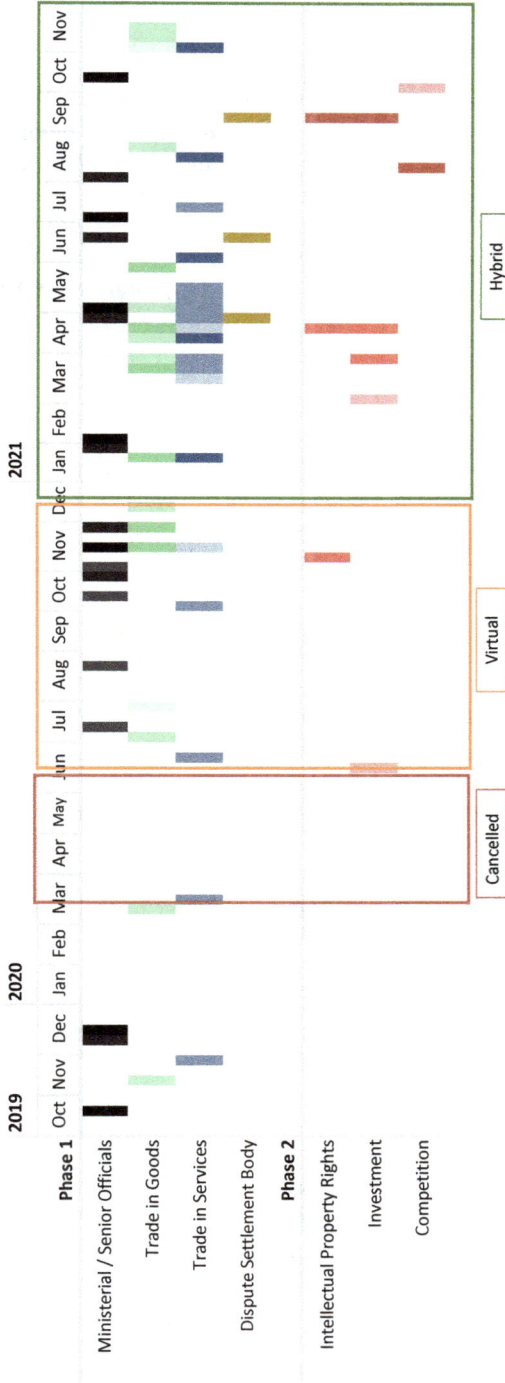

Source: Compiled by authors from AfCFTA Secretariat and AUC meeting reports and communications.
Notes: Negotiating meetings are shaded in accordance with three levels of hierarchy: capacity-building training or workshop (lightest); sub-committee, technical working group, or expert working group (medium); and committee or negotiating forum (darkest). If more than one meeting took place in a week, shading is accorded to the highest level.

commence trading by the start of 2021. The introduction of virtual platforms also enabled the initiation of capacity-building sessions and the first committee-level meetings on the phase II negotiating issues to be held in 2020.

The adjustment to virtual platforms was not without its challenges. Intelligent negotiators carefully craft the negotiating processes before negotiations over the substance of a trade agreement begin. The AfCFTA experience was no different, with four of the original negotiating forums dedicated to outlining the strict rules, regulations and terms of references guiding the participation, governance, transparency, reporting and observance of the negotiations. Such carefully crafted and agreed negotiating protocols were undermined over necessitated virtual platforms, with new challenges arising over issues such as the verification of accreditation, transparency and participation, including internet connection issues for some participants. Many negotiating forums were severely delayed due to technical issues as virtual negotiating systems were established. While some of these issues were eventually resolved with practice, others, such as internet connection disruptions, continued to affect negotiators.

The topics being negotiated in 2020 (and in many instances remaining unresolved and spilling over into 2021 and 2022) were also the most significant and sensitive, involving the product schedules of concessions, the rules of origin, and specific commitments in trade in services. These sensitive issues are commonly those requiring the most delicate discussions often resolved over more intimate 'coffee table' discussions or working lunches, rather than within the formalities of plenary-level negotiating meetings involving many negotiators. Such nuanced side discussions and caucuses are inherently more difficult to organise alongside virtual negotiations. Yet, as virtual negotiations – and options for virtual participation – became the 'new normal', they offered benefits, too. Asymmetry of representation in traditional physical negotiations can be stark: in the abovementioned sixth negotiating forum the sub-regional powerhouses South Africa and Kenya fielded at least 11 negotiators each, while Africa's LDCs averaged 2.9,[9] and its small island developing states just one each. The latter often would have to contend with time-consuming, expensive and exhausting flight connections to attend negotiations physically. However, virtual negotiations in general are also less satisfying, less effective and tend to be more protracted, suffering from reduced nuance and sensitivity in communication (Baltes et al. 2002). To get the most out of them, negotiators and negotiation secretariats must continue to learn new skills to improve the effectiveness of virtual negotiations. This can include employing frequent summarising language, labelling behaviour, and efforts in the preparation and planning around negotiations (Hughes 2020; Movius 2020).

Despite the considerable challenges posed by Covid-19 for the negotiation of the remaining issues of the AfCFTA, Africa made progress in the course of 2020 and 2021, including the establishment of the AfCFTA Secretariat (see Chapter 2). This achievement deserves due credit and demonstrates the commitment of policymakers to ensuring the success of the AfCFTA project.

Yet not all prerequisites for the effective commencement of trade under the AfCFTA could be finalised in this timeframe. The obstacle of Covid-19 perhaps also revealed some of the unrecognised opportunities in virtual negotiating methods. In his closing remarks at the Third Meeting of the AfCFTA Council of Ministers, in November 2020, the secretary-general of the AfCFTA Secretariat informed the meeting that, for future meetings, 'the hybrid virtual and in-person Meetings will be the mode of operation'.[10] This helps improve the accessibility to the negotiations of less well-resourced, capacity stretched, and remote countries in the continuing negotiating processes while allowing face-to-face discussions over the most sensitive issues.

Political commitment to the AfCFTA

The process of legal commitment to a treaty – such as trade agreements – typically involves two steps. A country first signs a treaty, indicating commitment to the terms of the treaty. Ratification then makes the terms of the treaty legally binding in that country. Before Covid-19, at the end of 2019, 54 African Union member states had signed the AfCFTA Agreement, of which a subset of 28 had at that point deposited their instruments of ratification with the African Union Commission. Momentum for the ratification of the AfCFTA seemed to have halted with the onset of Covid-19. From November 2019 to October 2020, just two African countries ratified the AfCFTA. To illustrate the severity of this slowdown in the pace of ratifications, nine instruments of ratification were deposited in 2018 and 19 were deposited in 2019 (Figure 6.18).

Figure 6.18: Cumulative number of AfCFTA ratifications over time

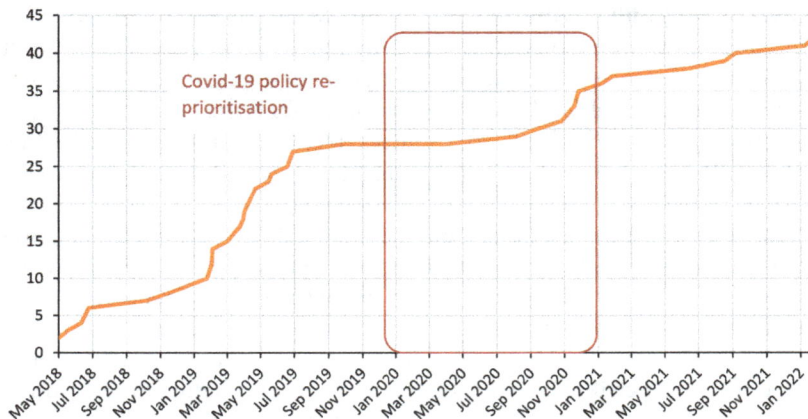

Source: Authors' calculations based on Tralac.

Why might progress have stalled so dramatically? Ratification entails processes through which a state reviews and shows its consent to be bound by a treaty, usually by parliamentary approval through the standard legislative procedure for passing a bill in that country. National consultations are frequently a prerequisite for such approvals. Covid-19 disrupted the hosting of national AfCFTA consultations and refocused legislative attention to emergency health and economic priorities. AfCFTA ratifications are also usually reserved for deposition at a ceremony within African Union summits. The postponement of the July 2020 summit denied member states this opportunity.

Despite the considerable impositions of Covid-19, African countries still managed to make progress with AfCFTA ratifications as the year 2020 drew to a close. In the lead-up to the 33rd Ordinary Assembly of the Heads of State and Government of the African Union, on 5 December 2020, six further ratifications were deposited with the African Union Commission, bringing the total to 32. A further 10 countries were able to conclude their ratification processes throughout 2021 and early 2022, bringing the total number of state parties to the AfCFTA to 42 as of December 2021. In comparison, the African Union Free Movement of Persons Protocol, launched at the same time as the AfCFTA in March 2018, had garnered only 33 signatories and just four ratifications as of early 2022. Still more ratifications are required to ensure the comprehensibility of the AfCFTA project for the African continent, yet the progress made in the face of Covid-19 is noteworthy, with the ratified state parties to the AfCFTA now comprising a considerable majority of the continent, and most of the large economies.

Government and business commitment to the AfCFTA

After giving the AfCFTA legal effect, practical preparations are required to implement and effectively utilise the AfCFTA. The Economic Commission for Africa worked with 43 African countries and five African regional economic communities to develop AfCFTA implementation strategies. Though each differs in accordance with country priorities, these strategies generally seek to establish the national-level institutions required for implementation, including creating national AfCFTA committees, identifying reforms required by the AfCFTA Agreement, and prioritising trade opportunities in AfCFTA partner markets.

Covid-19 disrupted the development of national AfCFTA implementation strategies. Work on 17 of the strategies was delayed, while the validation of a further six strategies that were already in an advanced stage of preparation at the start of 2020 was delayed or postponed.[11] By creating other critical challenges, Covid-19 distracted the attention of governments, but also business associations and civil society organisations, from contributing to such strategies. Nevertheless, as new teleworking and safety practices emerged throughout the year, governments began again reporting progress in finalising national AfCFTA implementation strategies, including validated strategies

Table 6.2: AfCFTA national implementation strategies: progress by March 2022

	Inception phase	Drafting/ consultations phase	Validated and/or under implementation
Countries	Benin, Central African Republic, Equatorial Guinea, Eswatini, Guinea-Bissau, Liberia, Libya, Cabo Verde, Sao Tome and Principe, Seychelles, Somalia, Sudan, South Sudan	Algeria, Botswana, Chad, Comoros, Djibouti, Mozambique, Nigeria, Rwanda, Mauritius, Tunisia	Burkina Faso, Burundi, Cameroon, Congo, Côte d'Ivoire, DRC, Gabon, Guinea, Kenya, Malawi, Mauritania, Namibia, Niger, Nigeria, Senegal, Sierra Leone, The Gambia, Togo, Zambia, Zimbabwe
No.	13	10	20
RECs	ECCAS, UMA	EAC, ECOWAS, IGAD	
No.	2	3	0

Source: Information shared directly by UN Economic Commission for Africa, by March 2022.

in Sierra Leone and Mauritania in early 2021. By March 2022, 20 AfCFTA implementation strategies had been validated or were in the process of being implemented (see Table 6.2).

It is not just governments that must prepare for the AfCFTA. Businesses must scout out market opportunities, identify related regulatory and quality standards requirements required for exporting, verify that they meet the AfCFTA rules of origin and determine payments and logistics options. In many sectors, Covid-19 refocused business attention from potential market expansion to survival. In a global business impact survey conducted by ITC through April to June 2020, 84 per cent of large businesses and 78 per cent of SMEs reported to either be following a 'resilience' strategy to 'weather the storm' or be in outright 'retreat', shedding assets, shutting down operations and accumulating debt just to survive (Figure 6.19). Just 16 per cent of large businesses and 21 per cent of SMEs were found to be proposing new products or business models in response to new market trends, identified as an 'agile' response strategy. The postures adopted by firms, of course, relate to the extent and way in which their broader industries were impacted by Covid-19: while some, such as airlines or hospitality businesses, may have experienced industry consolidation, others experienced sustained demand, such as telecoms. In banking, for example, there were signs of the emergence of 'digital-first' operating models as incumbents resized their branch networks and acquired smaller companies with technology capabilities (Jayaram et al. 2020).

Figure 6.19: Covid-19 response strategies, by business size

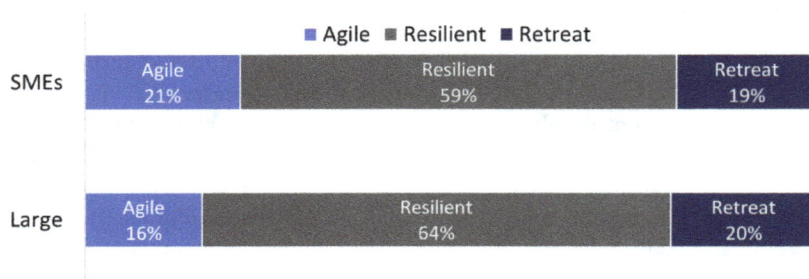

Source: ITC (2020). SME Competitiveness Outlook: Covid-19: The Great Lockdown and Its Impact on Small Business.

While fewer businesses may have been bullishly expanding into new products and markets, regional trade was reported to have emerged as an important 'backup' in business resilience strategies. In an ECA and IEC survey of 206 African businesses in June to July 2020, 56 per cent reported to have switched to national and regional suppliers in response to international supply shortages (UNECA and IEC 2020). Two-thirds of the surveyed firms further identified new opportunities in reaction to the crisis, of which 'growth in markets' was the most frequently cited.

Many African economies have been those least scathed, at least in economic terms, by Covid-19: of the 31 countries that remarkably experienced positive GDP growth in 2020, 16 were African (IMF 2022). African countries also have impressive medium-term market fundamentals, including a rapidly increasing, urbanising and maturing consumer population. Regional trade has been a legitimate solution to African business survival, recovery and longer-term growth post-Covid-19.

AfCFTA leadership

'When a state finds itself in crisis, it does not see beyond its nose', lamented Adebayo Adedeji in surveying the lost opportunities of Africa under the plague of economic crises it faced in the 1980s (United Nations African Renewal 2002). One of the lost opportunities at that time was economic integration; the 1980 Lagos Plan of Action – a systematic political programme for integration – collapsed as policymaking attention refocused on commodity price and debt stability challenges (Gérout, MacLeod and Desta 2019). Covid-19 likewise diverted the attention of leaders onto Covid-19 health and economic shocks, including (initially) falling commodity prices, domestic production and imported access to essential medical equipment, tax revenue, debt sustainability and unemployment. Policy attention consumed itself with new budgeting and funding priorities and crisis management, rather than implementing an economic project such as the AfCFTA that involves a longer-term vision and commitment.

In the marketplace of ideas, attention is the currency. Stakeholders continued to fight for the attention of the AfCFTA as a tool for the transformative growth of the African continent. Much effort was made to articulate the AfCFTA as a part of the Covid-19 'recovery package' for Africa:

> Many countries in Africa do not have the monetary policy space, the fiscal policy space to provide large bailouts in the trillions of dollars for economic recovery. Therefore, for Africa, the stimulus package is the actual AfCFTA, the implementation of this agreement. Increased intra-African trade is what will drive economic development post-COVID-19. (H.E. Wamkele Mene, secretary-general, AfCFTA Secretariat, cited in Ighobor 2020)

> Africa does not need a Marshall Plan to ride out the ongoing coronavirus crisis. It has a more powerful tool in the African Continental Free Trade Area (AfCFTA) to use in accelerating regional and economic integration and prepare for uncertain times. (Vera Songwe, executive secretary of the ECA and under-secretary-general for the UN, cited in Tralac 2020)

> While the operationalization of the Secretariat was postponed due to the Covid 19 pandemic, the same pandemic has also magnified the urgent need for speed to accelerate economic integration on the Continent. (H.E. Moussa Faki Mahamat, chairperson of the African Union Commission, cited in Mahamat 2020)

As of December 2022, with 44 African Union member states having now ratified the AfCFTA Agreement – and 42 having submitted their initial tariff offers – it appears that Africa's leaders agree as to the significant role of the AfCFTA in Africa's Covid-19 recovery.

Though it is likely that more progress on the AfCFTA may have been made without the Covid-19 distractions to policymaking attention, that such a crisis failed to upend the momentum of the AfCFTA is impressive. Covid-19 also enabled the introduction of new working practices such as the option of remote participation in negotiations, which has persisted even after physical travel became possible, and offers new possibilities for improved participation for some countries. The history of failed African economic integration under the economic crises of the 1980s fortunately appears to have been averted. The challenges of Covid-19 in Africa in 2020 reveal a story of the perseverance of African leadership and commitment to transformative economic policies.

Summary

Covid-19 created a sharp, but relatively short, crisis in African trade. The main determinant of the trade performance of African countries is revealing of their continued structural weaknesses. Successes, and failures, in exports from African countries closely charted the ebbing and flow of just a few commodity prices, and especially the prices of petroleum oil and gold. These goods and other metals continue to account for more than 60 per cent of Africa's exports. Africa's exports of services embodied a similar dependency challenge, being heavily concentrated in travel and tourism services, which plummeted in the crisis. A drought in international travel precipitated by the pandemic could not, as was the case in other countries in Europe and the US, be replaced by domestic tourism, which remains overly nascent in most of the continent. The brevity of the impact of Covid-19 on African trade, at least in commodities trade, and the rapid rebound in the value of African commodity exports, undermines the opportunity that the crisis could have created for deciding upon meaningful change. As commodity prices soared, they reinforced and entrenched the commodity dependencies of African countries that do little to serve longer-term goals of structural transformation, jobs creation and sustainable economic development.

Excitement over the potential for Covid-19 to shorten supply chains, localise production and bring some manufacturing from Asia to Africa appears to have been – in general – premature. Though Covid-19 did disrupt more complex global supply chains, such as those in the manufacturing sector, producers are reported to have considered many these changes to have been merely transitory. Covid-19 catalysed some investments by pharmaceutical companies for production facilities within the continent, but there have been challenges due to a reluctance of developed countries over the TRIPS waiver at the WTO and free Covid-19 vaccine donations, which undermined local production efforts. Further efforts are still needed to improve the business environment and better attract diversified export-oriented businesses to Africa. In summary, the Covid-19 crisis does not appear to have catalysed the substantial transformation of Africa's trade. Covid-19 is, however, also a story of African trade policymaking focus and persistence. The AfCFTA, as an initiative, amounts to a longer-term and slower-burning economic policy, rather than a 'quick fix'. That is exactly the kind of project that is most at risk of being forgotten in the throes of the sorts of emergency crises pressed upon African countries during the Covid-19 pandemic. Despite the redirection of policy and business attention towards health and economic urgencies, the longer-term vision of continental economic integration embodied by the AfCFTA has persisted. The momentum behind the AfCFTA has weathered a considerable storm, suggesting that this time policymakers have held fast and committed to its promise of economic development. African policymakers have also shown the willingness and value of policy efforts at the continental level. Pooled medical supplies procurement across the continent helped to alleviate the difficulties African countries, as some of the poorest in the world, faced in the global scramble for vaccines, medicines and medical products.

Notes

[1] Early versions of some figures in this chapter were first published in Luke, David and MacLeod, Jamie (2021) 'The impact of COVID-19 on trade in Africa', Africa at LSE blog. 3 December. https://blogs.lse.ac.uk/africaatlse/2021/12/03/the-impact-of-covid-19 -pandemic-on-trade-africa-afcfta/

[2] Authors' calculations based on ITC TradeMap Data.

[3] The Russian Federation, Vietnam and Myanmar, among others see (ECA 2020)

[4] Survey of 206 businesses with operations covering all 54 African countries over the period of 16 June to 20 July

[5] Manufactured value-added growth data comes from World Bank development indicators.

[6] Manufactured value-added growth data comes from World Bank development indicators.

[7] In the case of Benin, for example, we observe a decline in the growth of added value between 2019 and 2020 (11.25 per cent vs 3.36 per cent).

[8] List of participants. Sixth Meeting of the Continental Free Trade Area Negotiating Forum, 5–16 June 2017, Niamey, Niger.

[9] Average excludes the host country Niger.

[10] Report of the Third Meeting of the AfCFTA Council of Ministers, Accra, Ghana, 20 November 2020, AfCFTA/CoM/3/Decns 11.

[11] Updates on progress with the development of national AfCFTA strategies were supplied by Judith Ameso of the African Trade Policy Centre, at the UN Economic Commission for Africa, in November 2020.

References

Adepoju, Paul (2022) 'Lack of Orders Could Halt COVID-19 Vaccine Production in South Africa', Devex, 14 April. https://perma.cc/EWR5-H448

AmCham (2020) '2020 China Business Report'.

Baffes, John and Nagle, Peter (2020) 'The Commodity Markets Outlook in Eight Charts', World Bank Blogs, 22 October. https://perma.cc/P4LS-8XVR

Baker McKenzie (2022) 'Supply Chains Reimagined: Recovery and Renewal in Asia Pacific and Beyond', Report. https://perma.cc/33P5-M6GC

Baltes, Boris; Dickson, Marcus W.; Sherman, Michael; Bauer, Cara; and LaGanke, Jacqueline (2002) 'Computer-Mediated Communication and Group Decision Making: A Meta-analysis', *Organizational Behavior and Human Decision Processes*, vol.87, no.1, pp.156–79. https://doi.org/10.1006/obhd.2001.2961

Banga, Karishma; MacLeod, Jamie; and Mendez-Parra, Max (2021) 'Digital Trade Provisions in the AfCFTA: What Can We Learn from South-South Trade Agreements', ODI, Supporting Economic Transitions Working Paper Series. https://perma.cc/59U4-QKP9

BBC (2020) 'Brexit-UK Meeting to Go Ahead via Video Link'. https://perma.cc/QY58-VVM3

Cable, Jonathan and Kihara, Leika (2020) 'Asian Factories Recover Further from COVID-19 Crisis in November as China booms', *Business News*, 1 December. https://perma.cc/5FUT-3FK5

Committee for the Coordination of Statistical Analysis (2021) 'How COVID-19 Is Changing the World: A Statistical Perspective – Volume III', Report. https://perma.cc/D954-SKAF

Cordon, Carlos (2020) 'A Post COVID-19 Outlook: The Future of the Supply Chain', Institute of Management Development, Research & Knowledge blog post. https://perma.cc/PS25-VA6R

El Baz, Jamal and Ruel, Salomée (2021) 'Can Supply Chain Risk Management Practices Mitigate the Disruption Impacts on Supply Chains' Resilience and Robustness? Evidence from an Empirical Survey in a COVID-19 Outbreak Era', *International Journal of Production Economics*, vol.233, 1 March. https://doi.org/10.1016/j.ijpe.2020.107972

Financial Times (2020) 'African Health Officials Warn of Chronic Medical Shortages', 8 April. https://perma.cc/P357-JYEC

Gartner (2020) 'Future of Supply Chain', Survey. https://perma.cc/4YP4-44MK

Gérout, Guillaume; MacLeod, Jamie; and Desta, Melaku (2019) 'The AfCFTA as Yet Another Experiment towards Continental Integration: Retrospect and Prospect', in Luke, David and MacLeod, Jamie (eds) *Inclusive Trade in Africa: The Continental Free Trade Area in Comparative Perspective*, London: Routledge.

Giorgi, Emanuele; Cattaneo, Tiziano; Ni, Minqing; and Enríquez Alatriste, Renata (2020) 'Sustainability and Effectiveness of Chinese Outline for National Tourism and Leisure'. *Sustainability*, vol.12, no.3, p.1161. https://doi.org/10.3390/su12031161

Hughes, Tony (2020) 'Effective Virtual Negotiation', Huthwaite International. https://perma.cc/XD2D-MQP2

IEA (2019) 'Africa Energy Outlook', World Energy Outlook Special Report. https://perma.cc/UJH4-676E

Ighobor, Kingsley (2020) 'Implementing Africa's Free Trade Pact the Best Stimulus for Post-COVID-19 Economies', *Africa Renewal*, 15 May. https://perma.cc/Y4GH-T49T

IMF (2022) 'World Economic Outlook (April 2022)', Washington, DC: IMF Publications.

Ivanov, Dmitry (2021) 'Exiting the COVID-19 Pandemic: After-Shock Risks and Avoidance of Disruption Tails in Supply Chains', *Annals of Operations Research*. https://doi.org/10.1007/s10479-021-04047-7

Jayaram, Kartik; Leiby, Kevin; Leke, Acha; Ooko-Ombaka, Amandla; and Sunny Sun, Ying (2020) 'Reopening and Reimagining Africa', McKinsey, 29 May. https://perma.cc/S598-RMJJ

König, Michael and Winkler, Adalbert (2021) 'COVID-19: Lockdowns, Fatality Rates and GDP Growth', *Intereconomics*, vol.56, no.1, pp.32–39. https://doi.org/10.1007/s10272-021-0948-y

Kuteyi, Damilola and Winkler, Herwig (2022) 'Logistics Challenges in Sub-Saharan Africa and Opportunities for Digitalization', *Sustainability*, vol.14, no.4, pp.1–18 https://doi.org/10.3390/su14042399

Mahamat, Moussa Faki (2020) 'Statement by H.E. Moussa Faki Mahamat, Chairperson of the African Union Commission Delivered at the Handover Ceremony of the AfCFTA Buildings to AU 17 August, 2020 Accra, Ghana'.

Martin, Nicolas (2020) 'Africa to profit from global supply chains overhaul?', Deutsche Welle, 14 May. https://perma.cc/WRB9-URM6

Monnier, Oliver (2021) 'A Ticket to Recovery: Reinventing Africa's Tourism Industry', IFC News Release. https://perma.cc/LXD6-FNPY

Movius, Hal (2020) 'How to Negotiate Virtually', *Harvard Business Review*, 10 June. https://perma.cc/PFE8-7SXZ

OECD (2020) 'Coronavirus (Covid-19): Update on OECD tax work', 17 March. https://perma.cc/56U2-M7KN

Oke, Adekoke; Boso, Nathanial; and Marfo, John S. (2022) 'Out of Africa', *Supply Chain Management Review*, 5 January. https://perma.cc/W95Y-B64R

Tralac (2020) 'AfCFTA Africa's Plan to Ride Out Crippling Coronavirus Crisis, Says Vera Songwe', 15 July. https://perma.cc/UZE6-48CY

UNECA (2020) 'Insights on African Businesses' Reaction and Outlook to COVID-19', UNECA Publications, Report. https://perma.cc/2A5N-YGBF

UNECA (2020a) 'COVID-19 in Africa: Protecting Lives and Economies', UNECA Publications, Report. https://perma.cc/PCJ2-97DS

UNECA (2020b) 'COVID-19 in Africa: Protecting Lives and Economies', UNECA Publications, Report. https://perma.cc/NL95-STFZ

UNECA (2020c) 'COVID-19: Lockdown Exit Strategies for Africa', UNECA Publications, Report. https://perma.cc/TG3S-WSXE

UNECA and IEC (2020) 'Reactions and Outlook to COVID-19 in Africa', UNECA Publications, Report. https://perma.cc/3BQT-828J

UNIDO (2022) 'World Manufacturing Production: Statistics for Quarter IV 2021', Report. https://perma.cc/62VC-SUJL

United Nations African Renewal (2002) 'You Must First Set Your House in Order'. https://perma.cc/W7JQ-L9XH

UNWTC (United Nations World Tourism Organization) (2019) 'Global Report on Women in Tourism'. https://perma.cc/XZ5M-2GFS

World Bank (2021a) 'Commodity Markets Outlook, April 2021: Causes and Consequences of Metal Price Shocks', Open Knowledge Repository. https://perma.cc/4BYK-MM9L

World Bank (2021b) 'World Development Indicators'.

WTTC (World Travel and Tourism Council) (2017) 'Domestic Tourism Importance and Economic Impact'. https://perma.cc/H5H4-5R2J

WTTC (World Travel and Tourism Council) (2021) 'Travel and Tourism Economic Impact 2021'. https://perma.cc/X433-B3VG

Zhao, Yanyun and Liu, Bingjie (2020) 'The Evolution and New Trends of China's Tourism Industry', National Accounting Review, vol.2, no.4, pp.337–53. https://doi.org/10.3934/NAR.2020020

7. How the Covid-19 crisis affected informal and digital trade

Kulani McCartan-Demie and Jamie MacLeod

The Covid-19 pandemic had significant consequences beyond the traditional aspects of Africa's trade in commodities, agricultural goods, manufactures or services. The first was the effects on informal cross-border trade, itself an area that has long been a persistently under-appreciated aspect of intra-African trade and policy. We show here that it was severely affected by the pandemic. Informal cross-border trade faced pressure to aggregate – in what became known as 'grouping' – to collectively satisfy border health requirements. And in doing so it often by necessity became more 'formalised'. But, in other instances, such trade was pushed to even more precarious informal routes, aggravated by the difficulties of complying with new pandemic-related 'safe trade' measures at borders.

The second dimension, by contrast, is digital trade, which attracted less attention in Africa before the pandemic, and then a lot of rhetoric and discussion once the crisis took hold. Covid-19 brought digital trade and digital means of trade facilitation to the attention of policymakers and the speeches of global panjandrums, but the new rhetoric about it surpassed a more muted reality on the ground. The second part of this chapter looks at digital trade and e-commerce, and whether Covid-19 contributed to the acceleration of digitalised forms of trade.

This chapter, like Chapter 6, assesses what Covid-19 changed about trade in Africa, with a particular interest in 'tipping points' and the 'sticking power' of those changes. It highlights persisting gaps in trade policy awareness within the continent and how policy priorities changed in the course of the pandemic.[1]

How to cite this book chapter:

McCartan-Demie, Kulani and MacLeod, Jamie (2023) 'How the Covid-19 crisis affected informal and digital trade', in: Luke, David (ed) *How Africa Trades*, London: LSE Press, pp. 177–208. https://doi.org/10.31389/lsepress.hat.g License: CC-BY-NC 4.0

7.1 Informal cross-border trade (ICBT)

In the wake of Covid-19 in 2020, efforts were made for formal cargo trade to flow by air, sea and land, helping to keep African economies afloat. Informal cross-border trade (ICBT), on the other hand, was substantially disrupted. Despite being a valuable (yet under-valued) source of intra-African trade, the policy landscape overlooked small-scale and informal cross-border trade. By its nature, ICBT requires functioning land borders, the physical movement of people, and access to markets – all of which were affected by Covid-19 restrictions. When 'safe trade' measures were introduced to keep trade flowing, they were conceived and targeted more with formal trade in mind, often under-appreciating the role of informal cross-border trade. Some of the safe trade measures restricted the movement of informal traders across borders, resulting in additional costs as well as delays in the delivery of goods. At the same time, they also gave rise to new aggregated forms of informal trade across the continent. A prime example was 'groupage', wherein informal traders grouped and transported consignments to satisfy border health requirements.

The picture across the continent has not been entirely bleak, however. Countries, regional economic communities (RECs), trade and information desk officers (TIDOs) and formal and informal traders, with time, adapted to the new normal of 'safe trade'. This section unearths the competing realities of cross-border trade during Covid-19 and the uneven experiences that policy interventions have shaped across different regions and countries. It looks to understand whether the 'safe trade' measures that were introduced during the pandemic are likely have a long-term impact on trade facilitation. Was Covid-19 a 'tipping point' for a transition to more formal and aggregated patterns of trade or did it reinforce the precariousness of informal trade?

ICBT is carried out both through unofficial crossings, where goods are smuggled across the border, and over official border points – where goods are not declared. The most salient drivers behind the informality of cross-border trade include cumbersome border procedures, shortages of commodities on either side of the border, and different taxation levels affecting prices and offering attractive arbitrage margins for smugglers (Titeca 2021). This type of trade in goods and services is still important, despite circumventing the regulatory framework set by the government. The composition of ICBT export and import baskets is predominantly low-value and takes place between border communities with strong mutual linkages and crucially ensures that there is food security across the border. Though it does not tend to extend too far in land, some traders move goods as far as three countries away. ICBT is gendered, owing to its flexibility and precarity. Women in ICBT play an integral role in sustaining Africa's informal economies and make up the largest share of informal traders, representing 70 per cent to 80 per cent in some countries, thanks to low start-up capital requirements and the earning potential it offers in border areas, where there could be limited employment.

The value of ICBT is significant across all African sub-regions but the availability of continent-wide data is weak by virtue of its inherent informality (Byiers et al. 2021). Recent estimates have found ICBT to be between 7 and 16 per cent of formal intra-African trade flows, and 30 and 72 per cent of formal trade between neighbouring countries – the equivalent of around $10 billion to $24 billion in pre-pandemic years (Gaarder, Luke and Sommer 2021). While the individual consignments of informal traders might be small in volume and value, the large number of daily transactions means that the aggregate value of imports and exports can sometimes exceeds formal trade (World Bank 2020a).

Policy responses to Covid-19 in Africa depended on capacity levels across both trade and health policy. Policy interactions between trade and health are not new; neither are weaknesses in their coordination. Trade-health policy enforcement at the border was often weak pre-pandemic, particularly in terms of sanitary and phytosanitary measures. In many instances, this stemmed from the prevalence and character of informal trade, the porosity of borders, and the sparsity of formal crossing points, or the relative ease with which formal crossings could be circumvented. The issuance of health certificates prior to the pandemic was in many instances more of a revenue-raising activity than a health measure (Gaarder 2022). With many traders and goods crossing unofficially, the effectiveness of such measures and safe trade more generally risked being undermined by the large presence of informal trade (Gaarder 2022). With this weak 'safe' trade regulatory backdrop that pre-existed the pandemic, new policy interventions during the crisis had a lot to make up for.

The stringency of Covid-19 health policy measures varied between African countries and evolved over time (see Chapter 6). Many lockdowns were announced with little notice given to traders about the timelines for lockdowns and this lack of communication did not consider the impact on the livelihoods of traders. Different types of measures had different impacts on traders (Resnick, Spencer and Siwale 2020). Some responses focused on creating an enabling environment in some cases, while others involved restrictive policies that worsened outcomes for traders. Informal traders in Africa had to navigate uneven enforcement of travel bans, border closures and testing across the borders of the countries where they operated. Health policy was often prioritised over trade activity, primarily due to the fragility of available health infrastructure. But some of the pressure to impose such stringent measures was external:

> You have these people sitting in Geneva who essentially modelled their crisis response for Africa based on what rich countries did and the type of measures they put in place. You can't have a one size fits all approach when the reality on the ground is so hugely different. If you didn't put in place travel or movement restrictions you were

seen as 'irresponsible' without contextualising whether this safe trade response was appropriate. (Gaarder 2022)

While new trade-health regulations on movement across borders disrupted and slowed the operations of larger-scale traders, in most cases informal traders were completely cut off. Many public health policies primarily restricted the movement of persons, allowing trucking traffic to continue the shipment of goods, largely unhampering commercial traders. For food and agricultural trade, additional sanitary controls for Covid-19 delayed the flow of traffic and goods, causing price increases for foodstuffs. In some border towns, restrictions led to price jumps as high as 50 per cent for certain commodities (Resnick, Spencer and Siwale 2020, p.5). In addition to sanitary controls, curfews disproportionally affected small producers and fresh food supply chains, which constitute a significant portion of ICBT. Serious delays at the border were also compounded by the lack of personal protective equipment for customs and other agencies' staff as well as quarantines imposed on truck drivers (Banga et al. 2020).

Land border closures and the response of informal traders

Land border closures were a primary way in which health and trade policy was implemented in the initial phases of the pandemic, though this changed over time, with borders opening at uneven rates across different regions. By March 2020, most African governments had closed their land borders, with restrictions peaking in May/June 2020. Though restrictions varied, land borders remained strictly closed in some countries for as long as two years. Figure 7.1 illustrates points of entry that were fully or partially closed and those that remained fully operational (land and blue borders) in February 2020 and February 2022. Though restrictions varied, land and blue borders (sea, river and lake ports) overall were strictly closed in most countries in 2020, before gradually opening over the following two years.

Land border restrictions varied regionally. In March 2022, the region with the highest global share of fully closed points of entry (including airports, land borders and blue borders), suggesting considerable restrictions to cross border trade, was Central and West Africa (24 per cent out of 588; see Figure 7.2) and the lowest was East and Horn of Africa (5 per cent out of 382). When this is disaggregated to land border crossing points, Central and West Africa was the region with the highest global share of fully closed land borders (120 out of 450, 27 per cent). Among the highest percentage of fully operational land border crossing points in Africa was Southern Africa (169 out of 226 locations, 77 per cent out of the total), and East and Horn of Africa (132 out of 213, 62 per cent) (IOM 2022).

Nevertheless, despite the relative degree of regional openness in Southern Africa, some states maintained stringent border closures for extended

Figure 7.1: Evolution of Covid-19 mobility restrictions – Africa, February 2020 (left) and February 2022 (right)

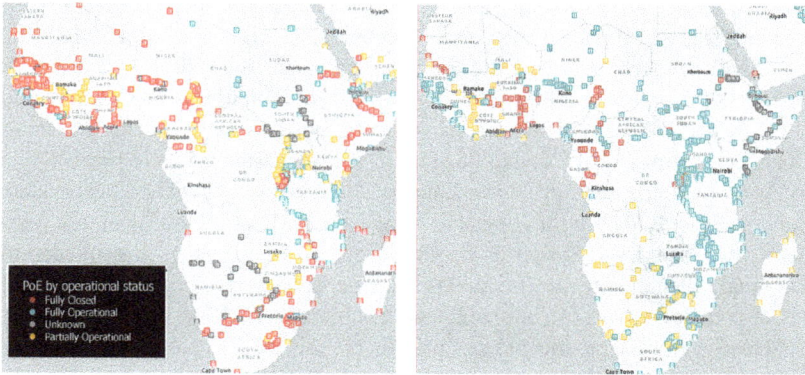

Source: IOM Mobility Restriction Tracker (2022), reproduced with permission.

Figure 7.2: Covid-19 mobility restrictions, West Africa, 2022

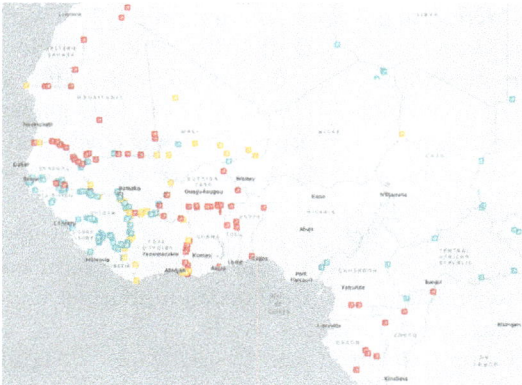

Source: IOM Mobility Restriction Tracker (2022), reproduced with permission.

periods. Zimbabwe only opened the borders for ICBT in February 2022. In essence, 'safe trade' here was taken to mean *no trade at all* for informal traders. This was not the case for other countries in Southern Africa: South Africa, Zambia and Botswana opened their borders much earlier. This trend cut across many borders in Africa: while border restrictions reduced in the course of 2020, aided by 'safe trade' facilitative measures, they remained more burdensome than pre-pandemic times in other countries (Luke and MacLeod 2021).

Border closures, delays and increased costs of trading drove informal traders to pivot to unregulated and more precarious informal crossing points in 'no man's lands' (Mvungu and Kunaka 2021). Increased trade costs have been a severe non-tariff barrier to informal traders. In the Great Lakes Region, pre-pandemic, a 'jeton' (day pass) was previously issued to small traders for free, but this was replaced with a 'laissez passer', which cost roughly US$10.00 for small traders crossing the borders between the DRC and Rwanda and 10,000 Uganda shillings (about US$2.75) for Ugandan small traders and US$5.00 for DRC small traders crossing the borders between the DRC and Uganda (Mvungu and Kunaka 2021). These circumstances were not isolated to Eastern Africa; in Zimbabwe, Zambia and Malawi, where the borders are quite porous, ICBT might appear to have dramatically fallen during the pandemic because it was absent at *formal* border posts. In reality, it displaced to informal, 'illegal' entry points owing to expensive compliance measures that acted as disincentives for informal traders (Mafurutu 2022).

Africa's regional economic communities (RECs) introduced a series of trade-health guidelines to harmonise measures. These were largely directed at large-scale formal trade and failed to appropriately integrate informal traders. In the initial stages, SADC, COMESA and the EAC developed regional guidelines to facilitate trade, which was followed by guidelines developed at the tripartite level. Some of the measures enforced by COMESA member states were recognised as punitive, especially towards small-scale traders, and, in response, the COMESA Secretariat developed guidelines to facilitate the movement of essential commodities, PPE and foodstuffs for member states (Onyango 2022). Most of the REC guidelines included regulations covering mandatory testing, sanitising trucks and limiting crew numbers, and were primarily focused on facilitating the movement of emergency essential supplies. One of the major shortcomings of these regionally articulated guidelines was how informal traders were overlooked in these trade-health policy responses – they did not tailor specific policy interventions to cater to, and assist the livelihoods of, informal traders (Onyango 2022; Sommer 2022).

The African Union took up the task of working towards a continental set of guidelines in 2020 that would better integrate small-scale cross-border trade facilitation – a task that had yet to be fulfilled by December 2022, with the guidelines remaining a work in progress, and increasingly irrelevant, more than two years on. The position of ICBT still had not received sufficient attention within the AU: 'Right now to tell you the truth, we did not have any activities focused on informal traders but the guidelines [recognise the need] to deal with small scale traders' (Kassee 2022). The AU guidelines were presented to the heads of customs authorities in 2021, who managed the trade facilitation component, and were then endorsed by the ministerial meeting responsible for trade in late 2021. While they focused on the broader scope of trade (beyond land borders and maritime trade), they did not dedicate a specific set of policy interventions for informal traders – 'we are not saying they are the best guidelines but at least we tried to come up with something' (Kassee 2022). The AU guidelines are perhaps better viewed as a 'live document', dynamic in nature, and updated and disseminated through recurring consultations and workshops with stakeholders as the Covid-19 pandemic transitions into the recovery period.

Some cross-border agencies did not speak to each other in the wake of the pandemic, whereas others harmonised interventions. In the DRC, cross-border agencies did not coordinate responses in the early phases with neighbouring countries. For example, PCR tests priced in the DRC were not recognised in Rwanda, and Congolese small-scale traders could not afford to test twice each time they crossed the border (Bashi 2022a). Most of the rules implemented were aimed at large traders not small traders, because they were not formally registered; this was despite data being given to the government: 'we provided the numbers: the ICBT association in Goma is made up of 7,000 people, in Bukavu it is 2,000 people', yet they were still excluded in any policy considerations (Bashi 2022a). In some cases, cross-border harmonisation improved once border agencies begun speaking to each other (Box 7.1).

'Safe trade' measures: here to stay?

For trade to operate in as safe an environment as possible, specific measures were introduced early in the pandemic. Many of these 'safe trade' measures were adapted by countries as the pandemic evolved into the recovery period. By

Box 7.1: Inter-agency harmonisation: the DRC and its neighbours

Some three months into the pandemic, regional talks took place on trade facilitation. The governor of North Kivu (DRC) and South Kivu (Rwanda) met and small cross-border traders were invited to share grievances from informal traders on both sides of the border: on the Rwandan side they said 'we are not making money anymore because the Congolese are not coming to buy our goods anymore and on the other side Congolese markets were empty because they couldn't bring goods from Rwanda' (Bashi 2022). This consultation process helped to develop a crucial policy to facilitate ICBT. The PCR test was reduced to $5 on the Rwandan side (previously costing as much as $60), recognised by both border communities, and made available to any informal trader registered with an ICBT association. This was a local authority and regional government-driven trade facilitation process. Despite greater inter-agency cross-border policy harmonisation, there was still some miscommunication on border openings: Rwanda and the DRC had different opening and closing schedules.

Source: Bashi (2022).

early 2022, borders had reopened in most cases but, overall, many health regulations remained in place, and time was needed for traders, customs authorities and immigration officials to familiarise themselves with new regulations
(Sommer 2022). In some countries, Covid-19 'safe trade' border restrictions
were lifted or adjusted. For example, law enforcement become more relaxed
in Uganda: travellers still needed to present a negative Covid-19 test issued
no more than 120 hours before travel, but in practice this was not enforced
for small-scale traders and cross-border mobility improved (Titeca 2021).

In some cases, 'safe trade' measures helped to improve the enabling environment for informal traders, especially in marketplaces during the height
of the pandemic (Resnick, Spencer and Siwale 2020, p.6). For example, in
response to market traders, who tend to operate in crowded environments
in border communities, authorities emphasised decongesting markets and
ensuring they operate with new health protocols. In Ghana, a partial lockdown exempted actors in the food value chain and markets in all regions (not
just cross-border communities). Marketplaces were cleaned and disinfected,
with some districts following an 'alternate products for alternate days' system.
This adaptation depended on building trust and dialogue with Ghana's 'market queens' – influential female traders in the wholesale/retail distribution of
food commodities (Resnick, Spencer and Siwale 2020). Measures were not
always adapted to the needs of informal traders (Box 7.2). In the DRC, informal traders were not able to take advantage of the facilitation measures put
in place by certain governments to mitigate the negative effects of Covid-19
on the country's economy, such as the three-month exemption of VAT on
the importation and sale of 'basic' goods and a financing scheme from the
Industry Promotion Fund (FPI – Fonds de Promotion de l'Industrie). These
were aimed at larger-scale traders (Bashi 2022a).

Box 7.2: Short-sighted public health measures: Zimbabwe

In Zimbabwe, a major challenge in terms of sectoral policy
coordination was the location of testing sites and their proximity to
informal traders. These test centres were not located at the borders
and it took time for these to be gradually decentralised. The government privatised the test centres and provided a list of authorised
private sector testing facilities. With no public facilities available,
complying with testing requirements was costly for informal traders.
At Beitbridge, the border post between Zimbabwe and South Africa,
and Chirundu (between Zimbabwe and Zambia), the amount it cost
to obtain a PCR test ranged from $60 to $120 – out of touch with the
economic realities of informal traders.

Source: Mafurutu (2022).

Many of these 'safe trade' measures are likely to persist. In the words of one interviewee, 'the thing about bureaucracy is that once you've introduced it, it's really hard to get rid of' (Gaarder 2022). Two years on since the announcement of land border closures, it had become standard practice to comply with sanitisation measures, Covid-19 testing and vaccination certification in order to trade across many borders. It would take more effort to debureaucratise this entire ecosystem, especially once parts of it had become digitally integrated with cross-border trade – among the positive longer-term policy outcomes of this period.

Did the STR ecosystem buffer informal traders from the pandemic?

Simplified trade regimes (STRs) are currently operational in two RECS: the EAC and COMESA. These intend to facilitate small-scale cross-border trade, by way of simplified clearance procedures (such as forgoing the requirement for a certificate of origin) for low-value consignments (for example, less than US$2,000) on applicable products. In COMESA these products are included in several 'common lists', which are bilaterally agreed upon between participating countries, whereas in the EAC products are agreed unilaterally. In reality, the STR merely 'eliminates a duty that those traders should not have been paying anyways' (Gaarder 2022). Traders still have to pay VAT, excise duty, obtain immigration documents and comply with a range of standards in order to benefit from the STRs.

Prior to the pandemic, STRs faced implementation weaknesses. In the EAC, many small-scale traders were unable take advantage of the STR owing to limited awareness of the procedures and regulations and inconsistent compliance by customs officers (Osoro 2022). In COMESA, the thresholds for goods were not harmonised across member states; for example, Zimbabwe applied the STR to consignments under $1,000, whereas Malawi applied the STR to consignments under $2,000. STR desk officers in Zambia and Zimbabwe spotlighted these challenges and the fact that the goods covered under the regime were last reviewed in 2013 (Mafurutu 2022). The utilisation rates of the STR by informal traders is hard to quantify owing to a lack of data but the picture across border posts is uneven. For example, the STR worked well at the Chirundu border between Zimbabwe and Zambia, but:

> the main reason it works there is pretty basic: the Zambezi River separates the two countries, the formal border crossing point is on the other side of a bridge, and it's in the middle of a national park with lions and elephants, incentivising people to trade formally. (Gaarder 2022)

Was the impact of Covid-19 less severe on informal traders who traded within the STRs? If it was the case that those borders with STRs affected informal traders less adversely during the pandemic, then this may well form a strong case to push for the roll out of STRs across the continent. The picture is not so simple. In the EAC, as long as informal traders were registered with associations and complied with the STR by passing official check points, they could benefit from the STR during the pandemic after the initial shock border closures (Osoro 2022). Yet, with the absence of testing facilities at the border posts, informal traders were still greatly affected, and the lack of appropriate decentralised safe trade measures hindered the abilities of informal traders to conduct trade officially through the STR.

In Southern Africa, the 'STR did not change anything' and for a significant period of time three countries belonging to this STR still banned the movement of informal traders despite the presence of an STR (Mafurutu 2022). In Zimbabwe, it took two years to open the formal border to informal traders, so it was impossible for them to benefit from preferential treatment despite the provisions for clearing of goods remaining in place throughout the entire pandemic for formal cross-border trade. Regardless of how simplified the trade regime is, if the 'safe trade' policy is border closure, the only thing this is going to simplify is the decision of informal traders to take more informal and possibly even illegal routes.

The STR ecosystem is made up of several components (Figure 7.3). TIDOs function to help small-scale traders understand the benefits of the STR and are sometimes embedded inside ICBT associations but are rarely self-funded by those associations. The impact of Covid-19 was often not less severe on informal traders at borders because STRs were in place. Rather, STR ecosystems (border agencies, TIDOs and CBTAs) helped foster creative solutions, such as the rise of 'groupage' trade in some regions. With the growth of aggregated patterns of ICBT, this improved the monitoring of small cross-border trade, since the more efficient flow of aggregated goods across borders allowed customs administrations to better identify goods from small cross-border trade and to apply the preferential tariff provided for them under the STR (Bashi 2022a).

Informal cross-border trade has not transformed because of Covid-19. While the substance of trade did not radically change, the aggregate value increased, groupage trade emerged, and traders pivoted and found new routes to access border markets, oftentimes resorting to more dangerous routes. The means by which a substantive proportion of ICBT was carried out did become more 'formalised' through the groupage mechanisms and 'formal patterns of informal trade' emerged. While some informal traders adopted more formal mechanisms to continue operating during the Covid-19 pandemic, 'for every trader that formalised in response to the crisis, there was another trader that became even more informal' (Gaarder 2022). The impact was especially gendered: 'safe trade' measures designed to buffer shocks to Covid-19 disproportionately impacted women engaged more frequently in informal trade than large-scale commercial traders. For example, at the height of the pandemic in the EAC's six member states, around 21.2 per cent of 260 women traders sampled reported that they were using informal routes to circumvent the existing Covid-19 measures in EAC partner states (TradeMark East Africa 2021, p.12).

Figure 7.3: The STR ecosystem

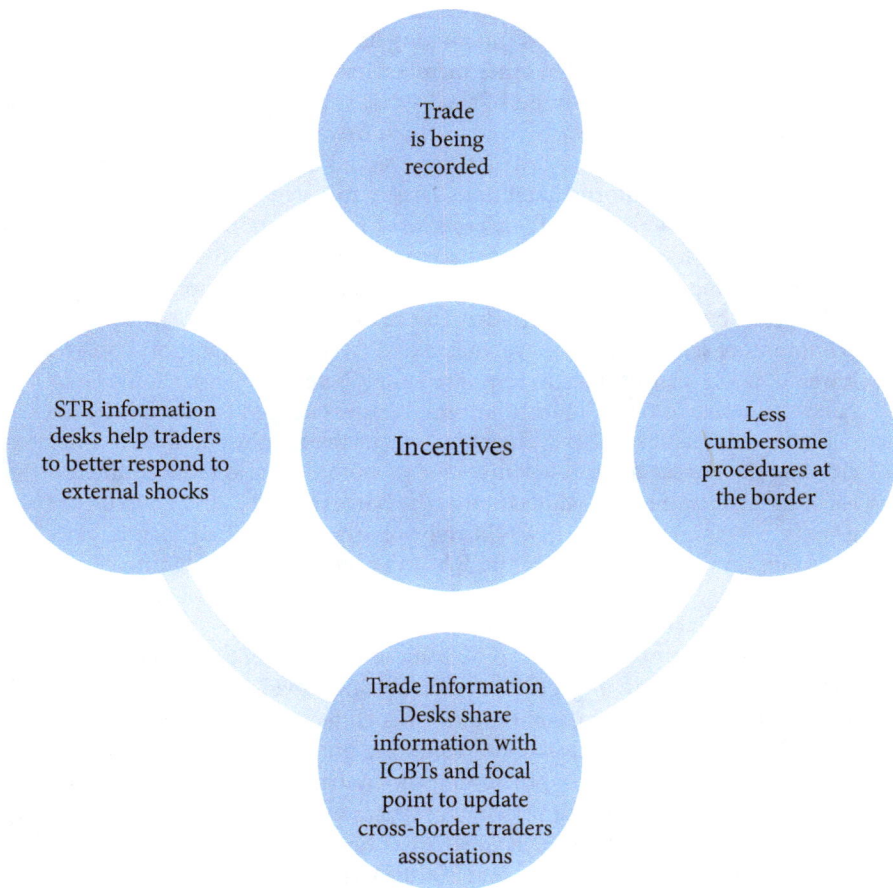

Source: Authors' own compilation.

Overall, the experience of Covid-19 revealed that, when traders could not easily pivot into new sectors/low-skilled employment/services or retrofit their consignments, they diverted trade through less safe routes or through groupage. Where borders were shut, some informal traders pivoted towards the scarce border posts that remained open, while others circumvented official border posts altogether. For example, in Malawi many informal traders pivoted towards the Mchinji border, between Malawi and Zambia. Two factors help to explain this: first, the Mchinji border is the nearest-to-destination border, so it is convenient to traders and, second, throughout the duration of the pandemic, the other key border posts such as Mwanza faced strict closures because of the measures taken by the destination countries. According to the TIDO, the increase in small-scale traders' passing through the Mchinji border post over recent years can also be attributed to the introduction of the

COMESA STR, which provides simplified customs clearance procedure for imports and exports (IOM 2021, p.11). In short, there was little harmonisation in which borders remained functioning during the pandemic in Malawi – a trend commonly spread in other member states.

There was an increasing trend of small-scale traders joining forces, aggregating their goods, and paying fees to truck drivers for transportation and clearance. Through this, informal trade was taking place in a more formal manner using informal solutions largely initiated through the nimble innovation of traders rather than because of concrete policy interventions. 'Groupage' involves organising the purchase, transport and delivery of goods in groups, using small trucks and vans, so reducing the operational costs typically borne by each individual trader. This made economic sense and created economies of scale: cargo was aggregated and the per unit transport cost was lowered. It was also an efficient response to new 'safe trade' costs; in the Great Lakes Region, two rather than 20 informal traders needed to take a PCR test (Mvunga and Kunaka 2021). The reduction in the number of small traders crossing the border to representatives for group orders also reduced the levels of harassment and illegal taxation at the borders (Bashi 2022a). However, groupage is not necessarily new. This type of arrangement had been in place for some time; for example, in the EAC, the bulking of consignments and shared delivery at the Busia border, where there is a very active cereal trade, was commonplace pre-pandemic (Osoro 2022).

Groupage systems were seen to be a more efficient and cheaper method considering the new stringent restrictions during Covid-19 at some, but not all, border posts. Certain commodities benefitted from this arrangement more than others. At the Nakonde–Tunduma border in Zambia, grain and potato consignments were predominately transported through groupage (Kanyanya 2022). This shift in trading practices may soon have the potential to accelerate the formalisation of small cross-border trade. At the Beitbridge border post between Zimbabwe and South Africa, an initiative of the revenue authority administratively encouraged informal traders to do groupage trade. Ten traders would group funds to send a driver with a seven-tonne truck to cross to Mesina and purchase goods, which would be sold back in Zimbabwe. However, the border authorities would clear those consignments as if they were commercial trucks passing through formal border posts and were less mindful of the fact that these were made up of aggregated smaller consignments of informal traders – trade data from this period needs to be scrutinised accordingly (Mafurutu 2022).

Trade data from the Covid-19 period needs to be read with appreciation for the rise of 'groupage', which was being recorded as formal by customs officials but would previously have crossed borders informally (and unrecorded). In the DRC, informal traders also started to buy goods in bulk and coordinate small cross-border trade to mitigate the effects of new policy regulations. In the absence of a clear distinction from the goods of large and commercial traders, groupage helps to explain the increase in the volume of formal imports during the pandemic. During the second quarter of 2020, an unexpected recovery took place in the eastern DRC, which recorded a 22 per cent increase in 2020 levels, compared to 2019 (Bashi 2022b). Goods imported using the groupage method were more closely monitored by customs administrations than had previously been the case for smaller informal consignments. The administration was less incentivised to disaggregate the flow of goods from small cross-border trade as 'informal' or 'formal' and blanket classified them as 'large' or 'commercial':

> The customs directorate were all so proud. Everyone was telling us: Covid-19 is going to crash our external trade and we're going to be in trouble. But look at the numbers, we even did better than 2019! But when asked how much is coming from informal groupage versus large-scale traders, they did not know, they just knew the numbers were good. (Bashi 2022a)

Elsewhere, the picture varied. For example, in Uganda, where ICBT was regularly recorded pre-pandemic, and stringent border health measures were imposed, the total ICBT in the second quarter of 2020 was a mere $3 million, a considerable drop from the $125 million recorded during the same period in 2019 (Gaarder, Luke and Sommer 2021, p.6), as shown in Figure 7.4.

Groupage cannot be taken as synonymous with formal trade as many informal traders engaged in groupage schemes were still not officially registered: 'by the end of our groupage trade facilitation project in the [DRC], less than 20 per cent had registered with the state' (Bashi 2022a). Incentives play a strong driving factor in this type of data collection for governments: first, to improve official trade flow statistics and the overall trade deficit, and, sec-

Figure 7.4: Ugandan informal exports, quarterly, $ millions

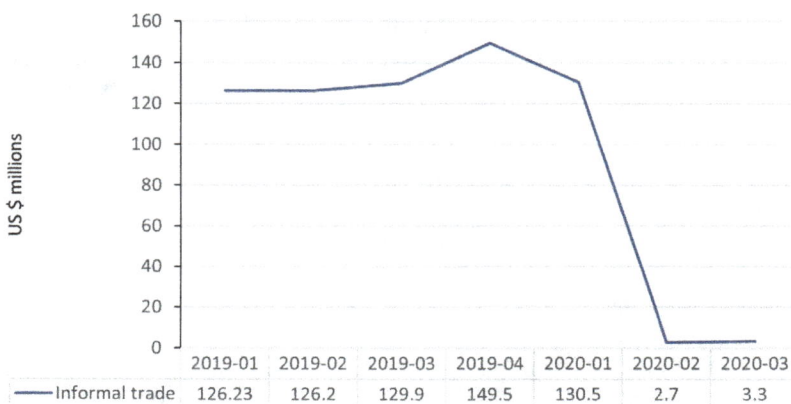

	2019-01	2019-02	2019-03	2019-04	2020-01	2020-02	2020-03
Informal trade	126.23	126.2	129.9	149.5	130.5	2.7	3.3

Source: Data from Bank of Uganda (2020).

Box 7.3: The hidden costs of groupage: informal traders subject to duties

In the DRC, groupage trade would pass through the 'large traders' entry point and be charged as 'commercial'. In response to these higher duties, informal traders put together a list where they disaggregated the consignments products, name of trader and the number of products included to prevent higher duties. However, this was done manually, with a large margin of human error, and the information provided was not recorded in the customs system. In Zimbabwe, a similar picture unfolded. Under the Zimbabwe Revenue Authority (ZIMRA), groupage did not qualify for preferential treatment at the STR facility because these were being cleared as commercial consignments. These STR benefits need to be restored for informal traders and revenue authorities should assist them with the free clearance of their groupage trade as a policy exception, during the pandemic.

Sources: Bashi (2022a); IOM (2021).

ond, to potentially reach a wider catchment for revenue mobilisation among unregistered traders. But, for informal traders, the incentives for groupage were not as clear-cut once their consignments were classified as 'commercial' and subject to certain duties (Box 7.3).

Did Covid-19 transform informal cross-border trade?

Covid-19 shifted the incentives around informal cross-border trade. In some instances, this 'pulled' formerly informal trade into larger and more formal groupage arrangements. In other instances, traders were 'pushed' by a combination of stringent policy interventions, 'safe trade' measures and border closures to either pivot routes or circumvent official border posts. Much of these trade dynamics spilled over into the economic recovery period. Public policy responses to Covid-19 varied drastically across regions and countries depending on the capacity levels to enforce policies that were tailored to informal traders. Policy responses from member states, RECs and the African Union were disproportionally aimed at large-scale cross-border trade and the lack of cross-border harmonisation between border agencies prolonged the unnecessary delays. Informal traders were acutely vulnerable to the pandemic, in both health and economic terms.

Covid-19 created shifts in policy, too. While new measures were imposed to make trade 'safe' at the border, these ranged from stringent land border closures to testing and health facilities, and in some instances long-overdue improvements to border hygiene and sanitation facilities. Some of the best of these measures, particularly those involving the digitalising and streamlining of processes, will likely endure to make trade easier long after the worst impacts of Covid-19 subside. Yet, in other instances, the pandemic created new bureaucratic obstacles that frustrate trade at border crossings, which also run the risk of persisting.

The pandemic was not necessarily the 'tipping point' for informal trade formalisation, but it introduced many traders to more formal and aggregated patterns of ICBT. These formal patterns of informal trade represent more than just a tongue-twister: groupage mechanisms were a result of nimble innovation 'from below', and not because of concrete policy inputs from countries or their RECs. Informal trade increasingly took place through more formal, aggregated patterns – a phenomenon distinct from 'formalisation', commonly associated with traders being registered and formally recognised by border agencies and revenue authorities. On the one hand, informal traders benefitted from scale efficiencies through bulk and transport costs of groupage; on the other, it is not clear whether this directly led to income gains for traders that outweigh their exclusion from the STR. In the absence of appropriate safe trade measures, some informal traders were able to advocate, facilitate and scale their trade.

One of the prevailing messages from the experience of informal trade through Covid-19 is that policy interventions to facilitate ICBT need to be informed by lived experiences on the ground in border communities. This requires dialogue and consultation *with* informal traders. Most policy interventions to date have been aimed at advancing the larger players in cross-border trade. But small players matter too – especially when the aggregate value of that 'small', presumed 'insignificant' informal trade may well tip the trade balance, and can even exceed that of formal intra-African trade.

7.2 Digital trade and e-commerce

Throughout the developed world, Covid-19 was considered to have been an accelerant for the uptake of digital technologies such as online banking, shopping, learning, leisure and doing business. With physical engagement impossible, Covid-19 nudged consumers, workers and businesses into virtual alternative forms of work and leisure. Was this phenomenon matched in Africa? We begin by summarising the 'starting point', showing the characteristics, foundations and trends in the African digital economy and digital trade in the lead-up to Covid-19. This is important because, as will be shown, these foundations (and in many instances there lack thereof) affected the trajectory of digitalisation in Africa inspired by Covid-19. This section then looks at data markers for economic behavioural changes in African countries in the course of 2020 and 2021. In doing so it focuses on three parts of the Covid-19 digital story: narratives, policies and emerging data, highlighting impressions of the nuanced reality of digital trade in Africa through Covid-19.

The internet, as well as other digital technologies, increasingly underpin international trade. A definition of the resulting 'digital trade' has gradually coalesced to describe 'digitally-enabled transactions of trade in goods and services' (González and Jouanjean 2017). Conceptually this is quite a broad idea: a product needs to be either 'digitally ordered, digitally-facilitated, or digitally delivered' to qualify (IMF 2018). In the parlance of international trade negotiations, digital trade has often been analogously termed 'electronic commerce' or 'e-commerce', stemming from an overlapping and explicit definition of the General Council of the World Trade Organization in 1998. There, e-commerce is considered to amount to 'the production, distribution, marketing, sale or delivery of goods and services by electronic means' (WTO 1998).

In trade policy and trade negotiations, negotiators often push and pull at the demarcation of the definitions of 'digital trade' and 'e-commerce' deliberately. For their intended negotiating outcomes, some wish to cast the boundaries to capture data governance issues, such as restrictions on cross-border data flows and limitations imposed on data processing, data transfers, or the legal rights and responsibilities of data owners and data subjects. In such instances, what is considered narrows down to trade specifically in *data*. Rather than how digital modes might affect trade in goods, for such negotiators it is bytes crossing borders that matters. Other negotiators seek to cast the definitions of digital trade and e-commerce to include the use of digital means for facilitating traditional trade in goods. This might be considered closer to digital forms of trade facilitation. This can include the use of electronic single windows for customs processing or encouraging the legal recognition of electronic signatures and authorisations as equivalent to their paper alternatives. In such an instance, the focus has been on the digital environment and *how* goods are traded digitally.

Even when the definitions of digital trade or e-commerce are agreed upon, its measurement remains elusive. The biennial UNCTAD Digital Economy Report in 2019 was dedicated to '*measuring* value in the digital economy'. This is challenging and diverges depending on whether its measurement is confined to narrow definitions, such as trade related to what might be considered a digital sector, like the information and communications technology sector, or trade strictly comprising digital goods and services. The digital sector can also be considered more broadly such as in instances where digital technologies are used in a wide range of sectors, such as the growing of crops using digitally designed or delivered agronomic services or the integration of computer-automated design processes into manufacturing. Even when the size of the net is determined, timely data is not always available either. This leads us to consider digital trade and e-commerce relatively broadly and to grasp a broad range of indirect means of its measurement to track its development during Covid-19, owing to a lack of any clear-cut definition and data sources. Digital trade provides both new opportunities and challenges for economic development. By reducing information costs and overcoming remoteness and distance, digitalisation is argued to help small businesses in developing countries to market and distribute to – and receive payment and make purchases from – a variety of international buyers (Lanz et al. 2018; Sandberg and Hakansson 2014; World Bank 2016). 'Developing countries, which exhibit the highest costs and biggest impediments to trade, stand to gain the most', according to the World Bank (2020b).

On the other hand, the same such businesses face a stark 'digital divide' and may risk being left behind by more sophisticated competitors (Foster et al. 2018). There are concerns that digital trade embodies network effects that can lead to market concentration and anti-competitive markets, meriting new approaches to cross-border competition regulation (Khan 2016; UNCTAD 2019). Digital trade may facilitate the distortion by international companies of their taxable income through transfer pricing (Banga 2019; OECD 2014). And, as unionisation potentially becomes less effective in fragmented and transitional work environments, digital trade may require greater policy involvement to ensure living wages and working standards (Graham, Hjorth and Lehdonvirta 2017; Vandaele 2018).

Digital trade governance gained prominence in the lead-up to the 11th Ministerial Conference of the World Trade Organization in 2017, with an escalation of controversial proposals for the negotiation of new multilateral rules in this area (Ismail 2020; MacLeod 2017). However, the seeds of those proposals emanated from earlier bilateral and regional trade negotiations, particularly the Trans-Pacific Partnership, the Regional Comprehensive and Economic Partnership and the Trade in Services Agreement negotiations (Berka 2017; Ismail 2020; Wolfe 2019). Three different visions for global digital trade governance can be considered to have since evolved. The first, led by the United States, emphasises openness and liberalisation (Azmeh, Foster and Echavarri 2020; Janow and Mavroidis 2019). The second, pushed principally by the European Union, prioritises consumer rights and protections, such as data privacy and cybersecurity (Aaronson and Leblond 2018). And the third, from China and Russia, promotes a narrower view of digital trade eschewing liberalisation and ensuring scope for substantive government interventions for purposes of surveillance and national security (Ferracane and Lee-Makiyama 2017; Gao 2018). This leaves a final camp, comprising many developing countries, including those in Africa, left falling in line with those respective visions, trying to define their own priorities or simply deferring commitment to different digital visions (Banga et al. 2020).[2]

It matters how African businesses, policymakers and traders engage with the digital economy and shape it on the continent. It is likely that it will not just increasingly reflect the way trade happens but also throw up unique challenges and opportunities that need to be addressed. Four characteristics help to understand the nature of the digital economy in Africa. Even before Covid-19, the digital economy had been, on average, growing rapidly in African countries, but doing so from a relatively low baseline compared to other regions. The breadth and depth of the use of the internet provides a straightforward but useful metric of the extent of digitalisation within an economy. By this measure, digitalisation in Africa is far behind that of the other regions of the world but it has been catching up rapidly. As Figure 7.5 shows, internet coverage across the continent has recently strengthened: 82 out of every 100 people in Africa were covered by at least 3G internet in 2021, up from 51 out of 100 in 2015. However, usage rates were lower. Nevertheless, Figure 7.6 shows that the share of the population actually using the internet in African countries remains much lower than all other world regions, even if it has been growing rapidly in recent years.

The second key characteristic to understand the African digital economy is the presence of stark inequalities within countries. There is a large digital divide, with urban individuals considerably more likely than rural populations to have access to, and use, the internet. To a smaller but noteworthy degree, there are also digital divides facing women and older demographic groupings, with men and youth (aged 15 to 24) significantly more likely to be internet users (see Figure 7.7). Increasingly addressing these gaps will be vital for the development of an equitable digital economy.

The third key characteristic is divisions between countries. The African digital economy remains geographically concentrated, with much more highly advanced hubs emerging in certain corners of the continent. Figures 7.8 and 7.9 give an impression of this by using data from the International Trade Centre on the presence and use of e-commerce platforms. The first simply shows the number of digital platforms present in each African countries in 2020, to demonstrate the breadth of e-commerce platforms. The second shows the average digital platform traffic for each country in the same year, to show a gauge of the usage of these platforms. Together they demonstrate considerable unevenness: outside of North Africa, and a few bright lights in South Africa, Kenya and Nigeria, Africa's digital economy remains in the dark.

The fourth key characteristic of the digital economy is its distinct form. African consumers are mobile-first digital adopters. Internet-enabled smartphone handsets are the most affordable and accessible avenue through which consumers can access and utilise the internet. Consumers can do this in the absence of fixed broadband connections and, because they are battery powered, even throughout intermittent electricity availability (Pankomera and van Greunen 2019). This in turn shapes the type of e-commerce that emerges within it, with mobile-optimised applications dominating growth in consumer usage.

The mobile digital economy does not always involve complex platforms with integrated delivery, payments or management services, like Amazon or Alibaba. In its most basic form, it involves vendors piggybacking on existing *communications* platforms – such as WhatsApp or Facebook – to market goods and communicate with prospective clients, before closing deals with physical goods and arranging transportation offline (BFA Global 2017). In parts of countries where internet coverage is limited, slow or comparatively expensive, mobile-first use can entail even simpler technologies, such as the use of USSD (unstructured supplementary service data) or basic telephony operations. In Niger, for example, the rollout of mobile phones to remote

Figure 7.5: Internet coverage rates: share of population covered by at least 3G

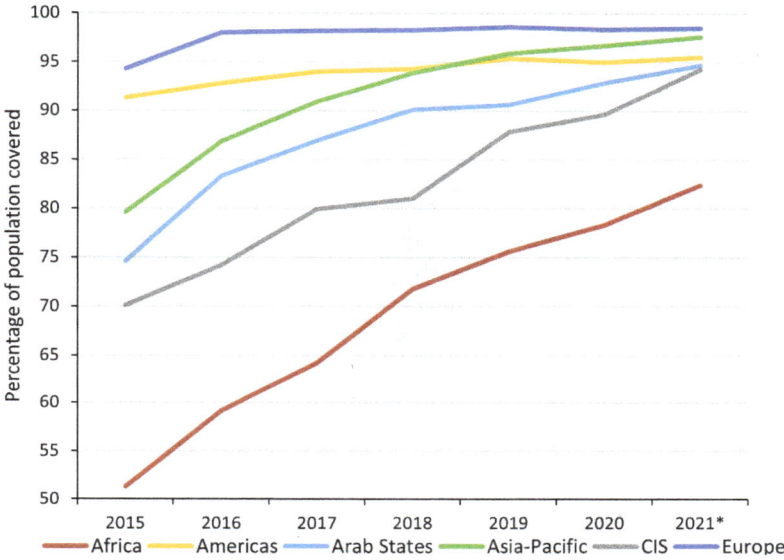

Source: Based on ITU (2022).
Notes: *Estimate. Data grouped by ITU world region. CIS is Commonwealth of Independent States (Armenia, Azerbaijan, Belarus, Kazakhstan, Kyrgyzstan, Russian Federation, Tajikistan, Turkmenistan and Uzbekistan).

Figure 7.6: Internet usage: share of population using the internet

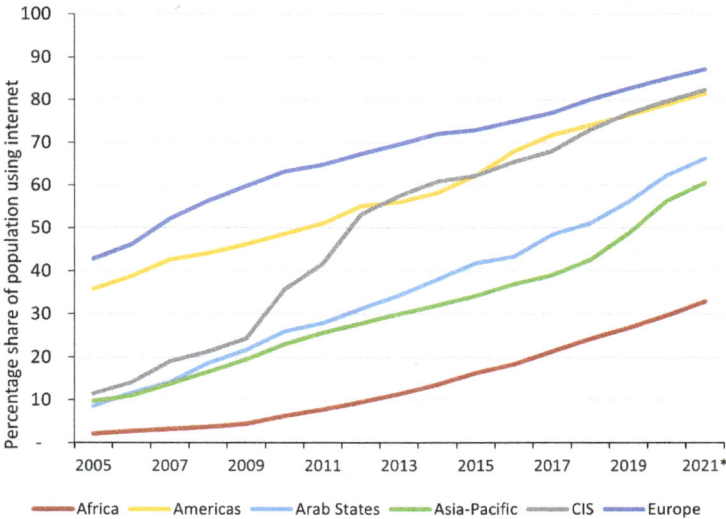

Source: Based on ITU (2022).
Notes: *Estimate. Data grouped by ITU world region. CIS is Commonwealth of Independent States (Armenia, Azerbaijan, Belarus, Kazakhstan, Kyrgyzstan, Russian Federation, Tajikistan, Turkmenistan and Uzbekistan).

Figure 7.7: Inequalities in the African digital economy: internet usage rates, by analytical grouping

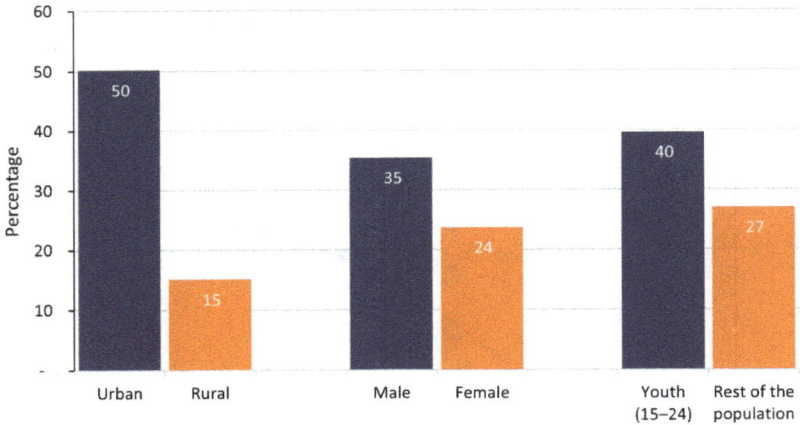

agricultural markets improved communication over grain deals, reducing the dispersal of grain prices by 10 to 16 per cent (Aker 2010). Owing to its inherent definitional and measurement difficulties, definitive data about the adoption of digital technologies is scarce. However, indirect measurements can give indications of how Covid-19 may have changed digital adoption in African countries.

Figure 7.10 shows changes in search behaviour on Google in the months leading up to the pandemic, in early 2020, and in the remainder of 2020. Trend lines are calculated for the world average and a selection of relatively more digitally developed African countries (Nigeria, Kenya, Uganda and Ghana). This shows relative changes in the popularity of 'online-' searches, the most popular of which were 'online-grocer' 'online-school', and 'online-casino'. Just as participation in physical spheres was constrained, we see a rise in search behaviour for online alternatives, demonstrating behavioural changes stimulated by the onset of Covid-19. Changing online search behaviours are visible and clear for the world average in Figure 7.10. It is also visible, though less smoothly, in data covering our selection of African countries. The Nigeria and Uganda trends more closely mirror the world average than do those for Ghana and Kenya. However, for many other African countries, the phenomenon is less clear, with trend lines reacting relatively chaotically.

Consumer behaviour changes during the course of Covid-19 are reported to have also resulted in the rapid growth of mobile money adoption in Africa. Mobile money grew about twice as fast in 2020 as pre-Covid-19 forecasts (Anderson-Manjang and Naghavi 2021). This was catalysed by both government and business policy changes, with government services in some African countries only available through mobile money payments and network operators offering reduced costs for mobile money transfers. In Kenya, electronic

Figure 7.8: Number of digital platforms per country, 2020

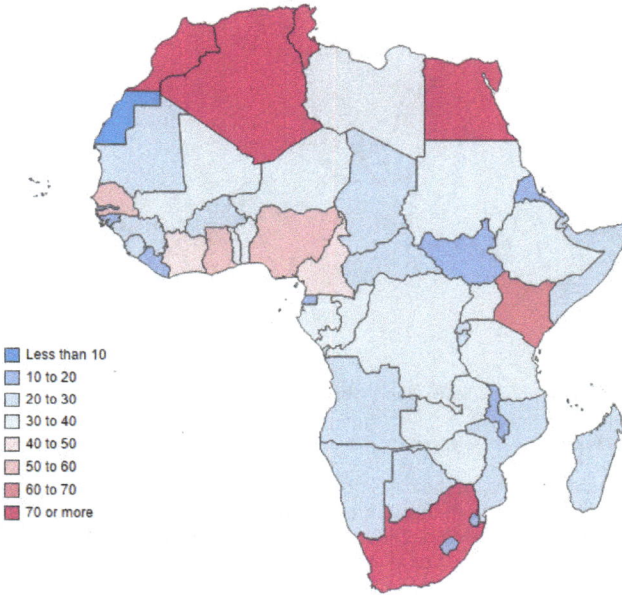

Less than 10
10 to 20
20 to 30
30 to 40
40 to 50
50 to 60
60 to 70
70 or more

Source: International Trade Centre (2020), p.6, reproduced with permission.

Figure 7.9: Average digital platform traffic per country, 2020

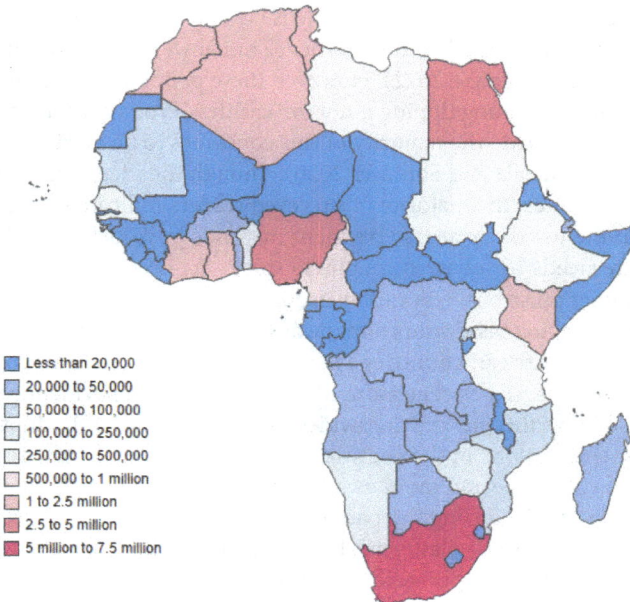

Less than 20,000
20,000 to 50,000
50,000 to 100,000
100,000 to 250,000
250,000 to 500,000
500,000 to 1 million
1 to 2.5 million
2.5 to 5 million
5 million to 7.5 million

Source: International Trade Centre (2020), p.7, reproduced with permission.

Figure 7.10: Trends in 'online'-something searches, for example 'online-shopping', in 2020

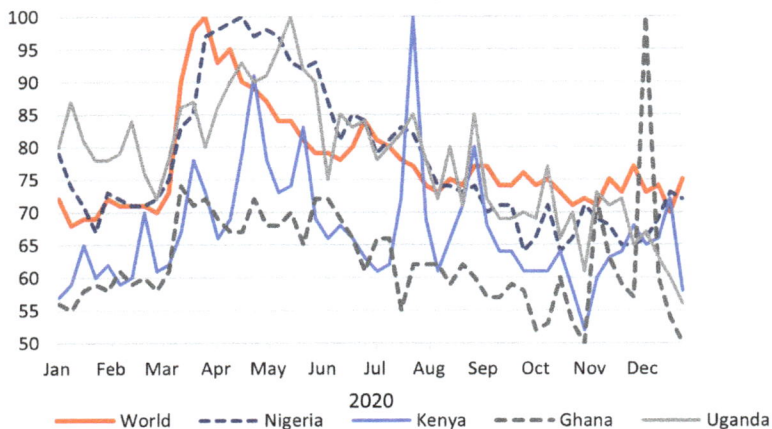

Source: Authors' calculations on the basis of data from Google Analytics.
Notes: Numbers represent search interest relative to the highest point on the chart for the given region and time. A value of 100 is the peak popularity for the term. A value of 50 means that the term is half as popular.

payments were facilitated through Safaricom's *temporary* fee waiver on M-Pesa transactions. Similarly, in Zambia, mobile payment platforms were presented as an opportunity for traders to go cashless, along with an electronic declaration form where traders could pre-declare goods before arrival at the border; one trader from Lusaka interviewed for the IOM's rapid assessments was able to digitally order from the Chirundu border (Zimbabwe) and go to collect the goods (Mvunga and Kunaka 2022). However, these policy interventions have not been the overwhelming tipping point for 'cashless' cross-border trade that might have been hoped. The majority of this continues to be carried out on a cash basis (Luke, Masila and Sommer 2020). Though the incentives are there in Lagos, for instance, the majority of surveyed traders indicated a high level of interest in the use of electronic payment methods post-lockdown, but the infrastructure needs to follow through (Resnick, Spencer and Siwale 2020, p.6). A consumer pulse business survey in 2020 identified a marked shift away from physical banking behaviours and towards online banking for consumers in several leading African countries (Table 7.1). Surveyed Kenyan consumers were as much as 55 per cent more likely to use mobile payment services – made feasible by the pre-existing widespread awareness and adoption of mobile payments options in the country. All of these countries saw reported rapid adoption of online and mobile banking services.

There was an uptake during the pandemic in use by African companies of Chinese e-commerce trade platforms. Following the China–Africa FOCAC-8 conference, e-commerce was facilitated through online shopping festivals to promote African products on Alibaba's eWTP. In January 2022, Ethiopia

Table 7.1: Consumer banking behaviour: consumer pulse survey reported changes in consumer behaviour, percentage, 2020

	South Africa	Kenya	Nigeria	Morocco
Online banking	+30	+37	+37	+18
Mobile banking	+30	+43	+44	+17
Mobile payment	−9	+55	+19	−1
Meeting with your financial adviser in the branch	−32	−28	−18	−9
Phone call with your branch advisers or branch staff	−29	−20	−32	−20

Source: McKinsey & Company (2020), as cited in Futi and MacLeod (2021).
Note: dark blue cells indicate reductions in activity of more than 10%; pale blue cells a reduction of between 1 and 10%; white cells indicate a growth in activity in 2020.

successfully listed a new range of domestic value-added coffee products on TMall Global (one of the Alibaba Group's cross-border online shopping platforms) and, using AntChain's track and trace technology, the coffee was airfreighted from Ethiopia direct to Chinese consumers.

The preceding data points could rightly be criticised as partial. They aggregate information on behavioural changes from the minority of individuals in the continent who are already online, who already receive financial services in some form, and who are from the more digitally developed African countries. As discussed in the previous section, this does not reflect a representative picture, but shows how Covid-19 may have accelerated digital uptake among those for whom access was not an inhibitive barrier.

If we widen our perspective, we see partial evidence that this accelerant effect of Covid-19 on digitalisation in Africa was not necessarily comprehensive. Figures 7.11 and 7.12 draw from the ITC eMarketplace explorer database to show how in aggregate internet traffic actually declined on e-commerce platforms with the onset of Covid-19. This phenomenon was consistent across five African regions (North Africa, Central Africa, East Africa, West Africa and Southern Africa). These trends are likely driven by the broader economic challenges imposed by Covid-19 upon economies in Africa, which affected entire economies and incomes of individuals who might have otherwise engaged in e-commerce.

Figure 7.12 shows how this internet traffic slowdown was not equal. Less sophisticated 'classifieds' platforms, which offer merely a site for product marketing and which account for a larger share of platforms in Africa, struggled more than the relatively more sophisticated 'transactional' platforms. The latter include integrated services, such as options for online payments, delivery, or warehouse management. Their relative performance suggests a maturation

Figure 7.11: Digital platform internet traffic index (January 2017 = 100)

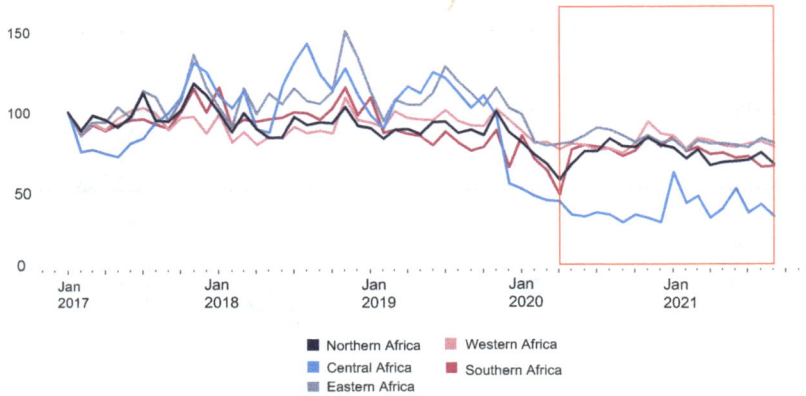

Source: International Trade Centre (2022), reproduced with permission.

Figure 7.12: More sophisticated 'transactional' platforms have weathered the Covid-19 storm better than simple 'classifieds' (index January 2017 = 100))

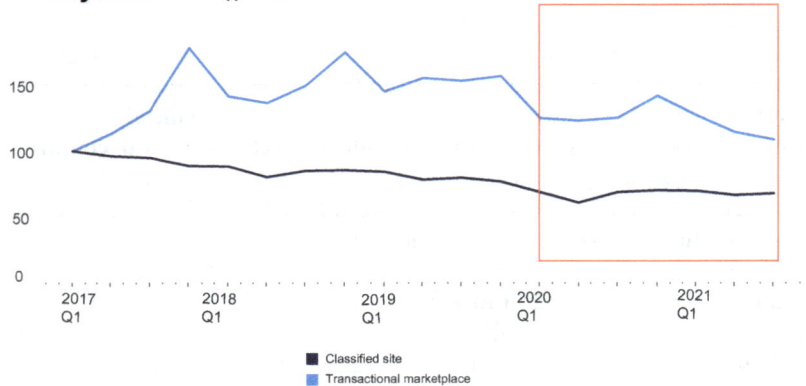

Source: ITC (2022), reproduced with permission.

of e-commerce platforms across the continent, with Covid-19 leading consumers and vendors to increasingly turn to more sophisticated platforms.

Another way to measure perceptions about the performance of the digital economy is through stock evaluations. During Covid-19, the stock market capitalisation of global tech companies, such as those captured by the tech-heavy NASDAQ-100, soared as investors perceived a shift in the future of global market value as a result of Covid-19. There is only one publicly listed company operating exclusively in the African continent: Jumia Technologies. It too was buoyed by the global tech investor wave by the end of 2021 but struggled by 2022, as shown in Figure 7.13. Too much should not be read into

Figure 7.13: Jumia – Africa's publicly listed tech bellwether: bumpy stock performance

Source: Authors' compilation; data from Google Finance.

the performance of a single company, yet the performance of Jumia stock is not indicative of easy times for e-commerce in Africa with Covid-19. As a publicly listed company, Jumia issue regular public financial reports. Their 2020 full-year financial report explained that '[o]verall, Covid-19 had a net negative effect on the business in 2020' and that 'the pandemic did not lead to a drastic change in consumer behaviour nor meaningful acceleration in consumer adoption of e-commerce at a pan-African level'.

Where the impact of Covid-19 has been more dramatic has been in the crafting of narratives and the attraction of policy and business attention to digital challenges and opportunities. The following five quotations are demonstrative of what might be considered a broader *techno-euphoria* catalysed by Covid-19:

> The COVID-19 crisis could be a catalyst [for] accelerating digital transformation. (McKinsey, May 2020, cited in Jayaram et al. 2020)

> There is no doubt that 2020 was a watershed year for the digital transition. (Oxford Business Group, April 2021)

> Africa goes digital. (IMF, spring 2021, cited in Duarte 2021)

> The Covid-19 pandemic is accelerating the arrival of the future in Africa. (Minney [*Africa Business*], November 2021)

> [T]he COVID-19 crisis builds momentum for Africa's digital transformation. (OECD, May 2022)

Such optimism should be considered cautiously. The consulting profession, in need of recurring hot marketing topics, will always have a vested interest in hype to some degree. Policy institutions, too, use hot topics to garner policymaking interest to pre-existing and structural policy issues; if not digital development, that might include food security crises, inflation or unemployment. Crises are useful moments at which to attract attention with which to attempt to drive change. There is evidence that the attention brought to digitalisation is however having an effect on policy attention in African countries:

> The digital economy was not a high priority before COVID-19. Ecommerce was mentioned in policy papers and priority documents but that did not always translate into reality. There are a lot of legal frameworks but few concrete actionable measures. COVID-19 has shown us the infrastructure deficit we face. (ECCAS 2020, cited in Futi and MacLeod 2021)

Since the start of the pandemic, the African Union Commission has launched a Digital Transformation Strategy for Africa 2020–2030. Negotiations for a protocol on e-commerce under the AfCFTA were effectively fast-tracked. The First Africa Heads of State Summit on Cybersecurity was held in March 2022. At the continental level, Covid-19 does seem to have brought the importance of digitalisation and digital trade into the policymaking spheres of attention.

Box 7.4: Digitalising border processes in the Democratic Republic of the Congo

In the DRC, the 'Animal and Plant Quarantine Services' (SCAV) border agency collects a tax on products that the COMESA simplified trade regime (STR) does not provide on exemption on. During Covid-19 this process became digitalised: traders would register and declare the numbers of goods and SCAV would send an automated text with the amount to pay at the bank to clear the goods. Traders appreciated this digital policy move and assessment of goods: 'before they used to pay and did not know where the money went ... now there is less paperwork, it saves time and it feels safer' (Bashi 2022a). However, the mobile platform only supported documentation and clearance of the tax certificate; it did not integrate sanitary and phytosanitary measures – 'going digital' did not satisfy all aspects of 'safe trade'. This is just one service that went digital and a number of other customs procedures could still be combined in a more integrated manner and harmonised across borders.

Source: Bashi (2022a).

Digital solutions have also played a role in enabling 'safe trade', reducing the need for physical human contact at borders (Box 7.4). These have ranged from the digitalisation of permits and certificates to cashless payments at the border. While the motivation was to improve public health measures, these government initiatives often entailed secondary benefits, such as improved efficiency or transparency. In some countries processes such as pre-registrations and pre-arrival clearance of consignments were adopted to enable a trader to register and enter goods for clearance on a mobile app ahead of arriving at the border (Mvunga and Kunaka 2021, p.8).

Summary

The prevailing stories thrown up by Covid-19 in African countries are of creativity, ingenuity and resourcefulness, and in general demonstrate a capacity for African trade policy to evolve and to be delivered nimbly. As the pandemic necessitated border health measures, 'safe trade' practices emerged to enable goods trade to flow. When those practices diverged, and made trade difficult between neighbouring countries, regional economic communities demonstrated their agility in harmonising such measures. That provides a lesson for trade policymaking at the continental level, where similar efforts for AU harmonised guidelines on safe trade measures did not deliver on time. If efforts to consolidate African trade policymaking at the continental level are to be successful, they will have to evolve to be more responsive.

Covid-19 interventions did not always work seamlessly or without issues. Safe trade measures frequently overlooked the importance of informal cross-border trade, despite this trade continuing to be a critical feature of intra-African trade and a source of livelihoods. With borders either closed or requiring stringent health measures to be satisfied, some of these informal traders adapted by aggregating their goods into more formalised 'pooled' consignments, while others were pushed to even more perilous informal crossings points to circumvent those measures. These changes seem unlikely to have a substantial and persisting 'sticking power' beyond Covid-19, with traders reportedly likely to return to informal trade routes to reduce tax and regulatory burdens.

Enthusiasm over the opportunity of Covid-19 for accelerating digitalisation and e-commerce – which appeared valid in many more developed parts of the world – seems in African countries to have put the cart before the horse. Covid-19 shifted digital narratives and sparked policy and business attention, possibly more than it transformed digital realities, outside of a few potent examples. Yet that shift in policy attention may yet be harnessed to build momentum and effectively change policies to boost digitalisation in African countries, as demonstrated by the fast-tracking of the AfCFTA negotiations on digital trade and the efforts to adopt digital trade facilitation measures at border points across Africa.

Notes

[1]   Early versions of some figures in this chapter were first published in Luke, David and MacLeod, Jamie (2021) 'The impact of COVID-19 on trade in Africa', Africa at LSE blog. 3 December. https://blogs.lse.ac.uk/africaatlse/2021/12/03/the-impact-of-covid-19 -pandemic-on-trade-africa-afcfta/

[2]   See Statement by the Africa Group, 'The Work Programme on Electronic Commerce: 20 October 2017', JOB/GC/144 (20 October 2017).

References

Aaronson, Susan A. and Leblond, Patrick (2018) 'Another Digital Divide: The Rise of Data Realms and Its Implications for the WTO', *Journal of International Economic Law*, vol.21, no.2, pp.245–72. https://doi.org/10.1093/jiel/jgy019

Aker, Jenny C. (2010) 'Information from Markets Near and Far: Mobile Phones and Agricultural Markets in Niger', *American Economic Journal: Applied Economics*, vol.2, no.3, pp.46–59. https://doi.org/10.1257/app.2.3.46

Anderson-Manjang, Simon K. and Naghavi Nika (2021) 'State of the Industry Report on Mobile Money 2021', GSMA, Report. https://perma.cc/DPG4-TYCE

Azmeh, Shamel; Foster, Christopher; and Echavarri, Jaime (2020) 'The International Trade Regime and the Quest for Free Digital Trade', *International Studies Review*, vol.22, no.3, pp.671–92. https://doi.org/10.1093/isr/viz033

Banga, Karishma; Keane, Jodie; Mendez-Parra, Maximiliano; Pettinotti, Laetitia; and Sommer, Lily (2020) 'Africa Trade and Covid-19: The Supply Chain Dimension', Overseas Development Institute, Working Paper. https://perma.cc/VY47-XLGL

Banga, Rashmi (2019) 'Growing Trade in Electronic Transmissions: Implications for the South', UNCTAD Research Paper, no. 29. https://perma.cc/5Y4C-CESY

Bashi, Jonathan (2022a) ATPR Key Informant Interview.

Bashi, Jonathan (2022b) 'COVID-19 Border Measures in the DRC Have Encouraged Informal Cross-Border Traders to Group Together', Africa at LSE, 1 March. https://perma.cc/RV3G-29QR

Berka, Walter (2017) 'CETA, TTIP, TiSA, and Data Protection', in Griller, Stefan; Obwexer, Walter; and Vranes, Erich (eds), *Mega-Regional Trade Agreements: CETA, TTIP, and Tisa: New Orientations for EU*

External Economic Relations, Oxford: Oxford University Press.
https://doi.org/10.1093/oso/9780198808893.001.0001

BFA Global (2017) 'Inclusive Digital Ecosystems of the Future', Fibr Project
White Paper no. 2. https://perma.cc/HLT7-DZFP

Byiers, Bruce; Apiko, Philomena; Karkare, Poorva and Kane, Mounirou
(2021) 'A system, not an error: Informal cross-border trade in West
Africa', Paper, ECDPM. https://perma.cc/6B8K-95J9

Duarte, Cristina (2021) 'Africa Goes Digital', International Monetary Fund.
https://www.imf.org/external/pubs/ft/fandd/2021/03/africas-digital
-future-after-COVID19-duarte.htm

Ferracane, Martina F. and Lee-Makiyama, Hosuk (2017) 'China's
Technology Protectionism and Its Non-negotiable Rationales',
European Centre for International Political Economy, Trade Working
Paper. https://perma.cc/PLN5-CSSE

Foster, Christopher; Graham, Mark; Mann, Laura; Waema, Timothy; and
Friederici, Nicolas (2018) 'Digital Control in Value Chains: Challenges of
Connectivity for East African Firms', *Economic Geography*, vol.94, no.1,
pp.68–86. https://doi.org/10.1080/00130095.2017.1350104. OA:
http://eprints.whiterose.ac.uk/117030

Futi, Guy and MacLeod, Jamie (2021) 'Covid-19 Impact on E-commerce in
Africa', UNECA, Report. https://perma.cc/3GVE-CE4D

Gaarder, Edwin (2022) ATPR Key Informant Interview.

Gaarder, Edwin; Luke, David; and Sommer, Lily (2021) 'Towards an
Estimate of Informal Cross-Border Trade in Africa', United Nations
Economic Commission for Africa. https://perma.cc/T3YD-FBVY

Gao, Henry S. (2018) 'Digital or Trade? The Contrasting Approaches of
China and US to Digital Trade', *Journal of International Economic Law*,
vol.21, no.2, pp.297–321. https://doi.org/10.1093/jiel/jgy015. OA:
https://core.ac.uk/download/pdf/200253693.pdf

González, Javier L. and Jouanjean, Marie-Agnes (2017) 'Digital Trade:
Developing a Framework for Analysis', OECD, Trade Policy Papers,
no. 205. https://doi.org/10.1787/524c8c83-en

Graham, Mark; Hjorth, Isis; and Lehdonvirta, Vili (2017) 'Digital Labour
and Development: Impacts of Global Digital Labour
Platforms and the Gig Economy on Worker Livelihoods', *European
Review of Labour and Research*, vol.23, no.2, pp.135–62.
https://doi.org/10.1177/1024258916687250

IMF (2018) 'Towards a Handbook on Measuring Digital Trade: Status
Update', Washington, DC.

International Trade Centre (2020) 'Business and Policy Insights: Mapping e-Marketplaces in Africa', ITC. https://perma.cc/G9FT-EGJF

International Trade Centre (2021) 'Business and Policy Insights: Mapping e-Marketplaces in Africa', ITC Publications, Working Paper. https://perma.cc/4JFE-CM8W

International Trade Centre (2022) 'African Marketplace Explorer'. https://ecomconnect.org/page/african-marketplace-explorer

IOM (2021) 'Rapid Situation and Needs Assessment at Mchinji Border in Malawi during the COVID-19 Pandemic', Report, 13 October. https://perma.cc/9KGR-2D2F

IOM (2022) 'IOM COVID-19 Impact on Points of Entry: Monthly Analysis, March 2022', Report, 7 April. https://perma.cc/ZLF8-MKF7

Ismail, Yasmin (2020) 'E-commerce in the World Trade Organization: History and Latest Developments in the Negotiations under the Joint Statement', International Institute for Sustainable Development and CUTS International, Report. https://perma.cc/97SM-V4WJ

ITU (2022) 'Statistics and Indicators', World Telecommunication/ICT Indicators Database. https://perma.cc/H63K-QCKE

Janow, Merit and Mavroidis, Petros (2019) 'Digital Trade, E-commerce, the WTO and Regional Frameworks', *World Trade Review*, vol.18, no.S1, pp.S1–S7. https://doi.org/10.1017/S1474745618000526

Jayaram, Kartik; Leiby, Kevin; Leke, Acha; Ooko-Ombaka, Amandla; and Sunny Sun, Ying (2020) 'Reopening and Reimagining Africa', McKinsey, 29 May. https://perma.cc/S598-RMJJ

Kanyanya, Michael (2022) ATPR Key Informant Interview.

Kassee, Dhunraj (2022) ATPR Key Informant Interview.

Khan, Lina M. (2016) 'Amazon's Antitrust Paradox', *The Yale Law Journal*, vol.126, no.3, pp.710–805. https://perma.cc/DNU4-APHA

Lanz, Rainer; Lundquist, Kathryn; Mansio, Grégoire; Maurer, Andreas; and Teh, Robert (2018) 'E-commerce and Developing Country-SME Participation in Global Value Chains', WTO, Staff Working Paper, no. ERSD-2018-13. https://doi.org/10.30875/ec5f0f21-en

Luke, David and MacLeod, Jamie (2021) 'The Impact of COVID-19 on Trade in Africa', Africa at LSE, 12 March. https://perma.cc/7QB6-5VKU

Luke, David; Masila, Gerald; and Sommer, Lily (2020) 'Informal Traders: A Balancing Act of Survival', UNECA, Report, 12 May. https://perma.cc/2WB7-WA4C

MacLeod, Jamie (2017) 'E-commerce and the WTO: A Developmental Agenda', Africa Portal, Global Economic Governance Africa Discussion Paper. https://perma.cc/L7VM-E2YU

Mafurutu, Rwatida (2022) ATPR Key Informant Interview.

Minney, Tom (2021) 'Covid-19 Boosts Uptake of Digital Technologies in Africa', Africa Business, 15 November. https://perma.cc/DL92-RX9V

Mvunga, Nyembezi and Kunaka, Charles (2021) 'Eight Emerging Effects of the COVID-19 Pandemic on Small-Scale Cross-Border Trade in the Great Lakes Region', World Bank, Report, 17 February. https://perma.cc/3BUW-3DP3

OECD (2014) 'Addressing the Tax Challenges of the Digital Economy', OECD/G20 Base Erosion and Profit Shifting Project, OECD Publishing, Paris. https://doi.org/10.1787/9789264218789-en

OECD (2022) 'Africa's Development Dynamics 2022: Regional Value Chains for a Sustainable Recovery', Report. https://perma.cc/RT86-FL7P

Onyango, Christopher (2022) ATPR Key Informant Interview.

Osoro, Geoffrey (2022) ATPR Key Informant Interview.

Oxford Business Group (2021) 'E-commerce in Sub-Saharan Africa: Can Covid-19 Growth Be Sustained?', 15 April. https://perma.cc/39ES-E4RT

Pankomera, Richard and van Greunen, Darelle (2019) 'Opportunities, Barriers, and Adoption Factors of Mobile Commerce for the Informal Sector in Developing Countries in Africa: A Systematic Review', The Electronic Journal of Information Systems in Developing Countries, vol.85, no.5, pp. 1–18. https://doi.org/10.1002/isd2.12096

Resnick, Danielle; Spencer, Ella; and Siwale, Twivwe (2020) 'Informal Traders and COVID-19 in Africa: An Opportunity to Strengthen the Social Contract', International Growth Centre https://perma.cc/3A8H-MV86

Sandberg, Karl and Hakansson, Frederik (2014) 'Barriers to Adapt E-commerce by Rural Microenterprises in Sweden: A Case Study', International Journal of Knowledge and Research in Management and E-commerce, vol.4, no.1, pp.1–7. https://perma.cc/LV2G-C3EA

Sommer, Lily (2022) ATPR Key Informant Interview.

Titeca, Kristof (2021) 'How COVID-19 Affected Informal Cross-Border Trade between Uganda and DRC', The Conversation, 24 May. https://perma.cc/6MBU-W9HE

TradeMark East Africa (2021) 'The Effects of COVID-19 on Women: Cross Border Traders in East Africa', Report, 16 March. https://perma.cc/7DJC-4PZ7

UNCTAD (2019) 'Digital Economy Report 2019 – Value Creation and Capture: Implications for Developing Countries', Report. https://perma.cc/7996-AZ8T

UNECA (2020c) 'Facilitating Cross-Border Trade through a Coordinated African Response to COVID-19', UNECA Publications, Report. https://perma.cc/684G-X9KT

UNECA (2020d) 'Trade Policies for Africa to Tackle Covid-19. UNECA Publications', Report. https://perma.cc/LNK2-NQCQ

UNECA (2021) 'Towards an Estimate of Informal Cross-Border Trade in Africa', UNECA Publications, Report. https://perma.cc/3XSL-48YR

Vandaele, Kurt (2018) 'Will Trade Unions Survive in the Platform Economy: Emerging Patterns of Platform Workers' Collective Voice and Representation in Europe', European Trade Union Institute, Working Paper. https://perma.cc/6XZH-VFSH

Wolfe, Robert (2019) 'Learning about Digital Trade: Privacy and E-Commerce in CETA and TPP', European Union Trade Institute, Working Paper. https://perma.cc/N8E6-BFEQ

World Bank (2016) 'World Development Report 2016: Digital Dividends', Report. https://perma.cc/Y43G-EQSH

World Bank (2020a) 'Monitoring Small Scale Cross Border Trade in Africa: Issues, Approaches, and Lessons', Report, 2 December. https://perma.cc/2SU6-VZYL

World Bank (2020b) 'World Development Report 2020: Trading for Development in the Age of Global Value Chains', Report. https://perma.cc/2SU6-VZYL

WTO (1998) 'Work Programme on E-Commerce', 30 September. https://perma.cc/H9WV-K4N7

8. Conclusion: it's in the world's interest to give Africa a new trade deal

David Luke

This book set out to examine *what* Africa trades, with *whom*, *where* and under *which* trade regimes, and also to assess and explain how the Covid-19 pandemic impacted how Africa trades. A normative framework that is pro-development and pro-equity provided the prism through which the issues were considered. This was complemented by an approach to trade policy analysis as applied to stages within the trade policy cycle to help identify what is working and what is not, and to concentrate analysis on the pressing issues at each stage.

We first set out the data on what Africa trades (Chapter 1) before reviewing the regimes, agreements and arrangements at continental, regional, bilateral and multilateral levels under which Africa trades (Chapters 2, 3, 4 and 5). Chapters 6 and 7 then explained the effect of Covid-19 on Africa's trade. Throughout the book, insights have demonstrated why Africa's trade is undersized and underperforms in contributing to the continent's development aspirations for industrialisation and economic transformation. The inherent limitations of commodity concentration in Africa's trade were weighed against the relative diversification of intra-African trade. This is why there has been so much interest in the AfCFTA, which entered into force on 30 May 2019. Yet the AfCFTA project is stutter-starting and to date trade has not substantively flowed under the arrangement as envisaged in the agreement. The asymmetrical trade relationship between Africa and its main trading partners and the WTO's 'one size fit all' rules raise questions of what concessions might be essential for Africa – the world's least-developed continent, accounting for only a tiny fraction of world trade – to help change its trade underperformance. Two key questions arise from these insights. First, what is the ideal trade deal that Africa requires from its partners and at the WTO to boost intra-African trade and incentivise trade deconcentration? Second, what are the most critical policy initiatives and reforms that are required from African stakeholders?

How to cite this book chapter:

Luke, David (2023) 'Conclusion: it's in the world's interest to give Africa a new trade deal', in: Luke, David (ed) *How Africa Trades*, London: LSE Press, pp. 209–217. https://doi.org/10.31389/lsepress.hat.h. License: CC-BY-NC 4.0

8.1 The ideal trade deal for Africa

Africa as the world's least developed region is increasingly where the last vestiges of extreme poverty reside, with 60 per cent of those living in extreme poverty now within the continent. With trade being a proven tool for growth, the advanced countries of the world can use it to help support Africa's self-chosen agenda for sustainable development. That would reduce global poverty, address instability and fragility, and make the world a more prosperous and secure place. But it would also be in the self-interest of those advanced countries of the world.

The African market will, in just 40 years, have more people in it than India and China combined. In the words of Janet Yellen, the US Treasury Secretary, at the Délégation Générale à l'Entrepreneuriat Rapide des Femmes et des Jeunes, in Senegal in 2023, 'Africa will shape the future of the global economy'. Reduced non-tariff barriers, lower intra-African tariffs, improved trade facilitation, and integrated markets can create a large, prosperous, peaceful, and more dynamic environment for trade and investment opportunities for Africa's partners as well as for Africa's own enterprises to grow. A more developed and integrated Africa is not merely philanthropy, but in everyone's best interest.

Yet, as discussed throughout the book, the trade relationships between Africa and its main trading partners are highly asymmetrical, a pattern observed in the bilateral relationships that were reviewed. In the case of the EU (the partner with the largest share of Africa's trade), asymmetry is compounded by the introduction of the EPAs, which are in effect reciprocal trade deals with gaps in their coverage of the RECs, resulting in hard borders for EU trade between African countries within the same customs union. In copying the EU's trade arrangements after Brexit, the UK (unlike Turkey, which as a member of the EU's customs union is obliged to maintain these arrangements) lost an opportunity to overcome the divisive implications of the EU's multiple trade regimes for Africa. China was shown to offer only a basic policy framework for guiding its trade with Africa. Overzealous implementation of its sanitary and phytosanitary regime, in which national quirks play a big role, limits the market access afforded by its duty-free, quota-free scheme for African LDCs. China is alone among the leading economies in not offering a generalised system of preferences scheme to African countries or a comparable programme such as the US's AGOA.

With positive elements such as non-reciprocity and uniform coverage among the eligible African countries, the US's AGOA was assessed to be a generous offer that is aligned to Africa's need for a tactical sequencing of trade opening with advanced country partners. That African beneficiaries have generally underperformed under AGOA illustrates the need for investment in productive capacity and other 'behind the border' reforms in African countries to complement the AGOA preferences; it is not an argument for shutting down AGOA, as some have advocated. However, AGOA is limited to the countries south of the Sahara. This has limited the incentives for the nascent intra-African supply chains that criss-cross the continent to be fully leveraged to boost internal and external trade. As a unilateral initiative, AGOA comes with political conditionalities that are determined by the US. This ushers an element of uncertainty into the deal. The other bilateral trade relationships that were briefly surveyed, such as Africa's trade with India, Turkey, Japan, Russia and Brazil, lacked ambition for leveraging trade for development.

The insights from the review of these trade relationships suggest that new trade deals are needed for Africa. Africa is the world's least-developed continent with the lowest global trade shares. It needs trade arrangements that incentivise and reward reduced commodity dependence, expanded productive capacities, interconnected supply chains, and diversified trade growth. The empirical evidence suggests that, for these goals to be met, two complementary measures are required: the right sequencing of trade policy that prioritises intra-African trade, which is already more diversified than Africa's external trade, and liberalised trade with harmonised trade rules between African countries as offered by the AfCFTA initiative. Evidence from economic modelling at the Economic Commission for Africa (ECA) was cited to illustrate this point in regard to Africa's trade arrangements with its biggest partner, the EU.

This evidence suggests that implementation of the EU (and other advanced country) reciprocal agreements ahead of the AfCFTA would result in losses in trade – or trade diversion – between African countries. On the other hand, if the AfCFTA were fully implemented before the reciprocal agreements, this negative impact would be mitigated. Trade gains by both African countries and the EU would be preserved, while intra-African trade would expand significantly, benefitting trade in industrial goods. African integration is in the world's interest. Reduced non-tariff barriers, lower intra-African tariffs, improved trade facilitation and integrated markets create a large, prosperous, peaceful and more dynamic environment for trade and investment opportunities for Africa's trading partners, as well as for African own enterprises to grow. This points to the need for strategic sequencing that prioritise implementation of the AfCFTA first.

The main elements of the ideal trade deal for Africa at this stage of its development can be sketched along the following lines: for a transitional period benchmarked against milestones in AfCFTA implementation and the gains emerging from it, a good development case can be made for Africa's trading partners to offer to all African countries unilateral market access that is duty-free and quota-free with a cumulative rules of origin regime. Concessions to Africa, as the world's poorest continent, that allow non-reciprocal access in goods and services to partner markets for a fixed transitional period, are strongly pro-development. With external market access secured for Africa's exports, they incentivise African countries to seek trade opportunities with each other and mitigate the risks of trade diversion. By ensuring such a deliberate sequencing for the AfCFTA, this will help Africa to build productive capacities and achieve its potential for strong and diversified growth in intra-African trade, with inclusive and transformational consequences. The ideal trade deal for Africa raises three immediate questions, centring on what might constitute a sufficient transition period, the justification for the inclusion of North African countries, and possible obstacles to a WTO waiver that would allow special treatment for Africa as a whole.

On the first question, of a sufficient transition period, the first clue is the AU's Agenda 2063, which envisages significant transformation of African economies by that year. The EU's Post-Cotonou Agreement (PCA), which was reviewed in Chapter 3, provides another clue. The EU's existing bilateral trade deal with sub-Saharan countries is for a period of 20 years from 2021. This suggests that, in the minds of the negotiators, it may take up to two decades for significant changes in Africa's trade to emerge, which at that point would warrant a review of the PCA. As regards the US's AGOA, 10 years from 2025 is understood to be the timeframe that is, as of late 2022, being considered for a renewal of this trade concession. Yet another clue comes from ECA modelling, cited earlier, which projects that, after full implementation of the AfCFTA, gains for Africa would essentially be concentrated in intra-African trade, which could see an increase of up to 33.8 per cent by 2045, as compared to a baseline without the AfCFTA. The data-driven ECA projection may be considered to be a judicious timeframe for the transition period.

On the second question, of the inclusion of North African countries, as was noted in Chapter 4, the August 2022 US Strategy Toward Sub-Saharan Africa announced by the Biden administration calls for the US to 'address the artificial bureaucratic division between North Africa and sub-Saharan Africa'. The EU too, with the 2018 Jean-Claude Juncker State of the Union address, raised the prospect of a 'continent-to-continent free trade agreement as an economic partnership between equals'. This appreciates that the value chains that are developing across the continent outdo artificial divisions and that trade integration on the continent as a whole provides a more dynamic market for both imports and exports. Egypt and Tunisia are already members of COMESA and Mauritania is in ECOWAS, while Morocco has sought ECOWAS membership. Algeria, Egypt, Mauritania, Morocco and Tunisia have ratified the AfCFTA Agreement, while at this point Libya has only signed it. It should also be noted that the ECA modelling results assume continent-wide implementation of the AfCFTA.

On the third question, of multilateral legitimisation through a WTO waiver, the precedent established by the US's AGOA in obtaining a WTO waiver suggests that this is not an insurmountable feat. Here it must be recognised that the WTO's 'one size fits all' rules require reimagination to meet the 21st-century realities and challenges facing late developers, such as African countries. As a member-driven organisation, with African countries accounting for a quarter of its membership, consensus on a special deal for Africa may not prove too difficult to achieve.

The ideal trade deal that assures non-reciprocal market access as sketched out above is conscious of the fact that African countries do not pose a threat to any of their trading partners in both goods and services. African countries account for just 2.3 per cent of world trade. This is underscored by the low levels of African participation in the WTO's dispute settlement system, which were discussed in Chapter 5. With insignificant shares of international trade, low-income countries have less economic heft to back up settlements whether as complainants or respondents in retaliating or absorbing retaliatory measures. This is compounded by the expense involved in litigation and by technical and capacity constraints at the African diplomatic missions in Geneva and at home in the capitals. The international trading system can accommodate a special trade deal for Africa with negligible systemic effect.

It further follows that African countries should rethink the merits of working through coalitions at the WTO that include other developing countries' groups such as the G90 or the Organisation of African, Caribbean and Pacific States (OACPS) as this does not allow for sufficient differentiation of Africa's specific needs. On some special and differential treatment (SDT) issues, for example, emerging economies or higher-income developing countries that have already acquired substantial market share in some sectors are unlikely to be granted policy space flexibilities, having already climbed some distance 'up the ladder'. As the region with the smallest (and declining share of world trade), African members should differentiate and pinpoint with finer clarity where SDT is required to support their growth. A related question concerns the distinction between 'least-developed countries' (LDCs) and 'developing countries'. With continental trade integration as the main strategy for boosting intra-African trade and global trade shares, this distinction between African countries is no longer tenable as it transcends the outworking of value chains on the ground. This is recognised in the AfCFTA protocols that require all signatories to assume the same obligations, with only a relatively short transition period granted to LDCs specifically with regard to the schedule for the liberalisation of trade in goods. In practice however, customs unions such as ECOWAS and EAC that encompass both LDCs and developing countries are following the same schedule for the liberalisation of trade in goods, which underscores the artificial distinction between the two categories of countries with respect to trade policy measures. Yet it is increasingly recognised by African policymakers that merely created exceptions to the general WTO rules, through SDT, has not in itself worked and is not sufficient (See communication of the Africa Group to the WTO General Council, WT/GC/W/868). The WTO needs to be wielded more proactively by African countries. This will involve pushing for provisions to the Agreement on Trade-Related Aspects of Intellectual Property Rights to encourage technological transfer, particularly of vital technologies needed for fighting climate change and catching up with digitalisation. African countries, as relatively small countries, must also fight for the equalising potential of the WTO in a world in which unilateralism is increasingly prevailing, even among advanced countries that were formally champions of multilateralism, such as the United States.

With dour realism the EU Parliament's 2021 resolution that was cited in Chapter 3 concluded that Africa requires a level playing field to reshape economic and trade relations and empower the continent. The ideal trade deal for Africa provides a basis for achieving the reasoning behind the resolution.

8.2 Critical responses required from African stakeholders

Three clusters of responses are required from African stakeholders. The first concerns implementation of the AfCFTA; the second is the importance of behind-the-border reforms that are also related to AfCFTA implementation; and the third is about strategic coordination in engaging with external partners. The responses required from African stakeholders are in line with the continent's industrial development aspirations and can help to drive diversification and ramp up trade performance.

AfCFTA implementation

The rationale of the AfCFTA is clear: it aims to boost intra-African trade and through doing so to diversify African economies, while contributing to their long-overdue industrialisation. It provides a platform for ambitious reforms that include elimination of nearly all tariffs, disciplining non-tariff barriers, harmonising approaches to services liberalisation and regulatory regimes, and ushering in a rules-based arrangement for trade governance across the continent. The AfCFTA enjoys broad consensus and strong political backing as a flagship project of the AU Agenda 2063, as discussed in Chapters 2 and 6. Covid-19 revealed the commitment of Africa's trade policymakers to the AfCFTA initiative, despite the considerable policy distractions of a global pandemic. With that commitment proven, it should be leveraged to broker the compromises needed to get the AfCFTA working to substantively transform trade in Africa.

The AfCFTA amounts to the crystallisation of decades of policy deliberation into an actionable and legally enforceable trade agreement. An increasing breadth of complementary projects, tools and initiatives such as the Pan-African Payments System and the Guided Trade Initiative have been put in place within the growing AfCFTA ecosystem to support implementation of the deal. However, with the start of trading stuck on technicalities, the AfCFTA is yet to substantively take off (beyond the products supported through the Guided Trade Initiative). Unlocking regional leadership could offer a solution, as has been the case with Kenya and South Africa in leading integration within EAC and SADC, respectively. Along with these countries, Egypt and Nigeria played a key role in bringing about the success that was achieved in the earlier phases of the AfCFTA negotiations. Rwanda, Senegal and Uganda were also active in these phases in brokering compromises. The message here is the need for leadership, creativity and compromise in realising the start of trade under the AfCFTA to help generate the momentum needed to get trade flowing across and transforming the continent.

AfCFTA implementation should take account of the RECs, which have a practical function in enabling trade integration and connecting a continent that is as vast as Africa. As also discussed in Chapter 2, the RECs are massively under-resourced, but they help to find and apply common solutions to mutual supply constraints. As was also seen in Chapters 6 and 7, it was at the level of the RECs that safe trade measures were designed and rapidly rolled out during the Covid-19 pandemic. In the preamble to the AfCFTA Treaty, and in Article 5 of the AfCFTA Framework Agreement, the eight AU-recognised RECs are designated as the AfCFTA's 'building blocks', meaning that their best practices and achievements are to be followed and incorporated into AfCFTA implementation. Article 12 confers an advisory role on them in AfCFTA deliberations. This complements the role accorded to the RECs as partners in the implementation of AU programmes.

As the AfCFTA is implemented, informal cross-border trade must not be overlooked, particularly in policymaking circles, as a critical source of trade and livelihoods. This was shown again during the Covid-19 crisis as border health measures often disregarded such traders, as discussed in Chapter 7. Frequently, trade policy measures are designed and implemented without sufficient assessment of the implications for these valuable traders. They can be better brought into each stage of the trade policymaking cycle. Improving and developing the existing simplified trade regimes provides the ideal avenue to use policy to interact with, and support, informal cross-border traders.

Behind-the-border reform

Turning now to behind-the-border measures which are also related to AfCFTA implementation, as discussed in Chapter 3, the insights from the Post-Cotonou Agreement (PCA) provide a ready-made agenda for policy and institutional reform. The PCA gives prominence to business environment reforms along with implementing effective competition policies, simplifying business regulations and processes including non-tariff measures, reducing and streamlining administrative formalities and other customs modernisation reforms, compliance with trade facilitation commitments, sanitary, phytosanitary and other standards, and more generally reducing trade costs. These are important reforms that should be complemented with open, transparent and clear regulatory frameworks for business and investment along with protection for property rights. The AfCFTA provisions on trade facilitation and protocols on investment, competition policy and intellectual property rights that were adopted in November 2022, if fully implemented, will lock in common obligations and requirements and provide a basis for benchmarking best practices.

Financial sector reforms are also crucial for improving trade performance as recognised in the PCA. In particular, sustainable and responsible investment – from domestic and foreign, public and private sources that focus on sectors that are essential for economic development – has high potential for job creation in value-adding sectors and foster environmental sustainability. At the same time appropriate measures are required that promote improved access to finance and financial services, especially for micro, small and medium-sized enterprises (MSMEs), the development and interconnectivity of financial markets, and the integration of capital markets to ensure the efficient allocation of savings to productive investment. Competition between financial service providers and strengthened mobile and digital financial services further helps to enhance access to finance, especially for MSMEs. Access to affordable finance is one of the drivers of the formalisation of informal cross-border trade (ICBT). As discussed in Chapter 7, the Covid-19 pandemic provided insights on how scale efficiencies can drive and transform ICBT.

There is evidence to suggest that African countries that work towards systematic improvements of behind-the-border measures are also performing better as traders. With regard to AGOA, for example, as discussed in Chapter 4, the strength of the trade support environment in African countries has determined whether or not they have been able to take advantage of AGOA. Countries with AGOA utilisation strategies have performed better. It is in this regard commendable that over 40 African countries are participating in programmes designed to enhance performance under the AfCFTA through national implementation schemes.

Strategic coordination

African Union resolutions frequently call upon its member states to consistently apply their own resolutions agreed under AU auspices 'to engage external partners as one … speaking with one voice'. As was noted, summits between African leaders in an AU configuration and partners now occur with regular frequency. In recent years, and in particular since 2013 when the AU's Agenda 2063 was adopted, the focus has turned towards how these partnerships can be leveraged to support long-term economic transformation in Africa. This can be seen in the increasing attention to support for overcoming supply-side constraints such as infrastructure, energy, human development and sustainability. Since Agenda 2063 shares many of the same aspirations as the UN's SDGs, it provides a ready-made basis for achieving consensus on priorities between Africa and its partners. Yet the AU Commission has no mandate to act on behalf of member states in trade negotiations or indeed in climate talks, although it is well established that Africa is disadvantaged in these two policy areas. Only ad hoc arrangements are put in place to coordinate negotiations.

Although the African Union maintains diplomatic representation in key capitals such as Washington, DC, Brussels and Beijing, African diplomatic missions struggle to engage strategically and coherently, and so underperform. Washington, DC, and Brussels offer multiple entry points for engagement through the diverse agencies of the US executive branch, the congressional caucus and committee system, and the EU Council, Commission and Parliament, respectively. Such pluralism may not be present in Beijing, but its concentrated power structures should perhaps make the task less onerous for coordinated African diplomatic activity. In Geneva, where an African Union office is also in place, as noted in Chapter 5, it lacks capacity to provide technical services to the WTO Africa Group including in drafting proposals and preparing responses to proposals from interlocutors. To enhance the role of the African Union in Geneva, it was suggested that it is essential it is given observer status at the WTO, which it is currently denied. It was recommended that to help ensure that African countries engage proactively on current and future questions that arise at the WTO, the African Union should set up a dedicated think tank on WTO issues to provide its member states with policy options that support African interests. One of the emerging issues that will impact how Africa trades concerns initiatives to decarbonise national economies and the role that border adjustment measures can play in reducing the risk of carbon leakage. It is essential that, from this early stage, African countries are able to shape new global rules on trade and climate.

Without effective coordination, African countries are vulnerable to being outmanoeuvred in trade negotiations and in their engagement with partners. In geoeconomics and geopolitics, individual African countries lack influence on their own to achieve meaningful outcomes that impact their development prospects. They should work together. The AU Commission must be given a mandate, direction and resources to secure outcomes that meet African aspirations. The stakes are high. A reliable revenue stream from trade is critical for development finance and sustainable debt management. Transforming how Africa trades will unlock structural changes in African economies that have proved elusive so far.

Final word

Informed deliberations on African trade policy need not be an activity for 'experts' alone. Trade affects the lives of ordinary Africans, shapes development outcomes, and impacts the continent's aspirations for economic transformation. *How Africa Trades* is packed with insights for interrogating the undersized and underperforming state of Africa's trade. The book is published on an open access basis to make it easily accessible and to enrich discussion and engagement on issues of trade policy reform. Researchers are encouraged to go deeper into the issues covered in this book. For teachers and educators, the book can be used in interdisciplinary courses on international development and across several disciplines in the social sciences including economics, law, politics and international relations. Most importantly, it is hoped that this book will help to bring about change in how Africa trades.